to
**from**

*Grandma*
*Christmas*
1976
all of us
K - B - T - S

# We Gather Together

# WE GATHER TOGETHER

## A Cook Book of Menus and Recipes

BY

*THE WIVES OF THE BISHOPS*
*OF THE EPISCOPAL CHURCH*

*With a Foreword by Ann Allin*

A CROSSROAD BOOK

*The Seabury Press · New York*

The Seabury Press
815 Second Avenue
New York, N.Y. 10017

Printed in the United States of America

Library of Congress Cataloging in Publication Data

Main entry under title:

We gather together.

"A Crossroad book."
Includes index.
1.  Cookery.  I.  Allin, Ann.
TX715.W353     641.5     76-15167
ISBN 0-8164-0320-1

# CONTENTS

# Recipes from the Bishops' Wives 129

*Favorite recipes from dioceses in every province—
for family fare and potluck suppers, parish
receptions, guild meetings and ordinations—all
featuring ease, economy, and appetite appeal*

# FOREWORD

Just as interesting projects frequently originate in chance conversations with companions, friends, or one's own children, the idea for this cookbook came from a conversation with our daughter Kelly. Kelly, one of our two children who moved with us from Mississippi to Dover House, is a recent college graduate who decided to seek her fortune in the East. In one of our frequent conversations about opportunities, needs, and projects, Kelly suddenly said to me, "A good idea for a project for the wives of bishops would be to do a practical cook book. Heaven knows, bishops' wives are exposed to enough recipes." The wives at the Portland Meeting of the House of Bishops received the proposal enthusiastically and immediately went to work on the project.

The past two years have brought new and rewarding opportunities for me to get to know the bishops' wives better. This cook book is a wonderful example of a shared experience. It is sharing which has made this not just another cook book. Here, as the title suggests, we have gathered together these offerings of menus and recipes; not gourmet fare perhaps, but good tasting, healthy foods that suggest a relatively simple style of eating and entertaining. Being conscious of countless people who know hunger as an everyday experience and hoping that what we save we might share with them, the proceeds from this book will go to the World Hunger Fund. You should also know that The Seabury Press has offered its services in the production of this book as its contribution to the World Hunger Fund.

Much gratitude is due Pat Read, Roxana Laughlin, and the people at The Seabury Press who have given many hours of their professional talents to this project; Janet Morgan and Charlotte Turgeon, of Amherst, Massachusetts, whose help and moral support have been most appreciated; the committee of wives: Jeanne Baden, Alice Witcher, Martha Henton, Ann Wood, and Patti Browning; Frances Wetmore who contributed the artwork; and all of the wives, without whom, this book simply would never have appeared. Thanks.

This collection of menus and recipes from the wives of the bishops can be a meaningful souvenir of the sixty-fifth General Convention, as well as a valuable addition to the cook book collections of those interested in good food, world hunger, sharing, and hospitality.

ANN ALLIN

*The Feast of the Annunciation*
*March, 1976*

# Saints
# and Celebrations

---

*Saints' days, feast days and fast days of special significance in the church year, with some traditional recipes that mark their observance.*

# DECEMBER

Throughout history, mankind has marked important occasions by feasting. From the crowning of a king to the baptism of a tiny babe —birthdays, weddings, funerals—the significant days of life are often associated with food. We seem to find comfort as well as joy in sharing the basic act of eating.

We will start at the beginning—Advent. Actually, the Sunday "next before," as it is called in the Book of Common Prayer, is an even more appropriate time to start. This Sunday has also been called "Stir-Up Sunday" from the words of the Collect: "Stir up, we beseech Thee, O Lord, the wills of thy faithful people; that they, plenteously bringing forth the fruit of good works, may by thee be plenteously rewarded." And by a rather easy leap, the pleasant task of "stirring up" one's plum pudding, fruit cake, or mince meat was done on that day, thereby allowing five weeks in which to mellow and bring forth fruit. It's a nice time to invite a few friends over after church or for tea and ask them to give a good "stir" to the luscious mixtures. This makes for a very friendly and profitable occasion, as well as noting the symbolism of many different hands helping in the preparation of a feast-day cake.

Advent has one saint in particular whose day can be marked off by special treats—St. Nicholas, on December 6th. St. Nicholas is an endearing figure and not just because, through the years, he has been transmogrified into our Santa Claus. There are many charming

3

legends about him—how he became a bishop while still a boy; how he endowed three penniless maidens by tossing bags of gold through their window (the derivation of the three gold balls as the sign of the pawnbroker); how he calmed storms; and how he was especially kind to children, even, so the tale has it, reassembling three small boys who had been chopped up and salted down by a wicked innkeeper! So, naturally, he is the patron saint of children as well as thieves and pawnbrokers. But especially he watches over fishermen, which is why so many small seaside chapels bear his name in the old world.

In Holland and Belgium, particularly, this is the day when children put out their shoes in the hope of receiving a present from St. Nick—but they might find a lump of coal or a birch switch if they've been naughty! One of the traditional goodies for this day is *Speculaus*, a hard cooky which can be cut into any shape, but might, appropriately, be that of a wooden shoe. It is easy to make a cardboard template and cut around it with a sharp knife.

4

## Speculaus

½ cup butter
1 cup sugar
1 egg
½ lemon rind, grated

2½ cups cake flour
½ teaspoon salt
1 teaspoon cinnamon
½ teaspoon baking powder

Cream the butter and sugar, add the eggs and continue beating. Add the lemon rind and the flour, sifted with the salt, baking powder, and cinnamon. Let the dough rest, covered, overnight in a cool place. Roll out as thinly as possible, cut into desired shape and bake at 350 degrees for 15–20 minutes.

5

St. Lucy's day, December 13th (supposedly the darkest day of the year), is hardly a major church event. But an interesting Advent custom arose after her martyrdom. Threatened with violence and outrage, Lucy refused to move from the spot where she stood and neither boiling oil nor pitch had the slightest effect on her. She was finally dispatched with the sword. Perhaps because of her youth and virginity, the tradition for this day in Scandinavian countries is that of the daughters of a family bringing coffee and "Lucia Buns" to their parents while they are yet in bed. The girls are dressed in long white dresses with red sashes and wear evergreen wreathes in their hair, with lighted candles on it! Whether our young could ever be persuaded to this custom or not, the buns are evidently quite delicious.

# *Christmas*

*Now let us feast and make good cheer*
*For Christmas comes but once a year!*

So runs the old song—and many a weary parent silently adds, "Thank God." Yet, in spite of the fuss and fatigue which have accrued to this season, Christmas remains the one holy day which seems to have an appeal for everyone. Heretics, cynics, lofty agnostics, and just plain bone-weary folk caught in the secular trap of gift buying, office parties, card sending (which everyone dislikes but no one can do anything about)—even to such as these must come at midnight a glimmering of that love which is focused in a manger stall.

No one really knows the exact date of Christ's birth, but St. John Chrysostom, writing in 386, says that Julian, after extensive investigation, found that the churches in the West all considered that he was born on December 25th, although the Eastern Churches considered January 6th to be the date. So we have December 25th fixed by the Julian calendar, but there are still pockets of the "old style" which retain January 6th.

As with so many pagan feasts, the Church "adapted" to the existing situation and "Christianized" the wild Roman Saturnalia. So while Christmas has grown out of pagan beliefs and customs, to us it is a celebration of the "invincible sun" whose light shall lighten all the world.

Although many parents are too exhausted to go to church on Christmas Eve—knowing the early hour at which they will be aroused—it does seem the right and perfect way to start the holy day. In one church, it has become the tradition to follow the French custom of *reveillon*. After the service, the worshipers adjourn to the parish house for onion soup, a glass of wine, and a slice of the *buche de noel*—a rolled sponge cake, frosted with chocolate and/or mocha to resemble a Yule log. It is wonderful how all the fatigues and frustrations disappear under the spell of the candlelight, the carols, the glow of the Christ-Mass, and the warmth of good food and fellowship.

Of course, we all know of the contest between the holly and the ivy as to which should reign supreme in the wood; we marvel that at midnight on Christmas Eve all the animals can speak (and we can be sure that they do not talk of passing trials but of the goodness of God); and each year we read again the story of Tiny Tim—such a rich and goodly heritage—and we say with him: "God Bless everyone!"

## Weinacht Stollen (Christmas Bread)

2 cups milk
3 packages yeast in ½ cup warm
   water
8 cups flour
1 cup sugar
1 teaspoon salt
⅓ teaspoon nutmeg
½ teaspoon cardamon seeds,
   crushed

⅔ pound butter (may be part
   other shortening)
3 eggs
½ pound nuts, chopped
2 ounces lemon rind
5 ounces citron, cut fine
2 cups seedless raisins, washed
   and plumped

Scald milk and cool. Dissolve yeast in warm water; add to milk.
Add part of flour to make a sponge. Beat well. Let rise until light—
about 2 hours. Meanwhile, mix sugar, salt, nutmeg, and cardamon
seeds together and cream with shortening. Beat in eggs. Now beat
into the mixture the lemon rind, nuts, citron, and raisins. Add this
mixture to the sponge and mix in the rest of the flour. Knead well.
Let rise again until light. Knead again and shape into loaves. Let

8

rise again. Bake in 375-degree oven for 20 minutes, then turn oven down to 325 degrees and bake for 30 minutes. This is delicious when toasted.

Cary McNairy / *Diocese of Minnesota*

# Rich English Christmas Cake

¾ cup butter
1 cup soft brown sugar, firmly
    packed
3 or 4 eggs
1 tablespoon black treacle
    (molasses)
2¼ cups self-rising flour
½ teaspoon mixed spice

¼ teaspoon salt
¾ cup sultana raisins (white)
1 cup raisins (dark)
2 cups currants
¾ cup cherries, cut up
½ cup chopped almonds
1 tablespoon brandy

Cream butter and sugar, add eggs, treacle, flour, then all the fruits, nuts, and other ingredients. Pour into a 7- or 8-inch pan approximately 3 inches deep. Bake for one hour at 350 degrees then turn down to 275 degrees for another 1¾ to 2 hours. You can put halved almonds on the top in circles before baking; use a half cup more almonds, halved, to cover it; or spread marzipan and royal icing on it; or just eat it plain.

## *Royal Icing*

2 egg whites
1 pound confectioners sugar,
    sifted

Break up egg whites but do not beat. Add sugar gradually, beating well after each addition until all sugar is added and mixture feels velvety, like thick cream. Vigorous beating is important. If icing is left at any time, cover with a damp cloth to prevent it from becoming too hard. If a crusty icing is desired, add 2 or 3 drops of lemon juice or 1 teaspoon glycerin to prevent undue hardening.

Ann Wood / *Executive Council*

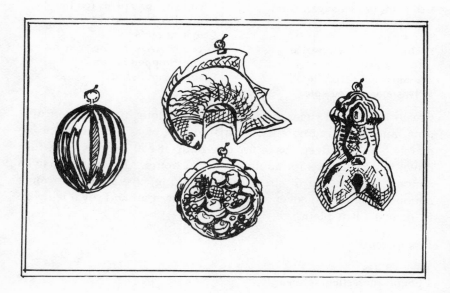

# JANUARY

Many churches have a "Watch Night" service on New Year's Eve and January 1 is the Feast of the Holy Name. People often have "Open House" on this day; it is a good way to see one's friends and neighbors and eat up what's left of the Christmas goodies.

In Greece, New Year's Day is also the feast of St. Basil and a special cake is made with a coin baked in it. The lucky person who finds it in his slice may expect great things during the year to come. It is thought that the custom of gift-giving at this time, which is in the Greek tradition, stems from the example of St. Basil, renowned for his generosity to children and the poor.

In Coventry, England, it used to be the custom for sponsors to send their godchildren special cakes on this day. This might be a fine tradition to revive even though many of us live too far apart to present the cake in person. Children were in the habit of visiting their godparents at New Year's and receiving a blessing as well as a "godcake."

## Coventry Godcakes

They should properly be made with puff paste, but a good rich pie crust pastry may be used. Roll it out to a thickness of ¼ inch and cut into 4-inch squares. Place in one corner two teaspoons of the

11

filling, moisten the edges and fold over to make a triangle. Press firmly with the tines of a fork to seal and bake in a hot oven, 425 degrees for 10–15 minutes.

*Filling for Godcakes*

¾ cup currants
⅓ cup lemon peel, finely
  chopped
½ teaspoon nutmeg

½ teaspoon allspice
¼ cup sugar
¼ cup butter

Mix all thoroughly and beat for a few minutes. Chill before using. This makes enough for 18 cakes, depending on size.

# The Epiphany
# Twelfth Night (or Day)

Twelfth Day comes, naturally enough, twelve days after Christmas and in medieval times marked the end of the long Christmas celebrations and feasting. Twelfth Night, the evening before, was the occasion of much merriment and a special cake was baked concealing a bean and a pea within its spicy richness. Whoever found the bean was crowned "King of the Revels" and his queen was designated by the pea. A mock court was set up and guests assigned to various offices and functions.

Religiously, the feast is called the Epiphany from the Greek word meaning "manifestation" or "showing forth." In our western tradition we associate this with the visit of the three kings, or magi, to the Christ child—whence another set of names: Kings' Day and Kings' Cake. In the Eastern Orthodox tradition, the association is more with Christ's baptism in the Jordan River and because of this the waters are blessed with much splendor and ceremony. A heavy cross is thrown into the sea or river by a priest or bishop and hardy young men dive in after it. This is still done in Florida by the Greek sponge fishermen. Also, because of the symbolism of the candle held during the eastern rite of baptism, the day is also called the "Feast of Lights" and many churches plan impressive, candlelit services on this day.

# Twelfth Night (or Day) Cake

1 cup butter
¾ cup sugar
3 eggs
¼ cup milk
3 cups flour
¾ cup each of currants and
  sultana raisins

4 tablespoons citron
4 tablespoons orange peel
1 teaspoon cinnamon
¼ teaspoon allspice
4 tablespoons shredded almonds

Cream the butter and sugar. Add eggs, one at a time, beating well after each. Add the milk and beat well. Mix the peels with a little of the flour and sift the rest with the spices. Fold the flour into the batter and, lastly, fold in the fruits and almonds. Bake in a pan lined with waxed paper for two hours in a slow oven at 250 degrees. It can be baked ahead of time as it keeps well. It should, tradition-ally, be covered with a thin coating of almond paste and then a thin white icing on top of that.

The beverage that was usually served with this splendid cake was called:

*Lamb's Wool*

Add the pulp of 6 baked apples to 1 quart of strong, hot ale. Add a small amount of freshly ground nutmeg and a bit of powdered ginger. Add sugar to taste, stir energetically, and serve hot.

# FEBRUARY

## *Shrove Tuesday*

Unless Easter is very late, Ash Wednesday comes in this month, and the day before that is called Shrove Tuesday—from the old requirement of confessing one's sins and being "shriven" before Lent. In the days of rigorous fasting, one used up all the fats in the house on this day and what better way than to concoct a large batch of pancakes. Even though fasting is not as common as it used to be, serving pancakes on this day has become a tradition. In the little town of Olney, England, they have revived the old pancake race which originated in 1445. Before the Reformation, the church bells rang to call people to confession but, in time, they became the signal to start flipping the pancakes!

> *Pancakes and fritters*
> *Say the bells of St. Peter's*

runs the old rhyme about the bells of London. And another:

> *Hark! I hear the pancake bell*
> *And fritters make a gallant smell!*

Of course, any kind of pancake will do.

14

## Shrove Tuesday Pancakes

2 cups plain flour
Pinch of salt
2 eggs

2½ cups milk
Lemon juice and verifine sugar

Put flour and salt in bowl. Add eggs and milk a little at a time, beating well until all milk is added. Let stand if possible for two hours. Heat a little oil in a frying pan. When hot, add enough pancake batter to thickly cover the pan. Cook until golden on both sides. Serve hot with lemon juice and fine sugar.

Ann Wood / *Executive Council*

*Almighty and everlasting God, who are always more ready to hear than we to pray, and art wont to give more than either we desire or deserve; Pour down upon us the abundance of thy mercy, forgiving us those things whereof our conscience is afraid, and giving us those things which we are not worthy to ask, but through the merits and mediation of Jesus Christ, thy Son, our Lord.  Amen.*

15

# MARCH/APRIL

## Mid-Lent
## *"Mothering Sunday"*

When the Lenten fast was more rigorous, a "break" was permitted halfway through, presumably to give the faithful courage for the last lap. This break, the fourth Sunday in Lent, usually comes in March and is called by several names, the nicest being "Laetare" from the opening Latin words of the Mass, "Rejoice!" It is also called "Refreshment Sunday" and "Mothering Sunday," possibly from the Epistle which refers to Jerusalem as the "Mother of us all." So, the custom arose of visiting one's cathedral, the "mother-church," and if possible one's own earthly mother. To her, one brought a small gift, often a "simnel cake." This is a truly delectable concoction, well worth the observance of this occasion. Robert Herrick, the seventeenth-century poet, refers to the day in these lines:

> *I'll to thee a simnel bring*
> *'Gainst thou go'st a-mothering;*
> *So that, when she blesseth thee*
> *Half that blessing thou'lt give me.*

There are many good rules for simnel cake. The word seems to come from the Latin *simila*, meaning "fine flour." Simnel Bread appears in many forms on the Fourth Sunday of Lent. In some

16

churches a large loaf is blessed and eaten as part of the Communion service, or it may be blessed at the service and shared at the coffee hour. The bread—in our day it has become more cake than bread—may be baked in cake tins of any desired size and frosted and decorated in any appropriate manner. The following recipe is a variation in the form of little cakes with almond paste filling.

*March 17—St. Patrick's Day*

## Simnel Cakes

3 sticks butter
2 cups sugar
6 eggs
2½ cups sifted flour

1 cup currants
1 cup golden raisins
½ cup candied mixed peel, chopped fine

Cream butter and sugar. Beat in the eggs one at a time. Add flour, currants, raisins, and peel. Make an almond paste, using:

¾ cup almond paste
2 eggs

¾ cup granulated sugar
6 tablespoons flour

17

Mix these ingredients together to a smooth, stiff paste. Using paper linings for tiny cupcake tins, place 1 teaspoon cake batter in the shell, then ½ teaspoon almond paste and top with a layer of cake batter. Bake in a 350-degree oven for 30 minutes. Makes 4 dozen cupcakes.

Martha Porteus / *Diocese of Connecticut*

# *Maundy Thursday*

On this day we commemorate the institution of the Eucharist, the Last Supper shared by our Lord with his disciples. At this time the Jewish Passover became the chief way in which Christians would "re-call" their Lord and Savior. In the Latin ritual for the ceremony of the foot washing, which is still done by the Pope in Rome, the antiphon begins: *Mandatum novum do vobis*—A New commandment I give you. It is believed that the word "maundy" comes from this phrase.

For some years now in a small New England college town, women from eight Protestant churches have been meeting to make the bread to be used in their Maundy Thursday services. One woman gets up early and "sets" the dough for its first rising. At about 10 A.M. the others appear. After a short prayer around the kitchen table, all take turns in kneading the dough, each shapes a round loaf and marks it with a cross. The loaves are then covered and left to rise for the last time. The hostess bakes them, leaving them to cool in her kitchen. During the day the others come by and take a loaf, not knowing who made which, as they like the symbolism. So, a local tradition has been born and becomes a very meaningful one in this community.

## Communion Bread

Pour 2 cups boiling water over:

| | |
|---|---|
| **1 cup All-Bran cereal** | **¾ cup sugar** |
| **¾ cup shortening** | **1 teaspoon salt** |

Cool this mixture to lukewarm.

| | |
|---|---|
| **2 packages dry yeast** | **2 eggs, slightly beaten** |
| **½ cup warm water** | **6½-7 cups flour** |

Dissolve dry yeast in ½ cup warm water. Add yeast mixture to other cooled mixture. Add eggs; then add 6½–7 cups flour. In greased bowl allow mixture to rise to twice its size. Put on greased cookie sheet or greased bread pan. Let rise about ½ hour. Bake at 350 degrees for about 30 minutes; be careful not to overdo. Makes 3 loaves.

If you do not want to use all the dough, you may keep it in the refrigerator covered with a damp cloth, for 4 days—no longer.

Martha Burt / *Diocese of Ohio*

19

# *Passover*

The Jewish Passover often comes during our Holy Week and sometimes coincides with Maundy Thursday. The "seder" is basically a family occasion, solemn but joyful. Through the ritual of questions (usually asked by the youngest child) and answers, readings, psalms and prayers, the mighty acts of God in history are recalled—how his angel "passed over" the houses of the Israelites in Egypt, sparing their first-born; how God led them out of slavery and bondage and formed them into a nation.

Some Christian churches emphasize the close connection between the Passover and the institution of the Lord's Supper by a short version of the seder ritual before the celebration of the Eucharist on Maundy Thursday. A table—lower and in front of the altar—is set with the traditional Passover foods, each rich with symbolism:

> 3 pieces of *matzo,* or unleavened bread, recalling the haste with which the Jews had to leave their homes;
> *maror,* the bitter herbs, to remember their days of bondage;
> *haroset,* a relish of chopped apples, nuts and wine, standing for the mortar used by the Jews in building for the Pharaohs;
> a roasted shankbone of lamb to symbolize the paschal lamb;
> a roasted egg which, with the shankbone, probably refers to the festival offering made by pilgrims to the temple in Jerusalem;
> a green vegetable, often parsley, to represent new life in the spring and a dish of salted water to dip it in, the water being a reminder of the tears of the oppressed people;
> a cup of wine.

---

*Set our hearts at liberty from the service of ourselves and let it be our meat and drink to do Thy will. Amen.*

# Good Friday

In a way it seems strange to mark such a solemn day in the church year with a special delicacy, but hot cross buns have long been a tradition. In fact, small loaves marked with a cross have been excavated at Herculaneum and archeologists say that in ancient Greece small cakes were offered to win the favor of the gods. So perhaps it was a natural step for Christians to take over this custom; they probably felt that the cross cancelled out the pagan

origin. It only goes to show that there is nothing new in the world and it's what is done with the tradition that gives it significance to each age.

It is too bad that our supermarkets begin to offer these buns as soon, or even before, Lent begins. Assuming you have fasted till sundown, what a pleasure to eat these on "God's Friday," as it was originally called. An ancient superstition has it that Good Friday buns will never grow stale or moldy—but that may be because they get eaten up so quickly. As Poor Robin wrote in his Almanack for 1733:

> *Good Friday comes this month, the old woman runs*
> *With one-a-penny, two-a-penny hot cross buns,*
> *Whose virtue is, if you believe what's said*
> *They'll not grow mouldy like the common bread!*

## Hot Cross Buns

½ cup seedless raisins or currants
1½ packages dry yeast
¼ cup lukewarm water
1 cup milk
½ cup sugar
½ cup shortening

3½–4 cups flour
¾ teaspoon salt
2 teaspoons cinnamon
1 teaspoon ginger
1 egg, beaten

Soften the raisins or currants in warm water for 15 minutes. Drain them. Soften the yeast in ¼ cup lukewarm water. Scald the milk with sugar and shortening. Then let it cool to lukewarm. Sift the flour, spices and salt in a large bowl. Add the raisins or currants.

Mix well. Add beaten egg, milk, sugar, yeast water, and shortening. Pour this mixture over the flour and knead lightly. Cover and let rise to double its size. Then shape the dough into 18 buns and place them on a greased baking pan. Let them rise again 1–2 hours. With a sharp knife, cut crosses on the tops. Bake them with powdered sugar while hot or frost the cut crosses with this icing.

2 tablespoons
  orange juice
1 tablespoon grated
  orange peel

1 cup confectioners
  sugar

Yield 1½ dozen

Dottie Hall / *Diocese of Virginia*

*April 23—St. George's Day*

# *Easter*

## (must be between March 22 and April 25)

English and German seem to be the only two languages where the word for Easter is not derived from the Hebrew *pesach*, or passover. Ours comes from the more pagan, anglo-saxon *oestre*, the name of the goddess of the dawn. Paques, Pasqua, Pascha, Pascua all recall the Hebrew original.

Roast lamb is the customary dish in many Mediteranean countries. In Greece, in the country, whole lambs are roasted over a bed of coals where they are turned on spits from early morning until ready to be served crackling and fragrant with wild herbs, dill, and oregano. Country bread, a big salad, oranges, and plenty of local wine complete this meal which, to the devout, is ample reward for the long weeks of fasting. The chief church service of the Orthodox Church is at midnight on Holy Saturday, and a wonderful and beautiful one it is. In the darkened church a new fire is kindled at the altar and spreads through the church from person to person as each holds his candle to receive the flame from his neighbor until the whole building is ablaze with light. After the service, each worshiper returns home, carefully wielding his candle in order to keep it lit until he is safely inside. There awaits a delicious hot soup, "mayaritza," made from rice, broth, herbs, and the chopped innards of the paschal lamb. Platters of blood-red eggs are on the table and are distributed to everyone. Holding it firmly, each turns to his neighbor and bangs his egg against the other's saying: "Christ is risen!" Whosoever egg remains uncracked is the winner and adds his opponent's egg to his own. In the days of royalty, the king always went to the barracks in Athens to crack eggs with the Evzones, the elite guard of the Greek army.

In our country there are not as many fixed traditions. Ham may be the main dish, or the ubiquitous turkey, or almost anything. Perhaps colored eggs are the only link with the older nations. Polish and Russian eggs are often intricately and beautifully decorated.

The egg, probably because of its secret, mystical life, is one of the oldest symbols of eternity.

A Russian *paska* makes a delectable dessert for the Easter feast and, in spite of its impressive appearance, is not at all difficult to make.

## Pashka

4 8-ounce packages cream cheese, softened
½ cup butter, softened
2 cups sifted confectioners sugar
3 egg yolks
2 teaspoons vanilla or vanilla cognac

¾ cup chopped citron, candied orange and lemon peel
Grated rind of 1 lemon
1 5-ounce can toasted slivered almonds
Fresh strawberries for garnish

Allow cheese and butter to stand at room temperature for 2 hours. With electric beater mix at low speed, adding sugar gradually, then egg yolks, one at a time, beating them well. Add vanilla or vanilla cognac. Stir in chopped peels, lemon rind, and almonds. Line a clay flower pot with double thickness of cheesecloth which has been

25

wrung out with cold water. Put mixture in the clay pot on a pan to catch any moisture. Refrigerate overnight. To unmold, pull cheesecloth very gently all around to loosen pashka. Place silver platter over pot and invert; very carefully remove pot, then gently pull off cheesecloth. Garnish with slightly sugared strawberries. Serves 14 to 16 people.

Marie Louise Creighton / *Diocese of Washington*

# Kulich (Easter Bread)

1 package active dry yeast
2 tablespoons lukewarm water
¾ cup scalded milk
3 cups sifted flour
2 egg yolks
⅓ cup sugar
½ teaspoon salt
½ cup melted butter

¼ teaspoon saffron (optional)
¾ cup currants
¼ cup chopped almonds
½ cup chopped candied lemon
    peel
¼ cup confectioners sugar
1 teaspoon water

Dissolve yeast in lukewarm water. Cool milk to lukewarm, add yeast and 1½ cups flour. Beat until smooth. Cover and let rise in warm place about 30 minutes, until doubled in bulk. Add egg yolks, sugar, salt, butter, and saffron (if used) to yeast mixture. Beat thoroughly until well blended. Add remaining 1½ cups flour, currants, almonds, and lemon peel. Knead lightly on floured board. Place in lightly greased bowl. Cover. Let rise 1½ hours until doubled. Shape dough to fit into well-greased 2-pound coffee can. Let rise in warm place 50–60 minutes until dough has doubled in bulk and has risen about 1 inch above can edge. Brush with melted butter. Bake in 350-degree oven for 50–60 minutes. Remove loaf from oven, let stand in can for 10 minutes, then remove to rack to cool. Mix confectioners sugar and water and drizzle on top of loaf.

Marge Gressle / *Diocese of Bethlehem (Pennsylvania)*

*Praised be my Lord*
*by all those who pardon one another*
    *for Thy love's sake;*
*and who endure weakness and tribulation.*

    *Blessed are they who peacably shall endure,*
*for thou, O Most Highest, shalt give them a*
*crown.*

—ST. FRANCIS OF ASSISI

# MAY

## *Pentecost or Whitsunday*

For Christians this is a very important day, commemorating the descent of the Holy Spirit upon the disciples. The Epistle for the day (Acts 2:1) tells of a great crowd gathered in Jerusalem, men from all those countries with such marvelous names—Parthia, Cappadocia, Phrygia, and Pamphilia—who were suddenly able to understand each others' languages. And so this day has always had great meaning for us in terms of "proclaiming the wonderful works of God." The early church baptized catechumens (candidates) on this day and from their white robes comes the alternate name of "Whitsunday." We do not have special dishes for this feast but in England it is common to eat gooseberries in some form—perhaps a Gooseberry Fool, which is basically a thick puree of stewed berries, sweetened and mixed with stiffly whipped cream. And there is nothing better or prettier than this simple dish—a pale pink or green cloud (depending on which kind of gooseberries) heaped in a glass bowl. There is also gooseberry pie (page 238). Perhaps because of the ecumenical character of this day—"men out of every nation under heaven" were in Jerusalem, they say—we might emphasize other-than-local dishes. Depending on where we live, we could invite guests from different ethnic backgrounds to share our table on this day, remembering the first Whitsunday when everyone could understand one another, and together praised God.

# JUNE

## *Midsummer's Day or St. John's Day*

Again we have to turn to Europe to find a celebration for this day, which seems a pity since St. John's Day, or Midsummer, could be a fine occasion for rejoicing in any country. June 24th is the saint's day and in spite of his rather exotic lifestyle, he is a great favorite in many places. Midsummer's Eve, especially in the northern countries where the nights are long and light at this time of year, provides the occasion for an excursion into the country, staying up all night, feasting and jumping over the bonfires which are lit on the hillsides. This custom certainly stems from pagan times when the arrival of the summer solstice was greeted with such joy, after the hard winter. And in many countries, the act of jumping over the fire was part of an ancient fertility rite.

Since St. John was supposed to subsist on honey and locusts, we have little to choose from in the way of food! To be sure, the "locusts" are not winged insects but the carob bean. These grow in long, dark brown pods which rattle persistently and are known as "St. John's Bread." They are used as a substitute for chocolate and so, perhaps one could make a favorite American cake for this day—though a "honey cake" might be a more appropriate way to remember St. John.

# JULY

In this month, of course, we have our own, very American Independence Day, which certainly should be a time not only to celebrate our national life but to remember the "faith of our fathers." All over our country there are festivities on this day—parades, speeches, fireworks, family celebrations such as picnics, cook-outs, and beach parties—all with a local or regional flavor (from salmon and green peas to the ubiquitous hot dog and hamburger).

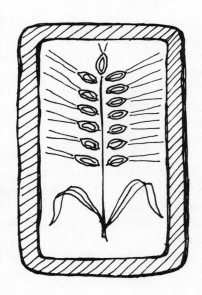

# AUGUST

One could keep very busy in this month. St. Lawrence's day is the 10th; St. Stephen of Hungary is remembered on the 20th; and in between, on the 15th, the Assumption of the Virgin is celebrated in countries where Roman Catholicism predominates. Even in many of our big cities with large ethnic groups, the streets are decorated, special foods are prepared, and all kinds of celebrations held in honor of Our Lady. In many countries, grapes and raisins are blessed on the Feast of the Transfiguration.

All through the Middle Ages and up to the eighteenth century, fairs were held throughout Europe and England. Some still exist today, although many became so rowdy that they had to be suppressed. The old nursery song runs:

> *O Dear! What can the matter be? Johnny's so long at the Fair!*
> *He promised to buy me a bunch of blue ribbons to tie up my*
> *bonny brown hair!*

It is more than likely that Johnny would bring his sweetheart "a-fairing" to make up for his lingering. It might be, indeed, a bunch of blue ribbons but it could also be gingerbread in some form, which was a specialty of these fairs. White or brown, cut into the shape of men or animals or stamped with the emblem of a saint, even made into primers for children—gingerbread was to be seen at every fair. A later form came to be known as "Fair Buttons," said to have gotten their name from the large buttons worn by British men down the front of their jackets.

31

## Brown Fair Buttons

2 cups butter
1½ cups sugar
1½ teaspoons ground ginger

1 cup dark corn syrup
8 cups sifted flour
¾ teaspoon baking soda

Cream butter, sugar, and ginger. Add syrup, then the flour which has been sifted with the soda. Roll out and bake at 375 degrees until lightly browned. If cut with a 1¼ inch cutter, the buttons will spread to 2 inches. This recipe makes a large quantity—about 200 "buttons." Store in an airtight tin.

# SEPTEMBER

We begin to think of harvests in this month and, since St. Fiacre is the patron saint of gardeners, we should at least give him a nod. He was an Irish nobleman of the seventh century who went to France and built a monastery in the province of Brie. What better way to honor him than by savoring a delicious brie cheese on his day, August 30th.

A rather obscure saint of the Greek Orthodox Church is remembered on September 11th. He is Saint Euphrosynos the Cook, who worked in the monastery kitchen all his life. Gentle and unlettered, he was often the butt of his fellow monks, but the Lord rewarded him with apples from the garden of Heaven. He used these to cure the sick and his saintliness was recognized by all. So an apple pie or pan dowdy on this day should serve to remind us that simplicity and faithfulness are virtues not to be despised!

Saint Michael is such a popular saint that it is a pity there are not more ways to celebrate him. In England, the Michaelmas goose is traditional. Although highly unlikely, the legend goes that Queen Elizabeth I was dining on goose when she heard the news of the defeat of the Spanish Armada. In her joy and triumph she decreed that, "hereafter, goose should be eaten on this day." Since, in our Prayer Book, all the angels are honored on the same day as is St. Michael—September 29—why not make an angel cake, light and airborne as a true angel?

Rosh ha-Shanah, the Jewish New Year, is apt to come in September. While there is no strictly traditional menu for this holiday, many delicious foods are prepared. The "hallah" or "challah" is one customary item. This is the braided loaf of bread which is made to grace the family table every Friday evening. Symbolic of basic human sustenance, and, if two loaves are made, of the twofold commandment given to the children of Israel—to preserve the Sabbath and to keep it holy—this bread is a beautiful sight. Its golden brown twists and fragrant richness remind all who partake, of God's goodness.

# Hallah

**6 cups sifted, unbleached flour**
**2 packages dry yeast**
**2 cups water, almost lukewarm**
**½ cup sugar**
**½ cup vegetable oil**
**3 beaten eggs (reserve a little for**
   **brushing)**
**1 teaspoon salt**

Put the flour in a large bowl, make a groove in it and add the yeast. Slowly beat about ¾ cup of the warm water into the yeast, absorbing some of the flour to make a loose paste. Add the sugar. After a few minutes the mixture will begin to bubble. Then add the oil, eggs, and salt. Beat in the remaining water slowly, making sure that all the flour is absorbed. The dough should be stiff; it may take another cup of flour. Put the dough on a floured board, knead well, cover with a cloth and let it rise for half an hour. Knead again, let rise for a second time, half an hour, in a warm area. Divide the dough into six parts and shape each into a long cylinder (with your hands). Braid three strips into a loaf, making two loaves, and tuck the ends under. Cover with a cloth and let rise again until almost double in size. Brush with the reserved egg and bake for about 40 minutes at 350 degrees.

---

*O Lord, we thank you for this food we are privileged to eat and beseech you to help us to speak the right words that we may not have to eat them later on. Amen.*

# OCTOBER

October 4th is the Feast of St. Francis. While still a young man, he led a most profligate life and undoubtedly feasted to excess. But after his call to follow Our Lord in a life of poverty, he gave little thought to eating. This might be a good day to fast and give a special offering to feed those who are less fortunate than we.

All Hallows' Eve, or Halloween, is perhaps the best known holiday in October and of very ancient origin. Dating from Druidic times, it was associated with all sorts of rites and runes, chanting and invocations. Evil spirits, goblins, and witches were supposed to be abroad on this night and the only way to placate them was to offer sweetmeats or other goodies, or to disguise oneself as one of them and join in their mischief. So arose our custom of dressing up and the modern cry of "trick or treat." The original cry on Halloween was "a-souling." Boys and girls would chant at each door:

*A soul cake, a soul cake,*
*Have mercy on all Christian souls;*
*For a soul cake.*

For the small consideration of a soul cake they, in turn, would pray for the dead of each family. The soul cake was originally a small round bun, best served warm with plenty of berry preserves.

## Soul Cakes

1 cake yeast
¼ cup lukewarm water
½ cup sugar
½ cup butter
2 cups scalded milk

6 cups flour
2 teaspoons salt
2 teaspoons cinnamon
1 egg, beaten

Dissolve yeast in water with 1 tablespoon of the sugar. Cover and allow to rise until light. Cream butter and remaining sugar. Add scalded milk. When mixture is lukewarm, add yeast and sifted dry ingredients. Knead into soft dough. Let rise until double in bulk. Shape into small round or oval buns. Brush tops with egg. Bake on greased cookie sheets at 400 degrees for 15 minutes. Turn oven down to 350 degrees and bake the cakes until golden brown.

Katherine Appleyard / *Diocese of Pittsburgh*

*For what we are about to receive may the Lord make us truly thankful. For Jesus Christ's sake. Amen.*

# NOVEMBER

November 1 is the day appointed for honoring all the saints in the church calendar. Actually, All Hallows' Eve, on October 31, and All Souls' Day, on November 2, merge with the Feast of All Saints into one remembrance—not only of the great band of witnesses, saints, and martyrs who faced death for the faith with a song on their lips and joy in their hearts, but also the long line of uncanonized "saints" whom we all have known in our families, church, and community. Not facing the fire, or the cross or the lion's den, many of them leading quiet, undramatic lives, they nonetheless testify to the love of God in a way that is perhaps easier for us to recognize than in those shadowy figures of the past.

## *Thanksgiving*

Our Thanksgiving dinners vary from region to region, but one standard item on the menu is the bird called in foreign tongues "french bird," "indian," or "turkey" in the mistaken belief that it came from these parts. The original wild turkey is a purely American product and was not introduced into Europe until after 1530. Corn and cranberries are also thought of as "ours," but we have so many good things in this diverse country that almost anything would serve to remind us of our blessings. See Turkey dinner from Virginia (page 100) or from Guatemala (page 103).

*November 30—St. Andrew's Day*

### THOUGHTS AFTER AN INORDINATE NUMBER OF PARISH SUPPERS

*Are there casseroles in Heaven?*
*Do they toss the salad high?*
*Will the biscuits need less leaven*
*For that banquet in the sky?*
*Do the angels wait on tables*
*While the coffee meekly drips*
*And the martyrs who are able*
*Fiercely wrestle with the chips?*

*O the hamburg and the noodles*
*And the transcendental bean!*
*May the Lord forgive the doodles*
*Of a scribe no longer lean!*

# "Come Again" Cranberry
## Thanksgiving Bread  .

2 cups sifted all purpose flour
1½ teaspoons baking powder
1 teaspoon salt
½ teaspoon soda
1 cup sugar
¼ cup shortening
2 teaspoons grated orange rind

½ cup orange juice
¼ cup water
1 egg, well beaten
1½ cups cranberries, coarsely
   ground
1 cup All-Bran cereal

Sift flour, baking powder, salt, soda, and sugar. Cut in shortening fine. Add orange rind. Combine orange juice, water, and egg; add to flour mixture and beat well. Add cranberries and bran. Pour batter into greased 9×5×3-inch loaf pan. Bake in slow oven at 325 degrees for 75–85 minutes. Store 24 hours before cutting. Makes 1 large loaf.

Martha Burt / *Diocese of Ohio*

Janet Morgan
*Amherst, Massachusetts*

39

# Menus from Near and Far

*From simple family fare to large buffets and formal dinners, a diverse collection of menus from every province of the Episcopal Church; including deliciously different contributions from dioceses in the Philippines, the Caribbean, Mexico, and Guatemala*

# LUNCH AND BRUNCH MENUS

(* Recipes for the starred dishes appear below the menus.)

## *A Brunch with a Punch for 8*

* Milk Punch
* Beef Rounds in Wine Sauce
* Garlic Cheese Grits
* Dried Fruit Compote
  Biscuits and Preserves

### Milk Punch

**1 quart milk**                    **1 pint bourbon**
**1 quart ice cream**

Mix and place in refrigerator several days ahead of the party. Stir occasionally. Sprinkle nutmeg on each serving.

43

## Beef Rounds in Wine Sauce

3 to 4 pounds round steak, ½
  inch thick
½ cup bacon drippings
½ cup flour
1 cup chopped onions
2 cups chopped green onions
1 cup chopped celery
1 cup chopped green peppers
2 cloves garlic, minced
2 cups canned tomatoes, chopped

¾ teaspoon thyme
1 cup water
1 cup red wine
3 teaspoons salt
½ teaspoon black pepper
2 bay leaves
½ teaspoon Tabasco
2 tablespoons Worcestershire
  sauce
3 tablespoons chopped parsley

Remove fat from meat. Cut meat into serving-size pieces. Pound to ¼-inch thick. Brown meat well in 4 tablespoons of the bacon fat in a black iron dutch oven. Remove meat, add remaining bacon fat and flour. Stir and brown flour well. Add onions, green onions, celery, green pepper, garlic; saute until clear. Add chopped tomatoes and thyme and cook for 3 minutes. Add water and wine. Stir for several minutes; add meat, salt and seasonings except for parsley. Simmer for about 2 hours, stirring occasionally. Remove bay leaves, add parsley. Cool, let sit overnight in refrigerator. Reheat before serving. Serves 8.

## Garlic Cheese Grits

1 cup yellow grits, uncooked
4 cups water
1 tablespoon salt
8 tablespoons butter

1 roll garlic cheese
½ pound sharp cheese, grated
2 tablespoons Worcestershire
  sauce

Cook grits in salted water. When cooked, add butter and remaining ingredients. Put in greased casserole and sprinkle with paprika. Bake in a 350 degree oven for 15 to 20 minutes.

## Dried Fruit Compote

1½ pounds mixed dried fruit,
  pears, peaches, apricots, prunes
3 cups water
3 cups sugar

3 whole cloves
1½-inch cinnamon sticks
Cointreau to taste
Fresh orange sections

Wash dried fruit and soak 12 hours in water. Place in a saucepan with sugar, cloves and cinnamon; simmer until fruit is soft. Remove fruit and boil the juice a few minutes longer until it is syrupy. Remove cloves and cinnamon; add Cointreau to taste. Pour over warm fruit, garnish with orange sections and serve. Also good served cold.

Alice Witcher / *Diocese of Long Island (New York)*

---

*When our family gathers at dinner we tend to break into song.*
*This French grace, sung as a round, is a favorite.*
*Pour ce repas et toutes joies, nous te louons, Seigneur.*

Pour|ce repas et|tout-es joies nous|te lou-ons Seigneur

# A Hamburger Menu From Dairyland

Serves 8

* Dairyland Hamburger Casserole
  Tossed Salad—Rolls
* Brockel Torte

## Dairyland Hamburger Casserole

1 8-ounce package of noodles, medium size
1½ pounds chopped beef
1 tablespoon butter
2 8-ounce cans tomato sauce
1 cup cottage cheese
½ cup sour cream
1 8-ounce package cream cheese
⅓ cup chopped green onions
1 tablespoon chopped green pepper
2 tablespoons melted butter

Cook noodles according to directions on package. Brown beef in butter. Add tomato sauce. Combine cottage cheese and sour cream with softened cream cheese, and add onions and green pepper. Butter a large casserole and spread half the noodles on the bottom. Cover with the cheese mixture. Put the remaining noodles on top of this and pour the melted butter over the noodles. Top with the tomato-beef mixture. Put casserole in 350-degree oven until heated through. This will be about 20 minutes if done immediately, or about 45 minutes if prepared ahead and heated later. Serves 8.

## Brockel Torte

6 eggs
1⅓ cups confectioners sugar
6 tablespoons bread crumbs
2 teaspoons baking powder
1 cup cut-up dates
1 cup broken walnuts
½ cup heavy cream, whipped

46

Beat eggs well. Add sugar, beat again. Add baking powder and bread crumbs to dates and nuts. Then add the beaten eggs and sugar to the date and nut mixture. Pour into a 9 × 9-inch ungreased pan. Bake at 350 degrees for 20 to 30 minutes. Test for doneness with a toothpick. Cake should be moist and not brown. When cake is cool, cut or break into 1½ × 1½-inch pieces. Whip the cream. Fold the broken cake into the whipped cream about 30 minutes before serving. Serves 8.

Mabel Gaskell / *Diocese of Milwaukee*

# A Hot Sandwich Lunch Before a Committee Meeting

Serves 4-6

* Hot Ham and Cheese Sandwiches
* Tang Salad
* Oatmeal Cookies

## Hot Ham and Cheese Sandwiches

1 package frozen broccoli
1 can cheddar cheese soup (or made-from-scratch cheese sauce)

1 3-ounce package pressed ham
4 to 6 slices toast

Cook broccoli according to package directions and drain. Heat soup with ⅓ can water until bubbly. Put ham, then broccoli on toast slices, then pour soup sauce over all. Serve very hot. Serves 4-6.

**47**

## Tang Salad

Mix 2 cups water and Tang according to package directions. Soften 1 envelope plain gelatin in small amount of mixed Tang. Heat remaining Tang to boiling point. Remove from heat and add gelatin solution. Mix well to dissolve gelatin and chill until thickening begins. Add canned fruit (peaches or apricots are especially good) and pour into molds. Serves 4-6.

## Oatmeal Cookies

| | |
|---|---|
| 1 cup shortening | ⅓ cup milk |
| 2 cups brown sugar | 1 cup flour |
| 2 teaspoons vanilla | ½ teaspoon salt |
| 2 eggs | 3 cups oatmeal |

Cream shortening, brown sugar and vanilla until fluffy. Add eggs and milk and beat well. Combine flour, salt and oatmeal in a separate bowl. Add to first mixture ⅓ at a time, stirring well after each addition. Drop by teaspoons on greased cookie sheet 2 inches apart. Bake about 10 minutes at 350 degrees.

Ruthie Gray / *Diocese of Mississippi*

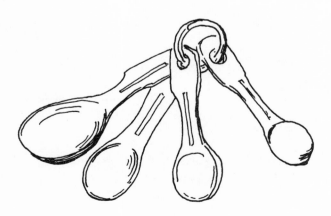

# Meatless Luncheon Menu for 6

* Garlic Grits
* Tossed Green Salad, Italian Dressing
* Bread Sticks
* Apple Cottage Pudding with Lemon
  Sauce

## Garlic Grits

Preheat oven to 300 degrees. Cook 1 cup grits according to directions on package, but using 3 cups water instead of 4. When grits are done, add:

| | |
|---|---|
| **1 roll Kraft garlic cheese** | **¼ cup milk** |
| **½ stick oleo** | **Red pepper, salt and black** |
| **2 eggs, well beaten** | **pepper to taste** |

Pour into greased baking dish and bake for 45 minutes at 300 degrees. Remove from oven and sprinkle on top:

| | |
|---|---|
| **¼ cup grated sharp cheese** | **Paprika** |

Return to oven and bake 15 minutes longer. Serves 6.

## Tossed Green Salad, Italian Dressing

Wash, dry thoroughly, tear into bite-size pieces and chill:

| | |
|---|---|
| **1 head iceberg lettuce** | **1 head romaine lettuce** |

Place in plastic bag in refrigerator. When ready to serve, place in salad bowl with

*Italian Dressing*
Place in bowl:

| | |
|---|---|
| **6 tablespoons olive oil** | **1 clove garlic, mashed** |

49

Mix well. Discard bits of garlic. Add and beat well with wire whisk:

**2 tablespoons wine vinegar**
**Juice of ½ lemon**

**1 teaspoon each salt and freshly**
**ground black pepper**

## Bread Sticks

Cut each slice of day-old regular sliced bread into 3 pieces. Dip lightly in melted oleo, place on cookie sheet, sprinkle with whole poppy seed, caraway seed and sesame seed. Place in 200-degree oven overnight.

## Apple Cottage Pudding With Lemon Sauce

Preheat oven to 350 degrees. Sift and set aside:

**¾ cup flour**
**2 teaspoons baking powder**
**¼ teaspoon salt**

**½ teaspoon ground cinnamon**
**¼ teaspoon ground cloves**

Beat until light and foamy:

**2 eggs**

Add and beat until lemon colored:

**1 cup sugar**

Stir in dry ingredients. Fold in:

**4 cups peeled chopped apples**

Turn into greased 6 × 10 × 2-inch baking dish. Bake at 350 degrees for 45 minutes or until it tests done. Serve with

*Lemon Sauce*
Blend in 3-cup saucepan

**1 tablespoon cornstarch**
**¼ cup cold water**

**½ cup sugar**

50

Stir in ¾ cup boiling water. Cook 1 minute until sauce thickens. Add and stir in

**1 tablespoon butter**
**2 tablespoons lemon juice**

**½ teaspoon grated lemon rind**

Serve hot over pudding. Serves 6.

Hazel Goddard / *Diocese of Texas*

# *Maida's Marvelous Macaroni Makes Memorable Meatless Menu*

### Serves 6 to 8

* Maida's Really Outstanding Macaroni
    Casserole
* Nedi's Delicious Herb Bread
  Lime-Pineapple Salad
  Lemon Sherbet with Chocolate Sauce

## Maida's Really Outstanding Macaroni Casserole

**12 ounces mostaccioli-type pasta**
**1 30-ounce can whole peeled**
  **tomatoes with liquid**
**12 ounces medium sharp cheddar**
  **cheese, coarsely shredded**

**9 ounces canned sliced**
  **mushrooms (or cuts and**
  **pieces), drained**

Cook pasta according to package directions to j-u-s-t this side of *al dente* consistency (it will cook further in the oven). Drain and rinse. Drop tomatoes into blender and "flick" once or twice (or chop into medium-size pieces with a knife). Toss all ingredients together and bake, uncovered, in 11½ × 7-inch casserole dish (or 2-quart size) in a 325-degree oven until warmed through and bubbly. If desired, reserve some of the cheese, shred finely and sprinkle over the top. Serves 6 to 8.

51

If casserole is tightly covered for storage in the refrigerator, it improves with age. It does not, however, freeze successfully. Cover casserole when reheating.

## Nedi's Delicious Herb Bread

1 large loaf sourdough French
  bread
½ cup soft butter
¼ teaspoon oregano
½ teaspoon dill

1 clove garlic, finely chopped or
  smashed
¼ cup finely chopped parsley
¼ cup grated Parmesan cheese

Mix together butter, oregano, dill, garlic and half the parsley. Spread on bread, which has been sliced down to but not through the bottom crust. Make a foil "boat" to hold bread in oven. Sprinkle Parmesan cheese and remaining parsley on top. Bake in a 400-degree oven for 10-15 minutes. Serve piping hot. Serves 6-8.

## Lime-Pineapple Salad

2 packages lime Jello
2 cups crushed pineapple,
  drained

16 ounces cream-style cottage
  cheese
12 ounces miniature marshmallows

Add Jello to 2 cups boiling water and stir to dissolve thoroughly. Add 2 cups ice and water and stir until ice melts. Chill until partially thickened. Fold in pineapple, cottage cheese and marshmallows. Pour into 2-quart mold and chill until firm. Unmold on lettuce leaves. Serve mayonnaise on the side. Serves 6-8.

Barbara Rivera / *Diocese of San Joaquin (California)*

# A Luncheon for 8 Guild Members

* Anita's Tuna and Asparagus Casserole
* Fresh Fruit Tray with Poppyseed
    Dressing
  Hot Buttered Biscuits or French Bread
  Lemon Squares (page 228)

## Anita's Tuna and Asparagus Casserole

6 ounces of *very fine* noodles
1 14-ounce can green asparagus, drained
2 7-ounce cans tuna fish
1 4-ounce can mushrooms, stems and pieces
1 cup grated sharp cheddar cheese

1 can condensed mushroom soup
1 can condensed cream of chicken soup
½ cup mayonnaise
½ cup pecans, chopped
Parmesan cheese

Cook and drain the noodles. Place a layer of noodles in a buttered 2-quart casserole, and on top of that place a layer of asparagus, then a layer of tuna, then the mushrooms and cheese. Heat the soups and mayonnaise together (or mix in blender) and pour over all and top with pecans and a sprinkling of Parmesan cheese. Bake at 350 degrees for about 45 minutes. Serves 8.

## Fresh Fruit Tray

Place lettuce on a large glass or silver tray and arrange grapefruit sections, orange sections, strawberries, if available, slices of avocado, apple, banana or whatever is available. It can be filled in with canned apricot halves or pineapple fingers. Amounts vary according to number to be served. Serve this with:

53

## Poppyseed Dressing

| | |
|---|---|
| 1 cup salad oil | ⅓ teaspoon or a very small |
| ⅓ cup sugar | amount of grated onion |
| 1 teaspoon salt | ½ cup vinegar |
| 1 teaspoon dry mustard | 1 tablespoon poppy seeds |

Shake all together in a jar and keep in the refrigerator.

Charlotte West / *Diocese of Florida*

For this food,
For all things,
For one another,
We thank you, Gracious Lord.
In Jesus' name. Amen.

# A Make-ahead Buffet Luncheon for 10

* Margarella Tuna Bake
  Rice
  Green Salad
* Frozen Strawberry Mousse

## Margarella Tuna Bake

6 tablespoons margarine
2 medium onions, chopped
2 diced green peppers
½ pound mushrooms, sliced
2 cans condensed tomato soup

½ pint coffee cream or
  evaporated milk
2 cans tuna (9¼-ounce size)
1 small jar pimientos
Salt and pepper

Melt margarine in skillet (electric fry pan works very well), add vegetables, stir and cook until onions are transparent. Add soup and cream mixed together. Cook at moderate heat for a few minutes. Add pimientos and tuna which has been drained and rinsed. Reheat. Serves 10.

## Frozen Strawberry Mousse

¼ cup milk
¼ cup sugar
4 cups miniature marshmallows
1 teaspoon vanilla

1-pound package frozen
  strawberries, partially defrosted
2 cups whipped dessert topping

Heat milk and sugar to the boiling point. Put marshmallows into blender, add hot milk, blend until smooth, about 25 seconds. Add vanilla and strawberries. Blend at medium speed for 15 seconds. Pour into large bowl and fold in whipped topping. Pour into 9×5×3-inch pan and freeze. Serves 10.

Maureen Atkins / *Diocese of Eau Claire (Wisconsin)*

55

# Lunch for 6 with a Golden Gate Air

* San Francisco Devilled Crab
* Barbecue Salad
  Hot Biscuits
* Frozen Pineapple Torte

## San Francisco Devilled Crab

1 pound crabmeat (or 2 6½-ounce
  cans or 2 6-ounce frozen
  packages)
1½ cups cracker crumbs
¾ cup chopped celery
¾ cup chopped onion
¼ cup chopped parsley

1 tablespoon chopped green
  pepper
1 teaspoon dry mustard
½ teaspoon salt
Dash cayenne pepper
⅔ cup butter
¼ cup heavy cream

Remove any cartilage from crabmeat. Crush crackers and chop all vegetables. Mix all ingredients together thoroughly. Spoon into 1½-quart greased casserole or greased shells or ramekins. Dot top with additional butter. Bake casserole in a 350-degree oven for 30-40 minutes. Bake shells for about 20 minutes. Serves 6.

## Barbecue Salad

1 package lemon or orange Jello
1¼ cup hot water
1 8-ounce can tomato sauce

1½ tablespoons vinegar
½ teaspoon salt
Dash of pepper

Dissolve Jello in hot water; add remaining ingredients. Pour into molds. Refrigerate. When firm, unmold on lettuce. Add mayonnaise or onion dressing. Serves 6-8.

## Frozen Pineapple Torte

| | |
|---|---|
| 3 egg yolks | 3 egg whites |
| Dash of salt | 2 tablespoons sugar |
| ½ cup sugar | 1 cup heavy cream |
| 1 9-ounce can crushed pineapple, drained | 2 cups vanilla wafer crumbs or graham cracker crumbs. |
| 2 tablespoons lemon juice | |

Beat egg yolks, salt and ½ cup sugar; add the syrup from your pineapple and the lemon juice. Cook over hot, not boiling water, until mixture coats spoon, stirring constantly. Add your crushed pineapple and set aside to cool. Whip your egg whites stiff and add 2 tablespoons sugar. Whip heavy cream. When your first custard mixture is cool, then fold in both the whipped egg whites and the whipped cream. Coat the sides of an oiled refrigerator tray with vanilla wafer or graham cracker crumbs. Spread half the wafers on bottom and sides of tray. Pour in your mixture; add remaining crumbs on top. Freeze firm, about 4 hours. Serves 6-8.

Kay Gilliam / *Diocese of Montana*

---

A BLESSING

*O thou who clothest the lilies*
*And feedest the birds of the sky*
*Who leadest the lambs to the pasture*
*And the hart to the waterside*
*Who has multiplied loaves and fishes*
*And converted water into wine*
*Do thou come to our table*
*As guest and giver to dine.   Amen.*

# A Light Luncheon Menu for an ECW Meeting

Serves 6

* Crab and Shrimp with Almonds
Spiced Apple Rings or Spiced Peaches
Salad of Two Kinds of Lettuce and
    Marinated Artichoke Hearts
* Judy's Brownies

## Crab and Shrimp with Almonds

1 generous cup crabmeat
1 generous cup shrimp, peeled
    and deveined
1 can condensed cream of
    mushroom soup
1 can condensed cream of shrimp
    soup

1 cup chopped celery
¼ cup minced green onions
1 3-ounce can Chinese fried
    noodles
1 2-ounce package slivered
    almonds

Combine first 6 ingredients and place in greased 2-quart casserole. Refrigerate. When ready to bake, fold in noodles, top with almonds, and bake at 375 degrees, uncovered, for 25 minutes or until piping hot. Can be made ahead. Serves 6.

## Judy's Brownies

2 sticks oleo
2 squares unsweetened chocolate
4 eggs
2 cups sugar

1 cup flour
2 teaspoons vanilla
1 cup chopped nuts

Melt oleo and chocolate. Beat eggs and sugar. Add flour, oleo, and chocolate. Add vanilla and nuts. Bake in large greased pan (about 9 × 13 inches) at 300 degrees for 45 minutes to 1 hour.

Marje Gosnell / *Diocese of West Texas*

# Philippine Lunch Menu—for Every Day and Special Days

Serves 6

Every Day Main Course:
* Paksiw na Isda (Braised fish)
    Special Day Main Course:
* Kari-Karing Pata (Calf's leg stew)
    Boiled Rice
* Leche Flan (Vanilla custard)

## Paksiw na Isda (Braised fish)

| | |
|---|---|
| 1 4-pound fish, well cleaned | 1 tablespoon salt pork lard |
| ¼ cup water | ¼ teaspoon ground black pepper |
| 1½ tablespoons vinegar | Salt to taste |
| 1-inch piece fresh ginger, crushed | ½ green pepper, sliced |

Place fish in pot and over it sprinkle the water, vinegar, ginger, lard, pepper and salt. Bring to a boil, then simmer, covered, until done. Add sliced green pepper before removing pan from fire. Do not overcook. Serves 6.

## Kari-Karing (Calf's leg stew)

1 calf's leg (pata) or 3 pounds
   boneless veal
5 tablespoons cooking oil
3 cloves garlic, crushed
1 big red onion, sliced
Salt to taste
1 heart of cooking banana (puso
   ng saging), sliced finely
20 string beans, cut in 4-inch
   pieces

4 small eggplants, cut in 1-inch
   cubes
3 small radishes, peeled and
   sliced
2 tablespoons seeds of Achuete or
   1 tablespoon red food coloring
⅓ cup toasted rice, powdered
½ cup toasted peanuts, ground,
   or peanut butter

Clean calf's leg, wash thoroughly, then cut into desired pieces. Pressure cook for 15 minutes, or until tender. Set aside. In a deep pan heat the cooking oil or lard and saute the garlic, onion and tender calf's leg for a few minutes. Add salt to taste and the sliced banana heart. When the banana heart is almost tender, add the string beans, then the eggplant and radish. Wash the seeds of achuete and soak in ½ cup water. Add this colored water or 1 tablespoon red food coloring to the mixture. Add the powdered rice and peanuts, stirring to avoid sticking. Serve with bagoong (anchovy) alamang sauted with pork, and with boiled rice. Serves 6.

## Leche Flan (Vanilla custard)

1 cup sugar
3 Grade A eggs
2¼ cups evaporated milk
1 teaspoon vanilla

Caramelize ¼ cup of the sugar by melting in a heavy pan until golden. Line a mold evenly with the caramelized sugar and let stand. Beat eggs well. Add the rest of the sugar 1 tablespoon at a time and continue to beat after each addition until all sugar is added. Pour evaporated milk and vanilla into the beaten eggs and beat for 2 minutes more. Pour into mold. Place mold in a bigger pan filled with water. Bake in a 325-degree oven until mixture becomes firm. Chill before unmolding. Serves 6.

Esther G. Manguramos / *Diocese of Southern Philippines*

# DINNER MENUS

## *A Dinner Menu for Just the Two of Us*

(and if friends stop by there's enough for them too)
Serves 2 to 6

  * A Wine Stew
    Noodles
    Tossed Green Salad
  * A Black Cherry Gelatin

### A Wine Stew

2 pounds of stew meat, cubed
2 cans condensed cream of
   mushroom soup

1 package Lipton's Onion Soup
   Mix
1 cup Chianti wine

Toss these ingredients into a 3-quart casserole, stir them up, put the cover on, and bake at 275 degrees for 4 or 5 hours, or until the meat is tender.

### A Black Cherry Gelatin

1 6-ounce package lemon or
   cherry gelatin
1 16-ounce can black cherries,
   pitted

1 15-ounce can sweetened
   condensed milk

Let the gelatin set until slightly thickened. Add the chilled condensed milk and beat until the mixture is light and fluffy. Add drained cherries. Chill and serve.

Nancy Burroughs / *Diocese of Ohio*

# A Sincerely Pleasing Dinner Menu

## Serves 4 to 6

* Beef Birds and Mushroom Gravy
* Mashed Potato Casserole
  Buttered Green Beans
* Skimmed Milk Sherbet
  Cookies

## Beef Birds and Mushroom Gravy

1½ to 2 pounds round steak or lean chuck roast, cut in thin strips 1½ to 2 inches wide by 5 to 6 inches long
Bacon strips, halved or quartered (same number as steak strips)
Onion wedges (same number as steak strips)
Fat for browning
1 10½-ounce can cream of mushroom soup
¼ pound fresh mushrooms, sliced, or 1 small can sliced mushrooms

Salt and pepper meat strips. Place bacon strips on the meat and an onion wedge at the end of each meat strip. Beginning at the onion end, roll the meat up and secure with toothpicks or string. Brown rolls in fat in large frying pan. Dilute soup with 1 can of water and add to frying pan. Simmer, covered, for about 2 hours. The meat should be very tender. Thin gravy if necessary. Add sliced mushrooms (if fresh, saute first in a little butter or bacon fat) and stir into gravy. When ready to serve, remove toothpicks or string. Allow 2 or 3 beef rolls per person. Serves 4-6.

## Mashed Potato Casserole

1 8-ounce package cream cheese
4 cups hot mashed potatoes
1 egg, beaten

⅓ cup finely chopped onion
1 teaspoon salt
Dash of pepper

Combine softened cream cheese and potatoes, mixing until well blended. Add remaining ingredients and place in 1-quart casserole. Bake at 350 degrees for 45 minutes. This can be prepared early in the day and placed in oven in time for dinner. Serves 4–6.

## Skimmed Milk Sherbet

2 cups skimmed milk
1 cup sugar

Juice of 2 lemons
½ can frozen orange juice

Bring milk and sugar to a boil, stirring to dissolve sugar. Place mixture in the freezer and freeze solid. Remove from freezer and mash with a potato masher. Add fruit juices, mix well and return to freezer. Can be made a day ahead. Serves 4-6.

Trudy Sheridan / *Diocese of Northern Indiana*

# A Distinctive Meat Loaf Dinner for 6

* Meat Loaf with Herbs
* Rice and Mushroom Pilau
* Glazed Julienne Carrots
  Mixed Green Salad
* Fruit Compote

## Meat Loaf with Herbs

1 pound very lean beef, ground
½ pound very lean veal, ground
½ cup bread crumbs
1 very small onion, minced
¼ teaspoon summer savory
⅛ teaspoon soy oil

½ teaspoon salt
¼ teaspoon black pepper
¼ cup skim milk
¼ cup red table wine

Place all ingredients into a mixing bowl, mix well and shape into loaf. Place on a baking sheet. Bake at 325 degrees for 1 hour or longer. Serves 6.

## Rice and Mushroom Pilau

¼ cup vegetable oil
½ pound mushrooms, sliced
½ cup chopped onions
2 cups canned tomatoes
½ cup water

1 cup uncooked rice
2 tablespoons chopped parsley
1½ teaspoon salt
Few grains pepper

Heat oil in deep skillet. Add mushrooms and onions. Cook very slowly until lightly browned. Add tomatoes and water; bring to a boil. Add rice and remaining ingredients. Cover and cook about 30 minutes until rice is tender. If drier rice is desired, cover may be removed for last 5 minutes. Serves 6.

## Glazed Julienne Carrots

3½ cups julienne carrot strips (1
   pound)
¼ cup water
½ teaspoon salt
2 tablespoons safflower margarine
3 tablespoons sugar
Nutmeg (fresh ground if possible)

Place carrots, water and salt in saucepan. Cover and cook over low heat for about 10 minutes (carrots should be firm). Add margarine and sugar. Cook, uncovered until carrots are tender and well glazed —stirring gently all the while. Sprinkle with nutmeg. Serves 6.

## Fruit Compote

Ripe strawberries
Peaches, quartered

Plums, quartered
Apricots, halved

Make a syrup of 1 part honey and 2 parts water and bring to boil; add lemon slice or lemon peel if desired. Pour boiling syrup over fruit, just enough to cover. Cover and refrigerate. Serve very cold.

Jeanne Bigliardi / *Diocese of Oregon*

# One of our Favorite Dinners at the Bishop's House

Serves 6 to 8

Cream of Crab Soup with hot bread
   sticks (dipped in melted butter
   and rolled in grated cheese)
Standing Rib Roast of Beef
Stuffed Baked Potatoes (chopped onion
   and parsley added to the mashed
   stuffing)
* Brussels Sprouts and Chestnuts
* Baked Dried Corn
Plum Pudding with brandy-flavored
   Hard Sauce

## Brussels Sprouts and Chestnuts

| | |
|---|---|
| ½ to 1 pound of chestnuts | 1 quart box of Brussels sprouts |
| ½ cup butter | 3 tablespoons of flour |
| 2 tablespoons sugar | Salt to taste |

Prepare the chestnuts for shelling. Cut a cross mark in the chestnuts and boil for 15 to 20 minutes. Then shell and remove the skin. Easier to do while hot. Melt half of the butter until brown with 2 tablespoons sugar. Let chestnuts simmer in this mixture.

Clean and boil the sprouts until tender. Reserve 1 cup of the liquid in which they were boiled. Melt the balance of the butter, stir in the flour, and add liquid from the sprouts. Cook until smooth. Add salt to taste, sprouts and chestnuts and simmer together. Hold in double boiler until ready to serve. Serves 6-8.

## Baked Dried Corn

| | |
|---|---|
| 1 cup dried corn | 2 tablespoons sugar |
| 3 cups milk | 2 eggs, well beaten |
| 2 tablespoons butter, melted | 1 teaspoon salt |

Grind the dried corn in a blender or food chopper. Add the other ingredients and mix thoroughly. Bake in a buttered casserole dish for 50 minutes in a 375-degree oven. Serves 6-8.

Alta Heistand / *Diocese of Harrisburg (Pennsylvania)*

# *Dinner at Bishop's House in Okinawa*

### Serves 6 to 8

Baked Ham
* Chinese Fried Rice
* Corn Pudding
Tomato Aspic
Tiny Hot Rolls
* Wine Jelly

## Chinese Fried Rice
### (As prepared by the Benedictine Sisters of Peking)

2½ tablespoons oil
2½ cups coarsely chopped onions
3 cups cold cooked rice
3 eggs
2 tablespoons soy sauce
¾ teaspoon salt

About 2 cups of any of the following, or a mixture, as desired: chopped cooked ham, chicken, beef, shrimp; green peas, sliced mushrooms, sliced green peppers, bean sprouts, peanuts

**67**

Heat pan, add oil, fry onions until brown. Add rice and saute. Combine eggs, soy sauce and salt, stir slightly and add to pan. Saute, stirring, as the 2 cups of optional ingredients are added. Keep on low heat, covered, until serving time. Serves 6-8.

# Corn Pudding

2 slices bread, generously
   buttered
2 cups drained corn liquid and
   evaporated milk

2 eggs, beaten
1 can whole kernel corn, drained
Salt and pepper to taste

Cut buttered bread into as tiny cubes as possible. Soak in the drained corn liquid with evaporated milk added to make 2 cups. Fold in beaten eggs. Fold in corn and seasonings. Put in greased casserole and bake in moderate oven, 350 degrees, for 45 minutes to 1 hour. It can stand when done about 45 minutes (while someone has an extra cocktail). Serves 6-8.

# Wine Jelly

1 package lemon Jello
1 cup boiling orange juice
¼ cup cold orange juice

¼ cup cold water
½ cup sherry

Dissolve Jello in boiling orange juice. Add cold orange juice and water. Cool slightly and add sherry. Pour in mold. Chill until firm. Unmold. Serve with cream or topping.

Dorothy Gilson / *Diocese of Honolulu*

---

*"Contribute to the needs of the saints, practice hospitality."*
*Romans 12:13*

# A Casual and not too costly Dinner for 8

* Tasty Triscuits
* Hamburger and Wild Rice Casserole
  Tossed Salad with Italian Dressing
  Buttered French Bread
* Fudge Cake

## Tasty Triscuits

Triscuits buttered, then sprinkled with lemon pepper, topped with your favorite cheese slice (we like hot pepper cheese) and run in a 400-degree oven for about 5 minutes.

## Hamburger and Wild Rice Casserole

2 cups boiling water
⅔ cups uncooked wild rice
1 10½-ounce can condensed
   chicken and rice soup
1 small can sliced mushrooms
½ cup water

1 bay leaf
¼ teaspoon each celery salt, garlic
   salt, onion salt, paprika, pepper
3 tablespoons salad oil
¾ pound lean ground beef
3 tablespoons chopped onion

Pour boiling water over wild rice; let stand 15 minutes, covered; drain. Place rice in a 2-quart casserole. Add soup, mushrooms, water, bay leaf and seasonings. Heat salad oil in a skillet and brown beef and onion. When brown, add to rice and refrigerate overnight —or all day long, if you make it in the morning—so the flavors can meld. Bake, covered, in a 325-degree oven for 2 hours. Serves 8.

69

## Fudge Cake

| | |
|---|---|
| 4 squares unsweetened chocolate | ½ cup coarsely chopped pecans |
| ½ pound butter | Pinch of salt |
| 2 cups sugar | 1 teaspoon vanilla |
| 4 eggs | ¼ cup Jamaica rum |
| 1½ cups sifted flour | |

Melt chocolate and butter in top of double boiler. Stir in sugar, then eggs one at a time, beating well after each addition. Dust ¼ cup of the flour on the nuts. Blend remaining flour, salt and vanilla into the chocolate-egg mixture, adding nuts last. Bake in 12 × 12 × 1½-inch pan, well greased and floured, in a 350-degree oven for 25 to 30 minutes. Let stand in pan for 10 minutes, then sprinkle with the rum. When cool, ice with:

*Fudge Frosting*

| | |
|---|---|
| 3 tablespoons butter | 2½ cups confectioners sugar |
| 3 squares unsweetened chocolate | 1 teaspoon vanilla |
| ¼ cup hot milk | Pinch of salt |

Melt butter and chocolate in top of double boiler over hot water. In a separate bowl, stir hot milk into sugar and beat until smooth. Add vanilla, chocolate-butter mixture and salt. Beat until smooth and thickened.

Emmy Cerveny / *Diocese of Florida*

# *A Carefree Cook-ahead Dinner for Family or Friends*

Serves 8

* Oven Stew
* Savoury Spinach Salad
  Bran Muffins (page 157)
  Applesauce Cake (page 223)

## Oven Stew

3 pounds beef chuck, cut in
  1-inch pieces
3 onions, sliced
3 carrots, sliced
1 small can baby peas, with
  liquid
2½ cups canned tomatoes, with
  liquid

½ cup pearl tapioca (do not use
  instant; pearl tapioca is the
  secret of the thickener)
2 teaspoons salt
½ teaspoon pepper

Toss all of this into a casserole or dutch oven. Cover and cook in a 250-degree oven for 4½ to 5 hours. Stir once or twice during the cooking. You may want to add more carrots or onions than called for, also potatoes, if desired. It is not necessary to brown the meat or wait until later to add vegetables. You will have brown gravy and the vegetables will not be overcooked.

This stew can be made ahead, frozen, and used later, whole or in parts. The flavor seems to improve with each reheating. Serves 8.

## Savoury Spinach Salad

½ cup oil
½ cup sugar
½ cup catsup
¼ cup wine vinegar
1 tablespoon Worcestershire sauce
1 onion, grated

1 10-ounce bag of spinach
1 16-ounce can of bean sprouts
1 8-ounce can of water chestnuts
4 hard-cooked eggs, sliced
8 strips of bacon, fried crisp and
  crumbled

Mix the first 6 ingredients and set aside. Wash the spinach, drain and chill the canned ingredients. Toss together with the eggs and bacon bits and dressing. The dressing is also good for use as barbecue sauce on beef short ribs. Serves 8.

Ginny Thornberry / *Diocese of Wyoming*

# Menu for a Relaxed Hostess: A Step-By-Step Buffet

Serves 8

* Cocktail Appetizers (Step 3)
* Beef Hash with Sherry (Steps 1 & 7)
  Rice (Steps 4 & 8)
  Tomato, Avocado and Watercress Salad
      (Step 5)
  Meringue Cookies (Step 2)

This is a good choice for a buffet supper. The food is already cut up into small pieces, so that guests need not juggle with knife and fork on a precariously tilted plate.

*STEP 1:* In the morning, prepare:

## Beef Hash with Sherry

4 pounds beef, chuck or round,
    diced
2 tablespoons fat
1 large onion, minced
2 cloves garlic, minced
2 green peppers, minced

1 teaspoon salt
3 large peeled tomatoes or 2½
    cups canned tomatoes, chopped
1 teaspoon minced parsley
1 cup sherry
2 cups water

Ask the butcher to cut the meat into 1-inch cubes, then cut it smaller yourself with a sharp knife or a pair of scissors. Leftover beef, lamb, or veal may be combined with fresh meat as an economy measure. Ground meat may also be used, either alone or in combination with cubed meat.

First melt the fat in a skillet or large, heavy aluminum kettle. (A pressure cooker may be used nicely.) Then add meat and minced onion, garlic, and green pepper to the fat, and brown lightly. Add chopped fresh or canned tomatoes, salt, and parsley. Simmer 10 minutes. Add sherry and water. Cover with tight-fitting cover. Simmer 1 hour, or until meat is tender. (If using a pressure cooker, follow directions for beef stew.) Cool. Leave on back of stove, or place in refrigerator, depending on how far away dinner time remains when you have finished this step. Serves 8. (This recipe can be cut in half for 4. A little more salt may be needed in proportion. Taste to make sure.)

*STEP 2:* Prepare the dessert. A very easy and impressive dessert for a buffet is:

## Meringue Cookies

Make refrigerator cookies, using a standard recipe or a prepared cookie mix. When thoroughly chilled, slice thin, bake according to directions. Next top each cookie with a scant half teaspoon jelly or jam, and spread stiffly beaten, sweetened egg white over the top. One egg white with 1 tablespoon confectioners sugar will make enough meringue for a dozen cookies. Place cookies in oven reduced to 325 degrees for 8 to 10 minutes.

*STEP 3:* Prepare cocktail appetizers. You might offer toasted coconut chips, Cheetos, and:

## Curried Sardine Canapes

1 can sardines
1 3-ounce package cream cheese
Few drops lemon juice

¼ teaspoon curry powder
1 teaspoon sweet or sour cream

Mash sardines with a fork, first removing backbone and ugly bits of skin. Keep light and fluffy. In a separate bowl, whip cream cheese, adding a little sour cream or heavy sweet cream to soften. Season with curry powder. Add lemon juice to taste, adding more if the first few drops don't seem to be enough. Go easy on the lemon at first, though. You could easily add too much. Serve in a bowl surrounded by potato chips and let people dunk, or serve with a butter spreader.

73

*STEP 4:* Wash 1½ cups rice through several waters, until water is clear. You will remove more starch (and the grains will be drier and more separate) if you stir the rice around briskly in a kettle instead of simply holding it under the faucet in a strainer. When rice is well cleaned, place in heavy kettle, one with a tight-fitting cover, add 4 cups water, ½ teaspoon salt. (Or follow directions on rice package.) Cover. Do not cook until 20 minutes before dinner is to be served.

*STEP 5:* Clean watercress. Place in bowl which has been rubbed with garlic. Chill tomato and avocado, but do not cut up until a short time before guests are due. Keep all salad ingredients in refrigerator. Mix French dressing, adding a pinch of curry powder.

*STEP 6:* Set table. Put coffee and water in pot. Arrange cookies on a plate and fruit in a serving bowl. Then have a nice, long bath and get yourself completely relaxed.

*STEP 7:* Make a paste of 2 tablespoons flour with a little water added slowly until it's the consistency of thin cream. Add this to hash. Reheat hash slowly. Have hash at a simmering temperature when guests are due. If a long wait appears possible, turn off the heat under the stew, and bring back to a simmer when everyone is ready to eat.

*STEP 8:* About the time the guests are enjoying a second round of cocktails, turn the heat on under the rice. Watch until it comes to a boil, then turn heat as low as possible. Consult your watch, and let the rice cook exactly 20 minutes. It should have absorbed all the liquid, leaving little "gopher holes" here and there.

Meantime, arrange salad for table. Reheat hash. By time rice is cooked, everything else should be ready, including your guests.

Dorothy Persell / *Diocese of Albany*

# Saturday Night Teens Buffet

Serves 8

* Beans and Burgers
  Slaw Savoy
* Blueberry Muffins
* Spanish Cream
* Walnut Clusters

## Beans and Burgers

1½ pounds ground chuck
1 small onion, minced
1 tablespoon bottled thick meat
  sauce
1 tablespoon snipped parsley
½ teaspoon dried oregano
½ teaspoon dried rosemary
Dash paprika
Salt

¼ teaspoon pepper
¼ cup dried bread crumbs
2 tablespoons salad oil
1 8-ounce can tomato sauce
⅓ cup catsup
½ cup sour cream
1 1-pound can red kidney beans,
  drained and rinsed

In large bowl thoroughly mix chuck, onion, meat sauce, parsley, oregano, rosemary, paprika, 1 teaspoon salt and pepper. Shape this mixture into small meatballs, roll in bread crumbs and saute in hot oil in large skillet until browned on all sides.

Meanwhile, stir together tomato sauce, catsup, sour cream and ¾ teaspoon salt. Add, with kidney beans, to browned meat balls in skillet. Simmer over low heat, uncovered, 15 minutes or until meat is done. Serve from skillet. Serves 8.

## Slaw Savoy

Carefully hollow out a good head of cabbage. Finely shred the center of cabbage, then toss with chopped unpeeled apple, ½ green pepper chopped, one small onion chopped, ½ cup grated carrot. Mix with 3 tablespoons Kraft Coleslaw dressing. Decorate with slivers of tomato. Serves 8.

75

## Blueberry Muffins

2 cups sifted all-purpose flour
3 teaspoons double-acting baking
   powder
1 teaspoon salt
2 tablespoons sugar

1 egg
1 cup milk
6 tablespoons melted shortening
1 cup frozen blueberries

Heat oven to 425 degrees. Grease 14 2½-inch muffin cups well. Sift flour, baking powder, salt and sugar into mixing bowl. Beat egg until frothy, add milk and melted shortening and mix well. Make small well in center of flour mixture, pour in milk mixture all at once. Stir quickly and lightly, DO NOT BEAT—until just mixed, but still lumpy. Quickly stir in berries. Fill muffin cups ⅔ full. Sprinkle tops with granulated sugar.

Bake 25 minutes or until cake tester comes out clean. Run spatula around each muffin to loosen, lift out into napkin-lined basket and serve piping hot.

## Spanish Cream

1 envelope unflavored gelatin
½ cup sugar
¼ teaspoon salt

3 eggs, separated
3 cups milk
1 teaspoon vanilla

In double boiler top, mix gelatin, ¼ cup sugar, salt. Stir in egg yolks, then slowly stir in milk. Cook over boiling water, stirring, until mixture covers spoon.

Refrigerate mixture until slightly thicker than unbeaten egg white, stir in vanilla.

Beat egg whites until they form moist peaks when beater is raised, gradually add ¼ cup sugar, continue beating until whites are stiff. Fold in gelatin mixture.

Refrigerate in bowl. To serve, spoon into sherbet glasses. Serve plain or topped with whipped cream. Serves 8.

### Walnut Clusters

½ cup sifted all purpose flour
¼ teaspoon double-acting baking
   powder
½ teaspoon salt
¼ cup soft butter or margarine
½ cup sugar

1 egg, unbeaten
½ teaspoon vanilla
1½ squares unsweetened
   chocolate, melted
1½ cups broken walnuts

Heat oven to 350 degrees. Sift together flour, baking powder and salt. In large bowl, with mixer at high speed, mix butter, sugar, egg and vanilla, until very light and fluffy. With mixer at low speed, mix in chocolate, then flour mixture. Fold in walnuts.

Drop by teaspoonsful, 1 inch apart, on greased cookie sheet and bake 10 minutes—NO LONGER. Makes approximately 2½ dozen.

Rene Dean / *Diocese of Upper South Carolina*

# A Hearty Mexican Dinner Menu

## Serves 8-10

* Chili
* Mexican Salad
* Hot buttered tortillas
  Relish dish of carrot and celery sticks
        hot peppers, etc.
  Your favorite cookie for dessert

## Chili

⅓ pound beef suet
3 pounds boneless chuck, cubed
   or coarsely ground
3 cloves garlic, finely minced
4 to 6 tablespoons of chili powder
8 tablespoons "masa harina" (if
   you have a Mexican market
   nearby) or

4 tablespoons flour mixed with a
   little corn meal
6 to 8 cups hot beef broth
1 tablespoon vinegar
2 or more hot dried red chilis,
   according to taste.

77

Cut suet in cubes, render to fat, discarding cubes. Add meat and brown. Add garlic, chili powder to taste, salt and pepper. Cook about 2 minutes and sprinkle in masa harina, stirring madly. If using flour, make a paste with broth before adding. Add remaining broth, vinegar and chilis. Cook, partially covered, about 2 hours. Stir occasionally and skim fat as desired. Add more broth if you like chili thinner. Real chili aficionados scorn the addition of tomatoes to chili.

## Mexican Salad

2 cups lettuce, shredded
1 can kidney beans, drained
2 tomatoes, chopped and drained

½ cup chopped ripe olives
1 tablespoon chopped green chilis

Mix and chill the above.
Blend and chill separately:

1 large avocado
½ cup sour cream
2 tablespoons Italian dressing

1 teaspoon chili powder
Salt and pepper to taste

When ready to serve, mix 2 mixtures together, top with grated sharp cheese and mashed Fritos.

## Hot Buttered Tortillas

I use canned tortillas, but if you have a tortilla press and Mexican flour available, make your own. In any case, heat cooked tortillas quickly in a little hot oil, spread with butter and keep in very hot covered dish.

Polly Keller / *Diocese of Arkansas*

*Almighty God, to whom our needs are known before we ask, help us to ask only what accords in your will and those good things which we dare not, or in our blindness cannot ask, grant us for the sake of your Son, Jesus Christ our Lord. Amen.*

# Brisket and Beans Make an Easy Supper

### Serves 10-12

* Brisket in Barbecue Sauce
* Million Dollar Bean Casserole
  Sliced Tomatoes
  Stuffed Mushrooms
  Hot Rolls (page 152)
  Toffee Torte (page 232)

## Brisket in Barbecue Sauce

5-6 pound brisket of beef
2 10½-ounce cans beef
  consomme
6 tablespoons vinegar

12 tablespoons soy sauce
2 tablespoons liquid smoke
Salt, pepper and garlic salt to
  taste

Combine sauce ingredients and pour over brisket. Let stand in refrigerator overnight. Bake at 250 degrees for 5 to 6 hours. Remove meat from sauce. Slice when cool. Before serving, skim fat from sauce, pour over slices and reheat. Serves 10-12.

## Million Dollar Bean Casserole

½ pound bacon, diced
2 medium onions, sliced into
  rings
½ cup vinegar
1 cup brown sugar
¼ teaspoon dry mustard
1 large 20-ounce can large lima
  beans, drained

1 small 10½-ounce can baby lima
  beans, drained
(or 1 package frozen lima beans,
  cooked)
1 small 10½-ounce can red
  kidney beans, drained
1 large 20-ounce can pork and
  beans

79

Fry bacon until crisp, remove from skillet. Remove some bacon fat if it seems too much. Saute onions in fat until soft and clear. Add vinegar, sugar, mustard and simmer 20 minutes. Add beans, diced bacon and pour into casserole. Bake 1 hour at 350 degrees. Serves 10-12.

Mary Davidson / *Diocese of Western Kansas*

# *Lenten Lasagne Dinner Menu*

### Serves 6-8

* Spinach Lasagne
  Tossed green salad or coleslaw
* Italian Bread
  Pecan Tarts (page 236)

## Spinach Lasagne

Prepare the tomato sauce:

**1 tablespoon cooking oil**
**½ cup chopped onions**

**1 clove garlic, minced**
**1 large can tomato sauce**

Heat oil and saute onion over medium heat until limp. Add garlic and tomato sauce. Simmer ½ hour. You may substitute your own favorite tomato sauce.

**½ pound lasagne noodles**
**1 cup cottage cheese**
**½ cup grated Parmesan cheese**
**1 egg**

**Dash of nutmeg**
**1 pound fresh spinach, cooked,**
**  drained and chopped**
**½ pound mozzarella cheese**

Cook the lasagne in a large amount of boiling, salted water. Drain. Mix together the cottage cheese, Parmesan cheese, egg, nutmeg and spinach. Set aside. Slice the mozzarella cheese.

80

To assemble: lay out cooked lasagne and spread with cheese-spinach mixture. Roll up jellyroll style and set on end in deep casserole dish. Pour sauce over all and top with slices of mozzarella cheese. Bake uncovered for 45 minutes at 350 degrees. It may be made the day before and refrigerated; bake 15 minutes longer in this case. Serves 6-8.

## Italian Bread

1 cake yeast or 1 package dry
  yeast
2 cups lukewarm water

1 tablespoon salt
6 cups flour

Combine ingredients in order given, mix well. Knead for 15 minutes. Let rise for 2 hours or until doubled in bulk. Knead for 5 minutes. Divide into 2 portions; cover and let stand for 10 minutes. Shape into oblong loaves; place on greased baking sheet. Let rise for 1 hour. Bake at 425 degrees for 10 minutes. Reduce heat to 350 degrees. Bake for 20 minutes.

Chris Folwell / *Diocese of Central Florida*

# An Easy Fix-Ahead Dinner for 6

* Turkey Casserole
* Curried Fruit Bake
* Chocolate Mousse

## Turkey Casserole

8 slices of buttered bread
2 cups cooked turkey, chicken,
  ham, or tuna
½ cup mayonnaise
1 onion, chopped
1 green pepper, chopped

1 cup chopped celery
3 cups milk
4 eggs, beaten
1 10½-ounce can mushroom soup
Cheddar cheese, grated

81

Dice four slices of buttered bread and put in 3-quart casserole or 9×13×12-inch baking pan. Mix turkey (or substitute), mayonnaise, onion, green pepper, and celery, and spread on bread cubes. Cube other four slices of bread and place on top of mixture. Mix eggs and milk and pour over all. Place in the refrigerator overnight.

Bake at 350 degrees for 45 minutes. Remove from oven and spoon mushroom soup over. Sprinkle with grated cheese and bake an additional 15 minutes. Serves 6

## Curried Fruit Bake

⅓ cup butter or margarine
¾ cup brown sugar, packed
4 teaspoons curry powder

2 cups peach or apricot halves
2 cups pear halves
2 cups pineapple slices or chunks

*Day before:* Heat oven to 325 degrees. Melt butter. Add sugar and curry. Drain and dry fruit, place in 1½-quart casserole. Add butter mixture. Bake one hour, uncovered. Refrigerate. Reheat, covered, for 30 minutes before serving.

## Chocolate Mousse

1 6-ounce package chocolate chips
2 eggs

3 tablespoons strong coffee
¾ cup scalded milk

Blend all ingredients in mixer for 2 minutes at high speed. Pour into mousse cups and chill. Serves 6.

Peg Wyatt / *Diocese of Spokane (Washington)*

# Turkey Crunch for a Bunch

### Serves 12

* Turkey Crunch Casserole
  Winter Squash
* Oriental Spinach Salad
  Rolls
  Grape and Nectarine Compote (page 245)

## Turkey Crunch Casserole

6 cups diced cooked turkey
4 hard-cooked eggs, chopped
2 4-ounce cans sliced mushrooms
1½ cups diced celery
1 cup slivered blanched almonds
3 tablespoons chopped onion

2 10½-ounce cans condensed
  cream of mushroom soup
1½ cups mayonnaise
Chow mein noodles or crushed
  potato chips

Mix together first 6 ingredients. Stir soup into mayonnaise and toss with turkey mixture. Turn into a large casserole or 2 2-quart casseroles. Sprinkle with noodles or crushed potato chips. Bake in a 350 degree oven for 40 minutes or until mixture is bubbling. Can be assembled ahead except for noodles or potato chips, which should be added just before baking. Serves 12.

## Oriental Spinach Salad

1 pound raw spinach with heavy
  center stems removed
1 can bean sprouts, drained
1 can water chestnuts, drained
  and sliced

6 hard-boiled eggs, sliced
8 slices bacon, fried crisp and
  crumbled

Toss the above in a large salad bowl, then toss with the following dressing:

83

⅔ cup oil
½ cup sugar
¼ cup vinegar
Small onion, grated

½ teaspoon salt
¼ cup catsup
1½ tablespoons Worcestershire
sauce

The salad can be assembled ahead and tossed with dressing at the last minute. Serves 12.

Both the above recipes can be divided or multiplied successfully.
Dorothy Belden / *Diocese of Rhode Island*

# A "Lemony" Chicken Dinner for 6

\* Chicken "Lemonade"
Rice
\* Tomato-Beans
Vanilla Ice Cream with Hot Chocolate
Sauce (page 249)

## Chicken "Lemonade"

Our children gave this dish its name and it has stuck! Prepare the Lemon Sauce the day before so flavors will blend.

**Lemon Sauce:**

1 cup fresh lemon juice
1 tablespoon grated lemon rind
4 tablespoons chopped onion
(grated, if not using blender)
2 cloves garlic, minced
1 teaspoon salt
½ teaspoon monosodium
glutamate
1 teaspoon fresh ground black

pepper (more if you like
pepper)
1 teaspoon leaf thyme
1 teaspoon leaf rosemary (we use
2 teaspoons, but rosemary is
strong and you might like to
start out easy)
½ cup corn or peanut oil

Place in blender in order given, blend and refrigerate. If not using a blender, mix garlic and salt together, then mix in herbs and seasonings and onion, adding lemon and mixing thoroughly before

84

adding oil. When ready to prepare dish, remove sauce from the refrigerator and allow it to warm up a bit before mixing it again and pouring over the chicken.

\* \* \*

| | |
|---|---|
| 2 3-pound chickens, cut up | 1 tablespoon paprika |
| 2 cups flour | 1 cup corn oil, margarine or |
| 1 teaspoon pepper |     butter |
| 1 teaspoon salt | Chicken broth |

Shake chicken pieces in bag with flour, pepper, salt and paprika. Brown chicken in oil. This can be done the day before actual baking. Place chicken in 15 × 11-inch baking pan. Pour Lemon Sauce over chicken and cover with foil. Bake at 350 degrees for 40 minutes. Baste once or twice and if it seems to be getting dry, add water or broth. After 40 minutes uncover and bake 20 to 30 minutes longer. If the chicken and sauce have been refrigerated, they will take longer to cook. Remove the cooked chicken from the pan and keep warm while you add broth or water to the pan to make gravy to serve with the rice. Serves 6.

---

LORD, *we thank you for this day. Grant that we may always find a measure of your holy joy as we go about our daily living. Let us not forget those who do not have your blessings of food, family, and friends as we do. Bless this food to our use and ourselves to your service. Through Jesus Christ our Lord. Amen.*

## Tomato-Beans

Our version of an Armenian dish we once were served.

1 medium onion, diced
1 clove garlic, minced
1 tablespoon corn oil, margarine
  or butter
1 16-ounce can green beans,
  undrained
1 16-ounce can small tomatoes, or
  tomato juice

1 beef bouillon cube
¼ teaspoon basil
¼ teaspoon oregano
¼ teaspoon monosodium
  glutamate
Fresh ground black pepper and
  salt to taste

Saute onion and garlic in oil until soft. Add beans with juice, tomatoes and bouillon cube. Stir in herbs and seasonings. Simmer, covered, for ½ hour. Will sit happily for hours if necessary; just reheat to serve. Serves 6.

Carol Joyce Hillestad / *Diocese of Springfield (Illinois)*

# *A Chicken Casserole Buffet for 8*

\* Chicken and Spaghetti Casserole
\* Caesar Salad
  French bread with garlic butter
\* Grasshopper Pie

## Chicken and Spaghetti Casserole

4-pound fryer or small hen
1 medium onion, chopped
1 small green pepper, chopped
½ stick oleo
1 10½-ounce can condensed
  mushroom soup

½ cup chicken broth
1 5-ounce jar Kraft Old English
  Cheese Spread
1 4-ounce can water chestnuts,
  chopped
1 7-ounce box thin spaghetti

Stew chicken, cool in broth, remove meat from bones and cut in bite-size pieces. Reserve broth. In a skillet saute the onion and green pepper in oleo. Add mushroom soup and ½ cup chicken broth. Stir until smooth. Add cheese spread and stir until melted. Remove from heat. Add water chestnuts.

Cook spaghetti in chicken broth (with sufficient water added). Drain spaghetti. In a greased 2-quart casserole, layer ½ of the spaghetti, ½ of the chicken pieces and ½ of the cheese sauce. Repeat. Bake in a 350-degree oven for 35-40 minutes, uncovered, until bubbly around the edges and heated through. May be made a day ahead of time; freezes well. Serves 8.

## Caesar Salad

1 clove garlic, quartered
¼ cup salad oil
1 large head romaine lettuce
1 large head iceberg lettuce
¼ cup grated Parmesan cheese
¼ cup crumbled blue cheese
½ cup salad oil
1 tablespoon Worcestershire sauce

¾ teaspoon salt
¼ teaspoon freshly ground
 pepper
1 raw egg
¼ cup lemon juice
2 cups croutons or toasted bread
 cubes

Let garlic stand in ¼ cup salad oil overnight. When ready to serve salad tear greens in bite-size pieces in salad bowl. Sprinkle cheeses on top. Combine ½ cup salad oil with Worcestershire, salt and pepper, pour over greens and toss gently. Break whole egg on to greens. Add lemon juice. Toss just until all the egg disappears. Pour garlic oil (remove garlic!) over croutons and toss. Sprinkle over greens. Toss and serve. Serves 8.

## Grasshopper Pie

Make Chocolate Crumb Crust with:

1⅓ cups chocolate cookie crumbs
 (I use Famous Chocolate
 Wafers)

3 teaspoons sugar
¼ cup melted oleo or butter

Mix well. Press on bottom and sides of ungreased 10-inch pie plate. Bake at 375 degrees for 8 minutes. Cool completely. Fill with

87

**Creme de Menthe Filling:**

16 large marshmallows
⅔ cup milk

3½ ounces creme de menthe
1 cup whipping cream

Melt marshmallows in milk over low heat. Stir well and cool. Add creme de menthe. Whip the cream and fold into marshmallow mixture. Pour into crust and chill at least 2 hours. May be served with a thin layer of whipped cream on top. Serves 8.

Jane Gates / *Diocese of Tennessee*

# Dinner for 8 with a Spanish Flavor

* Green Chicken Enchiladas
* Apricot Salad
* Icebox Cake

## Green Chicken Enchiladas

1 fryer
2 medium onions, chopped
2 tablespoons oil
2 10½-ounce cans Cream of
    Chicken soup

2 4-ounce cans sweet green chilis,
    chopped (use roasted peeled
    chilis, not jalapenos)
20 tortillas
2 cups grated Mozzarella cheese

Cook chicken in water, remove meat from bones and cut in pieces. Saute onions in oil until clear. Add soup, chilis and chicken meat. Dip tortillas in a little hot oil just to soften; do not let them get crisp. Layer tortillas, grated cheese and chicken soup mixture in 3 or 4 layers, ending with soup mix. Bake in a 2-quart deep casserole at 400 degrees for 30 minutes. Serves 8.

## Apricot Salad

2 packages orange Jello
½ pound dried apricots, cooked
   and strained
¼ cup slivered almonds
Small can crushed pineapple,
   well-drained

Pinch of salt
1 tablespoon lemon juice
½ cup sugar

Prepare Jello according to directions on box. Before pouring in mold to chill, add the remaining ingredients. When firm, unmold and serve on lettuce with homemade mayonnaise.

## Icebox Cake

1 pound confectioners sugar
¾ pound butter, softened
6 egg yolks, beaten
1 cup pecans, toasted and
   chopped

6 egg whites, beaten stiff
1 box vanilla wafers

Cream the sugar into ½ pound of the butter. Add egg yolks and pecans. Fold in egg whites. Spread into a 9 × 13-inch pyrex dish which has been lined with crushed vanilla wafers mixed with ¼ pound melted butter. Refrigerate at least 12 hours and cut in squares to serve.

Evelyn Bailey / *Diocese of West Texas*

# A Fish Menu for a Foursome

\* Turbot with Sour Cream
Baked acorn squash (page 208)
Steamed broccoli
Tossed lettuce, grapefruit, and avocado
    salad
\* Eggnog Pie

## Turbot with Sour Cream

1½ to 2 pounds turbot fillets
2 tablespoons finely chopped dill
   pickle
2 tablespoons finely chopped
   onion
2 tablespoons finely chopped
   green pepper

2 tablespoons chopped parsley
¼ teaspoon dry mustard
1 tablespoon lemon juice
¼ teaspoon dry basil
1 cup sour cream

Arrange fish fillets in buttered flat baking dish. Sprinkle with salt and pepper. Combine all other ingredients and spread on fish. Sprinkle with paprika. Bake, uncovered, at 375 degrees for 25 minutes. Serves 4.

## Eggnog Pie

| | |
|---|---|
| 1 baked 10-inch pie shell | 1 tablespoon unflavored gelatin |
| 3 egg yolks | 3 tablespoons cold water |
| 1 cup evaporated milk | ½ teaspoon vanilla |
| ½ cup water | 3 egg whites, beaten |
| ¼ teaspoon nutmeg | ¾ cup whipping cream |
| ½ cup sugar | 1 square bitter chocolate |
| Pinch of salt | |

Beat egg yolks slightly in top of double boiler. Add milk, water, nutmeg, sugar, and salt, and cook over simmering water until the consistency of heavy cream. Remove from heat and mix in the gelatin soaked in cold water. Stir until gelatin is dissolved. Cool. Add vanilla and beaten egg whites. Pour into baked shell. Chill until set. Whip cream and spread on top. Sprinkle with shaved bitter chocolate.

Louise Millard / *Diocese of California*

# "Northwest Corner" Salmon Supper

### Serves 6

In the spring, if the fisherman's luck was good and there is salmon —left over from the big Chinook baked the day before—I say, "Come over for a Salmon Loaf."

The menu is the same—if two come or twenty—and it is "Pure Northwest Corner":

> A white wine
> Tossed green salad
> Peas with tiny onions
> Bread Sticks
> * And—*Salmon Loaf,* with lemon wedges
>      and lots of tartar sauce, to one's
>      own taste.

Our freezer usually supplies the dessert—Oregon strawberries, blueberries, raspberries or rhubarb—for pies, or just topping for ice cream.

## The Salmon Loaf

3 cups left-over salmon (or, for the deprived ones who don't live here, canned salmon to make 3 cups)
1 egg
1 can cream of mushroom soup

¾ cup cracker crumbs
2 tablespoons diced celery
2 tablespoons diced onion
1 teaspoon salt
⅛ teaspoon pepper

Combine all ingredients, mixing well. Bake in regular size bread pan in moderate 350 degree oven for ¾ to 1 hour. One recipe serves 5 or 6.

Phyllis Carman / *Diocese of Oregon*

# *A Dinner to Make on a Fine Spring Day*

Serves 6

* Escalloped Salmon and Potatoes
* Oatmeal Bread
* Dandelion Greens with Bacon
    Dressing
  Fresh fruit

## Escalloped Salmon and Potatoes

4 cups mashed potatoes
2 cups flaked salmon
1 cup small boiled onions
2 eggs, beaten
½ cup milk

3 tablespoons butter
3 tablespoons flour
1½ cups milk
Salt and pepper to taste

Line a Pyrex bread-loaf dish with the mashed potatoes. Add salmon and onions. Beat eggs with the ½ cup milk. Set aside. Make a white sauce of the flour, butter and 1½ cups milk and cook for about 3 minutes. Add eggs beaten with milk, salt and pepper to taste, and pour over fish. Bake at 375 degrees for 30 minutes. This dish can be made in the morning and refrigerated until dinner, but freezing is not recommended. Serves 6.

## Oatmeal Bread

3 cups uncooked oats
1½ cups raisins
1 quart boiling water
1 scant cup molasses

1 tablespoon salt
1 yeast cake
¼ cup warm water
7 cups flour

Pour boiling water over oats and raisins. Add molasses and salt. Cool to lukewarm. Dissolve yeast in ¼ cup warm water and add to oats. Mix in flour, let rise (preferably in oven that has a pilot light), covered. When double in bulk, divide into 2 large bread pans or 3 smaller ones. Let rise for an hour or more. Bake in 350-degree oven for 1 hour. The last 15 minutes cover with brown paper to prevent the bread from becoming too brown.

Oatmeal bread is better when made on a fine day.

## Dandelion Greens with Bacon Dressing

3 or 4 strips bacon
2 cloves garlic, finely chopped
½ cup fresh mint, coarsely
   chopped

2 tablespoons red wine vinegar
1 quart dandelion greens, picked
   before they blossom in spring
Salt and freshly ground pepper

Cut bacon into ½-inch bits and saute with the garlic. Add mint, wine vinegar and greens. Toss as you would a salad. Taste for seasoning; add more vinegar if needed. Serves 6.

Esther Burgess / *Diocese of Massachusetts*

# A Florida Dinner with Shrimp and Key Limes

Serves 6

* Shrimp in Shells
  Fresh green beans
  Tomato Aspic
  Hot rolls
* Key Lime Pie

## Shrimp in Shells

1½ pounds cooked shrimp, shelled and deveined
3 tablespoons butter
3 tablespoons flour
1½ cups milk
2 tablespoons sauterne

Lemon juice, salt and pepper to taste
1 egg yolk
½ cup grated Swiss cheese
6 shells or ramekins

Melt butter, add flour and stir. Add milk, sauterne, lemon juice, salt and pepper. Stir until smooth. Beat egg yolk with small amount of milk mixture—add to the remainder. Add cheese and shrimp. Pour into individual shells or ramekins and heat in moderate oven just until hot.

## Key Lime Pie

4 eggs, separated
⅛ teaspoon cream of tartar
⅓ cup sugar
1 can sweetened condensed milk
½ cup Key lime juice

Grated lime rind
1 teaspoon gelatin in ½ cup cold
  water
1 9-inch crumb pie crust

Beat egg whites stiff; add cream of tartar, then sugar slowly, beating at high speed. Beat yolks lightly, beat in condensed milk, add lime juice and rind. Soften gelatin in water and heat until gelatin is dissolved, then add to egg yolk mixture. Fold in egg whites and fill pie crust; chill.

Elaine Duncan / *Diocese of Southeast Florida*

# Intriguing Flavor Makes this Fish Dinner a Winner

### Serves 6 to 8

* Whiskey Sour Fish
* Artichoke Hearts Casserole
* Mystery Salad
* Wine Cake

## Whiskey Sour Fish

3 pounds halibut, bass, sole or
  other firm fish
1 6-ounce can concentrated frozen
  lemonade
1 8-ounce can tomato sauce
2 tablespoons bourbon

1 medium onion, sliced
½ green pepper, sliced
¼ teaspoon salt
¼ teaspoon pepper
¼ teaspoon seasoned salt

Defrost frozen lemonade and mix with tomato sauce and bourbon. Put the onion and green pepper slices on the bottom of a casserole. Lay fish on the onions and peppers. Sprinkle with seasonings and pour sauce over the fish. Bake in a 400-degree oven for 20 minutes or until the fish is done. Baste frequently. Serves 6-8.

95

# Artichoke Hearts Casserole

2 packages frozen artichoke hearts
¼ cup butter
⅓ cup flour
¼ teaspoon dry mustard
¾ teaspoon onion salt
1½ cups milk

1 egg, slightly beaten
½ cup Swiss cheese, grated
1 tablespoon bread crumbs
Salt and pepper to taste
Paprika

Cook the artichoke hearts according to directions on package, and reserve the liquid (½ cup). Melt butter, add flour, mustard, onion salt and mix well. Gradually add artichoke liquid and milk. Stir and cook until smooth and thick. Add egg and ½ of the cheese. Place hearts in a casserole, cover with sauce, and sprinkle with the rest of the cheese and breadcrumbs. Bake in 400-degree oven for 15 minutes. Can be made ahead and baked just before serving. Serves 6-8.

# Mystery Salad

2 packages raspberry Jello
3 cups canned stewed tomatoes
6 drops Tabasco sauce

1 cup sour cream
1 teaspoon horseradish

Dissolve Jello in 1 cup boiling water. Add tomatoes, breaking large pieces with a spoon. Add Tabasco sauce. Pour into a large ring mold, chill, and serve with dressing of sour cream and horseradish. Can be made a day ahead. Serves 6-8.

# Wine Cake

1 package yellow cake mix
1 small package instant vanilla
   pudding
4 eggs

¾ cup oil
¾ cup dry sherry wine
1 teaspoon nutmeg

Combine all ingredients, mix at medium speed with electric mixer for a good 5 minutes. Bake in a well-greased angelfood tube pan. Bake about 45 minutes or until done. Remove from oven and let cool 10 minutes. Turn out on rack and dust with powdered sugar. Best made ahead. Serves 6-8.

Helen Wolterstorff / *Diocese of San Diego (California)*

# A Shrimp Curry Dinner for 8

\* Shrimp Curry with assorted
    condiments
Steamed Rice
Tossed salad (A semi-sweet salad—
    assorted greens, orange sections,
    croutons, and oil and vinegar
    dressing)
Dry white wine
Sherbert served on fresh fruit
Currant cookies (page 229)

## Shrimp Curry

2 tablespoons shortening or oil
2 large onions, finely minced
1 medium green pepper, finely
    minced

2 tablespoons curry powder
1 cup water
2 pounds cleaned raw shrimp
1 13-ounce can evaporated milk

Heat oil in large skillet. Add onions and green pepper. Fry until light brown. Add curry powder and mix well for at least one minute. Add the water a little at a time and cook until it evaporates and grease comes to the surface. Continue this process until water is finished. This gives a rich gravy. Add shrimp and spoon gravy over each. Simmer until shrimp cook firm. Add the milk and stir constantly. When the grease comes to the top again, curry is done. This may be made ahead and reheated in time for serving.

Profer in small bowls five or six of the following:

Chopped walnuts
Chopped raisins
Chopped hard-boiled egg
Coconut (the fine-shredded or
    grated fresh)

Crisp bacon, crumbled
Raw zucchini or cucumber in
    small cubes
Chutney
Very finely chopped sweet onions

Ruth Ogilby / *Diocese of Pennsylvania*

# A Favorite Lunch or Supper Menu Starring Crabmeat, Charleston-Style

Serves 8

* Crabmeat Casserole with *Curried Rice
* V-8 Aspic with Artichoke Hearts
  Hot Rolls (page 152)
* Mary Barney's Pots de Creme

## Crabmeat Casserole

1 pound crabmeat—or 1½
  pounds, the more the better
4 cups thick white sauce
Salt and pepper
2 tablespoons Worcestershire
  sauce
2 tablespoons sherry

½ cup finely cut bell pepper
½ cup chopped pimiento
1 cup finely cut celery
1½ cups coarsely grated sharp
  cheese
Paprika

Season sauce with salt, pepper, Worcestershire and sherry. Combine all ingredients in casserole, reserving ½ cup cheese for top of dish. Sprinkle paprika over top and bake 1 hour in a 350-degree oven. Serve with curried rice. Serves 8.

## Curried Rice

2 cups uncooked rice
2 cups chicken stock

1 tablespoon curry powder
Salt to taste

Combine ingredients in top of double boiler and steam over simmering water for 1 hour. Serves 8.

## V-8 Aspic with Artichoke Hearts

2 cups V-8 juice          **Canned artichoke hearts**
1 envelope unflavored gelatin

Soften gelatin in ½ cup V-8. Heat remaining V-8 just to simmering. Stir gelatin mix into hot liquid until gelatin is dissolved. Divide among individual molds into which you have put 1 artichoke heart each, or pour into 1 ring mold. Chill until firm. Unmold on lettuce leaves and serve mayonnaise on the side. Serves 8.

TIP
To get aspic out of individual molds fairly easily, try the following method: Hold a mold upside down in your left hand and run water as hot as is comfortable over the bottom of the mold just for a few seconds, letting the water run off between your fingers. Then take the mold in your right hand, still upside down, and give a quick pop onto your left palm. The aspic usually comes right out whole into your hand and can then be quickly slipped onto the plate.

## Mary Barney's Pots de Creme

8-ounce package chocolate chips    2 tablespoons sugar
2 eggs                      2 tablespoons sherry, rum,
¾ cup milk, scalded         brandy or creme de menthe

Put all ingredients in blender and blend for 2 minutes. Divide into 8 individual serving dishes—pot de creme pots, demitasse cups or short-stemmed cocktail glasses. Refrigerate overnight. Top with a dollop of Cool Whip and serve—with demitasse spoons. Serves 8.

This dessert is easy, economical and less fattening than the French version.

**Maria Temple** / *Diocese of South Carolina*

---

OUR FATHER, *for the privilege of being not only guests at thy table, but members of thy family, we offer thanks in the name of our lord Jesus Christ. Amen.*

# BUFFETS AND SPECIAL OCCASION MENUS

## *Shenandoah Valley Thanksgiving Dinner for 12*

- * Baked Turkey with Dressing and Gravy
- * Sauerkraut
- * Sweet potatoes with pineapple
- * Blushing Apples
- Cranberry jelly
- Pickles
- * Pumpkin pie

## Baked Turkey

| | |
|---|---|
| **16–20 pound turkey (if frozen allow 36 hours to thaw in refrigerator)** | **1½ teaspoon salt**<br>**½ teaspoon pepper** |

Take out neck, gizzard, liver and heart, cover with water. Add ½ teaspoon salt and ½ teaspoon pepper and cook slowly for about 1½ hours. When cool, dice or cut up giblets, removing neck bones and slicing away thick lining of gizzard. Refrigerate with stock until ready to add to gravy.

Keep turkey cold until ready to cook. Remove lungs, small organs in bones at base of backbone and rinse out cavities, then sprinkle with 1 teaspoon salt. Stuff neck and body cavity lightly with dressing. Allow 20 minutes to a pound of turkey. If weight is 18 pounds, allow 6 hours. Place in 350 degree oven. Use a pan with a top. After 4 hours remove top to brown breast, pour off juices and fat in bottom of pan. Pour one cup over bottom of pan and reserve 1 cup for extra stuffing in casserole. Raise heat to 400 degrees until as brown as desired. Put top back on to finish cooking.

*Turkey Dressing*

| | |
|---|---|
| 4 cups dried bread, cubed | 1 teaspoon salt |
| 1/2 cup onion, diced | 1 teaspoon pepper |
| 1 cup celery, chopped | 1/4 cup minced parsley |
| 1/2 cup raisins | 1/4 cup minced celery leaves |
| 1 teaspoon sage | 2 eggs |
| 1 teaspoon poultry dressing | 1 cup milk |

Night before cut up dried bread and crusts. Add all other ingredients except eggs and milk. Keep in cool place. When ready to stuff turkey, add eggs beaten into milk. Save 3 cups dressing to bake and brown in a flat casserole dish.

*Turkey Gravy*

| | |
|---|---|
| 1/2 cup turkey fat | 1 1/2 cups turkey stock |
| 4 tablespoons flour | Giblets and neck meat, cut-up |

Dissolve flour in turkey fat and brown in frying pan. Add turkey stock and more water if necessary. Add giblets and neck meat. Allow to bubble slowly until thick and of consistency desired.

## Sauerkraut

| | |
|---|---|
| 2 large size cans sauerkraut | 1 cup water |
| 1 cup turkey fat and liquid | |

Combine and simmer for at least 1 hour.

## Sweet Potatoes with Pineapple

2 large size cans sweet potatoes      6 slices pineapple, cut in halves
½ cup honey

Combine ingredients in glass casserole dish. Use ½ cup liquid from sweet potatoes or ½ cup pineapple juice. Bake 1 hour.

## Blushing Apples

12 yellow Delicious apples, pared      ½ teaspoon nutmeg
¼ cup water                           or ¼ cup red cinnamon hearts
¼ cup sugar                              instead of nutmeg and food
1 drop red food coloring                 coloring

Quarter and slice apples into baking dish. Add other ingredients and bake 1 hour.

Serve turkey with the above dishes and with cranberry jelly (1 can) and cucumber pickles (1 jar).

## Pumpkin Pie

3½ cups pumpkin                       1 teaspoon ginger
½ cup honey or brown sugar            1 teaspoon allspice
1 tablespoon cinnamon                 4 eggs
1 teaspoon nutmeg                     2 cups evaporated milk
or 2 tablespoon pumpkin pie          2 unbaked 9-inch pie shells
   spice

Two days before baking turkey, cut pumpkin into about 6 sections and scrape out seeds. Place upside down in flat pan and bake 2 hours in slow oven (200 to 225 degrees). Peel away outside skin. Slice into small pieces and cook slowly, about 45 minutes. Do not add water. When soft, mash with potato masher or put through food mill. Allow juice to accumulate and pour off. (May be added to vegetable soup). Pumpkin may be placed in colander to drain. Refrigerate until ready to bake.

Measure pumpkin into large bowl and add all other ingredients, beating in eggs and mix very well. Pour into prepared pie shells. Bake at 450 degrees for 10 minutes to brown crusts on bottom, then lower temperature to 350 degrees. Bake 1 hour or until custard in middle of pie is set. Makes 2 pies.

Jeanne Baden / *Diocese of Virginia*

# Guatemalan Style Turkey Dinner for 10

* Roast Turkey Guatemalan Style
* Green Rice
* String Beans à la Guatemala
* Baked Bananas

## Roast Turkey Guatemalan Style

| | |
|---|---|
| 10 to 12 pound turkey | 4 ounces butter or margarine |
| Salt and pepper to taste | Bay leaves |
| 2 tablespoons mustard | Basil leaves |
| 1 big onion, chopped | Juice of 15 sweet oranges |

Wash turkey, then prick with fork or icepick. Rub in salt and pepper and leave in refrigerator overnight. Next day rub in mustard and leave in refrigerator another night. The following day rub with butter or margarine and large amount of chopped onion. Add bay leaves, basil and orange juice. Roast in 325 degree oven until well done, about 15 minutes per pound, basting several times during the roasting.

103

## Green Rice

3 tablespoons shortening
3 cups uncooked rice
6 green peppers, cored and
 seeded
4 or 5 parsley leaves
2 onions, chopped

2 cloves garlic, chopped
3 or 4 peppercorns
1½ cups broth or water
1 cup cream
2 ounces Parmesan cheese

Fry rice in shortening and when half way through frying, add the peppers which have been boiled and ground with the parsley. Add onion, garlic and peppercorns and finish frying. Add sufficient broth or water, cover and cook over a low flame until liquid is absorbed and rice is cooked. Before serving, the cream is mixed in with the rice and half the cheese. The other half of cheese is sprinkled on top. Serves 10.

## String Beans à la Guatemala

2 pounds string beans, trimmed
Salt to taste

5 beaten eggs
Shortening to fry

Cook the string beans whole in salted water. Remove and dry very well. Roll bunches (about 6) of the beans in beaten egg batter and fry in hot fat. If desired, serve covered with a sauce of tomatoes, minced onion, and chili sauteed in butter or a little shortening, seasoned with salt and pepper. Serves 10.

## Baked Bananas

2 bananas per person
Butter

Brown sugar
Juice of 1 lime

Use medium-size ripe bananas. Peel, removing long fibres. Place in buttered baking dish. Put dabs of butter on the bananas. Sprinkle liberally with brown sugar. Add juice of 1 lime. Cook approximately 40 minutes in 250-degree oven. Turn bananas once when about ⅔ done. Serve on hot plates.

Berta Carral / *Diocese of Guatemala*

# Supper for 8 To 45 People

with recipes that double, triple, quadruple, etc. very well

* Curried Chicken Casserole
  White Rice
* Spinach Supreme
  Fruit Salad
  Rolls

## Curried Chicken Casserole

1 hen, stewed and boned
2 tablespoons Worcestershire
  sauce
1 10½-ounce can condensed
  mushroom soup
1 10½-ounce can condensed
  celery soup

1 cup mayonnaise
3 tablespoons curry powder
¼ cup dry vermouth
2 hard-boiled eggs, chopped
1 small onion, chopped
1 4-ounce can sliced mushrooms

Cut chicken meat in bite-size pieces. Mix Worcestershire sauce, undiluted soups, mayonnaise, curry powder and vermouth. Pour small amount of this sauce in bottom of a 2-quart casserole. Add alternate layers of chicken, eggs, onion and mushrooms. Cover with rest of sauce. Bake in 350 degree oven for 20 to 30 minutes or until heated through and bubbling. Serves 8.

## Spinach Supreme

5 packages frozen chopped
  spinach
1 pint sour cream
1 8-ounce can tomato sauce

1 small can mushroom stems and
  pieces
1 14-ounce can artichoke hearts
¾ cup grated sharp cheese

105

Cook and drain spinach. Put into buttered casserole, add remaining ingredients except cheese and mix. Cover with grated cheese. If desired, sprinkle with paprika. Bake in a 350-degree oven until heated through and cheese melts, about 20 minutes. Serves 8 to 10.

Margaret Stough / *Diocese of Alabama*

# *Philippine Style Sunday Lunch*
### Serves 8 to 10

* Chicken Caldereta
* Pancit Bihon (pork, chicken and
      shrimp with noodles)
  Rice
  Buttered sweet peas
  Hot garlic bread
* Tropical Fruit Salad
* Mango Pie

## Chicken Caldereta

½ cup seasoned flour
4 pounds chicken legs or breasts
½ cup fat
1 clove garlic, minced
½ cup tomato sauce
1 cup mushrooms, halved

3 potatoes, peeled and quartered
2 medium onions, chopped
½ cup chopped green pepper
¼ teaspoon black pepper
2 pieces bay leaf
Salt to taste

Put seasoned flour in paper bag, add chicken pieces and shake well till each piece is coated. Brown on all sides in hot fat. Add remaining ingredients. Simmer, covered, for 1 hour. Serves 8-10.

## Pancit Bihon (Pork, chicken and shrimp with noodles)

1 pound boneless pork
1 medium-size chicken
1 pound bihon noodles (or
   Chinese egg noodles or
   "cellophane" noodles)
½ cup oil or bacon fat
1 clove garlic, minced

1 onion, chopped
1 cup fresh shrimp, shelled and
   deveined
2 cups finely sliced cabbage
Soy sauce and salt to taste
½ teaspoon black pepper
Sliced hard-boiled egg for garnish

Boil pork and chicken separately until tender. Reserve chicken broth. Break noodles into small pieces. Shred chicken and slice pork into thin pieces. Heat oil or bacon fat and saute garlic and onion until brown. Add the shrimps, stir to cook them, then add the pork and chicken. Mix in the noodles with about a cup of chicken broth, stirring constantly for about 5 minutes. Add the cabbage, soy sauce, salt and black pepper and stir for 3 minutes. Serve hot with hard-boiled egg garnish. Serves 8-10.

## Tropical Fruit Salad

5 bananas, peeled and sliced
¼ cup pineapple juice
3 cups pineapple cubes
3 cups avocado cubes

3 ounces cream cheese
2 tablespoons lemon juice
Salad greens

Cover sliced bananas with pineapple juice. Drain, reserving juice. Mix bananas with pineapple and avocado cubes. Mash cheese and add lemon and pineapple juices gradually. Beat until creamy. Pour over the fruits, arranged on salad greens. Serves 8-10.

## Mango Pie

5 ripe mangoes, peeled
1 teaspoon lemon juice
1 tablespoon flour

½ cup sugar
Double crust for 9-inch pie

Cut mangoes in long narrow pieces as for peach or apple pie. Sprinkle with lemon juice. Mix flour with sugar and sprinkle over each layer as you arrange the mangoes in the unbaked pie shell. Cover with top crust and bake for 45 minutes at 375 degrees. Serves 8-10.

Serafia Cabanban / *Diocese of Central Philippines*

# A "Finger-Food" Picnic—At Home or Outdoors

### Serves 6 to 8

Fun to serve for a picnic in summer or for a small group around the fire on a stormy winter night. Arrange main course on a large platter; knives and forks should not be required.

Soup or bouillon in mugs
* Brisket of Beef
* Finger-Baked Potatoes
* Cold Broccoli with Green Onion Dip
* Miniature Macaroons

## Brisket of Beef

1 4-pound brisket of beef
1 package onion soup mix

1 12-ounce bottle chili sauce
1 12-ounce can beer

Put brisket in roasting pan, uncovered, and roast for 20 minutes on each side in a 400-degree oven. Add the remaining ingredients. Reduce heat to 350 degrees and bake, covered, for 1 hour. Turn meat and continue baking for 1½ hours longer. Remove and cool. Refrigerate overnight. Serve thinly sliced. Serves 6-8.

## Finger-Baked Potatoes

Bake 6 or 8 potatoes for 45 minutes in a 350-degree oven. Remove and cut in half horizontally, then again vertically. Brush cut sides with melted butter, and return to oven for 20 minutes; brush again with butter and Parmesan cheese and bake until browned. Serve warm. Serves 6-8.

## Cold Broccoli with Green Onion Dip

Trim best parts of a large head of fresh broccoli into bite-size pieces. Cook in boiling salted water until just tender. Drain and refrigerate for 3 or 4 hours. Serve with

*Green Onion Dip*

**1 pint sour cream**
**1 envelope green onion dip**
   **seasoning**

Mix together and refrigerate until needed. May also be served with potato chips or crackers. Serves 6-8.

## Miniature Macaroons

Mix together:

**16 single-square saltine crackers,**      **½ cup pecans, chopped**
   **rolled fine**                          **1 cup sugar**
**16 dates, cut up fine**

Beat together until stiff but not dry:

**3 egg whites**                **¼ teaspoon baking powder**

Fold egg white mixture into dry mixture, then pour into smallest muffin tins and bake in a 350-degree oven for about 25 to 30 minutes. Freeze or refrigerate. Nice with a dab of whipped cream. Serves 6-8.

Martha Burt / *Diocese of Ohio*

# Curry Suppers Are Always Fun

### Serves 10

* Beef Curry with condiments
  Steamed Rice
  A Simple Green Salad
  Bread Sticks
* Hot Fruit Compote
  Tea or Coffee

Curry suppers provide their own decoration in the artistic arrange-
ment of condiments and create conversation. The main curry dish
can be prepared the day before, and the condiments may be fixed
ahead and kept tightly covered in the refrigerator. However, one of
our liveliest curry parties happened when we all came back after a
day out, and the guests each prepared a condiment in the kitchen
while the rice cooked. Everyone had fun grating, chopping, slicing,
and took a proprietary interest in the meal.

For the condiments, use anywhere from 6-12 of the following:

Chopped dry-roasted peanuts
Chopped green pepper
Chopped celery
Chopped pickles
Chopped parsley
Chopped chives
Chopped whites of hard-boiled
  eggs
Grated yolk of hard-boiled egg
Grated coconut

Thin onion rings
Toasted slivered almonds
Crisp crumbled bacon
Slivered ham, salami, tongue
Slivered smoked fish
Chutneys
Sliced cherry tomatoes
Marinated raisins (sprinkle
  with vinegar)

110

## Beef Curry

| | |
|---|---|
| 3 pounds of good stewing beef, or a small pot roast cut into cubes (left-over turkey or lamb with gravy make good curries too) | 3 tablespoons flour<br>1½ teaspoons salt<br>Dash of pepper<br>3 tablespoons margarine or oil |

Dredge meat cubes in mixture of flour, salt, and pepper and brown them in the hot fat in a dutch oven or heavy skillet with cover. Stir the cubes gently until well browned. Add 2 cups water, cover and let it braise a few minutes. Turn to low heat and let the meat simmer gently for an hour or more, until really tender. Add more water if it tends to stick; i.e., watch the pot! Don't let the gravy cook away.

Meanwhile saute in 2 tablespoons butter or margarine:

| | |
|---|---|
| 2 apples, pared and chopped | Handful of cauliflower pieces |
| 2 onions, sliced | Handful of chopped celery |
| 1 small turnip, chopped | Handful of thin-sliced carrots |

Add a little water or stock and cook until tender. When the meat is well done in its gravy, add the vegetables. (You can vary them according to what is available.)

When you are ready to serve, add:

| | |
|---|---|
| 1 teaspoon lemon juice | 2 teaspoons curry powder |

Stir well. Serve piping hot, but don't boil unduly. Serves 10.

## Hot Fruit Compote

These ingredients can be varied, according to taste, or to the contents of the pantry shelf.

| | |
|---|---|
| Juice and grated rind of 1 orange | 1 16-ounce can bing cherries, with juice |
| Juice and grated rind of 1 lemon | |
| 1 16-ounce can peaches, drained | 1 16-ounce can pears, drained |
| ½ pound dried apricots, or a 16-ounce can apricots, drained | ½ cup brown sugar |

Put everything in a large baking dish, layering or sectioning if you wish. Don't stir. Bake at 350 degrees for 1 hour. Serve with dollop of sour cream, or have it available.

Rosemary Clark / *Diocese of Delaware*

# Stew is International, This Nicaraguan Menu Shows Us

### Serves 8 to 10

* Baho (meat and vegetable stew)
  Steamed rice
  A salad of shredded cabbage, peeled
      sliced tomatoes with a vinegar
      dressing
  Vanilla flan

## Baho

This typical Nicaraguan dish of meat and vegetables should be cooked immediately before serving. If the cooking begins at 8:00 A.M. the dish will be ready by noon.

6 pounds cured meat with some
    fat (for extra flavor), cut up
4 big tomatoes (approximately 3½
    pounds), thickly sliced
3 big onions (approximately 1¼
    pounds), thickly sliced
5 pounds cassava, peeled and cut
    in 3-inch pieces
1 2½-pound cabbage, thickly
    sliced

5 ripe plantains, peeled and
    sliced
4 unripe plantains, peeled and
    sliced
3 tablespoons salt
6 sour (Seville) oranges, thinly
    sliced

Prepare stove with firewood. In the bottom of a 2-gallon pot pour 1 liter water. Over the water place a few dried branches (preferably from a mango tree) and cover the bottom and sides of the pot with banana tree leaves. From the bottom of the pot layer ingredients in the following order:

Ripe plantains
Cassava
Cabbage

Onions
Tomatoes
Meat

| | |
|---|---|
| Salt | Tomatoes |
| Cassava | Cassava |
| Oranges | Meat |
| Unripe plantains | Salt |
| Cabbage | Oranges |
| Onions | |

Cover the pot and cook over a low fire for about 4 hours. Do not uncover until done. The smell tells you it is ready. Serve immediately. Do not freeze. Serves 8 generously.

Babbie Haynsworth / *Diocese of Nicaragua*

# *Comida Tipica, A Typical Menu from the Dominican Republic*

### Serves 12

* Carne Mechada (Beef larded with ham strips)
* Moros con Cristianos (Rice and beans)
* Ensalata Mixta (Tossed Salad)
* Fritura de Plátanos Maduros (Fried ripe plantains)
* Quesillo de Piña (Pineapple custard)

## Carne Mechada (Beef larded with ham strips)

| | |
|---|---|
| 5 pounds beef pot roast | 4 tablespoons chopped parsley |
| ½ pound ham, in strips | 1 bay leaf |
| Olives and capers | Salt, to taste |
| 1 medium onion, chopped | 3 tablespoons oil or fat |
| 1 medium sweet pepper, chopped | 2 tablespoons tomato paste |
| 2 cloves garlic, minced | ½ cup dry red wine |
| 2 tablespoons vinegar | |

113

Clean and wash meat properly. Cut to make deep holes in various sections and fill with ham strips, olives, capers, chopped onion, peppers, garlic. Marinate in mixture of vinegar, parsley, bay leaf and salt for about 1 hour. Heat oil thoroughly and brown meat on all sides. Add tomato paste, wine and water in sufficient quantity for cooking. Cover and cook on slow fire for 3 hours or more until meat is tender. Slice for serving. Serves 12.

## Moros con Cristianos (Rice and Beans)

½ pound red kidney beans
3 slices bacon, diced
2 ounces ham, diced
2 cloves garlic, minced
1 large onion, chopped
1 large sweet pepper, chopped

2 tablespoons tomato paste
1 tablespoon vinegar
1½ pounds rice
Chopped parsley or chopped
   fresh coriander
Salt, to taste

Cook beans in sufficient water till tender. Cook bacon till crisp; add ham, garlic, onion, pepper and saute for a few minutes. Add tomato paste, vinegar, beans (with 4 cups of the water they were cooked in) and rice. Stir all together, then add parsley or coriander and salt to taste. Cook on slow fire till rice grains begin to open, then cover and simmer till done. Serves 12.

## Ensalata Mixta (Tossed Salad)

⅓ cup vinegar
1 cup olive oil
Salt, to taste
1 medium onion, chopped
½ cabbage, chopped

2 heads lettuce
1 large avocado, peeled and sliced
2 tomatoes, peeled and sliced
2 cucumbers, peeled and sliced
1 bunch radishes, sliced

Mix vinegar, olive oil and salt. Place ½ cup of dressing in bowl with onion and cabbage and toss. Surround with lettuce, torn in bite-sized pieces. Place avocado on top of cabbage and surround with alternating rows of tomatoes, cucumbers and radishes. Add remaining dressing before serving. Serves 12.

## Fritura de Plátanos Maduros (Fried ripe plantains)

6 large ripe plantains                    Oil for frying

Peel plantains and slice in ¼-inch slices. Fry in hot oil until golden.

## Quesillo de Piña (Pineapple custard)

2½ cups sugar                             10 eggs
1 quart pineapple juice                   2 egg yolks

Caramelize ½ cup of the sugar by melting in a heavy pan and adding ¼ cup hot water. Line a mold with the caramel syrup. Heat the pineapple juice, add remaining sugar and stir until sugar is dissolved. Cool. Lightly beat eggs and egg yolks and add to pineapple juice. Strain and pour into mold. Cook over hot—not boiling—water until firm, or place mold in a pan of hot water in a 325-degree oven until a knife placed in the center of the custard comes out clean. Chill and unmold. Serves 12.

Juanita Isaac / *Diocese of the Dominican Republic*

# *Supper for 12 On A Warm Sunday Night*

* Bloody Marys, served with *Pickled
  Mushrooms and *Garlic Cheese
* Avocados stuffed with Turkey Salad
* Hot Rolls
* Chocolate Mousse

## Bloody Marys

18 ounces vodka, 1 large can tomato juice, juice of 4 lemons, ¼ teaspoon each: salt, pepper and celery salt. 2 tablespoons Worcester-

115

shire sauce. 1 tablespoon powdered sugar. Dash of Tabasco. Mix all together. Serve over ice. This serves 12 people, one drink each. It keeps well in refrigerator.

### Pickled Mushrooms

Drain 2 4-ounce cans button mushrooms and put in glass jar. Fill jar ⅔ full with Italian Wishbone dressing; ⅓ wine vinegar. Refrigerate for about 2 days. Have toothpicks to spear them with for serving.

### Garlic Cheese

¾ pound sharp cheese. 1 3-ounce package cream cheese. 1 garlic clove, minced. ½ cup chopped pecans. 1 tablespoon Worcestershire sauce. Dash of Tabasco. Salt and pepper to taste. Paprika. Mix all except paprika together. (I put cheese through meat chopper.) Shape into 4 rolls, about 6 inches long. Roll in paprika, coating well. Roll in plastic wrap and store in refrigerator. Slice and serve on crackers.

# Turkey Salad

I cook a whole turkey in turkey roaster on top of stove, on low heat, adding 1 quart water, 1 onion, 1 carrot, 1 stalk celery. Cook until tender. Let cool, then skin and bone, and cut up. (I store mine in 2-cup packages in freezer until needed.) To make salad: 8 cups chopped turkey; add 4 cups chopped celery, and salt and mayonnaise to taste. Fill halves of ripe avocados with turkey salad and serve on bed of lettuce. Add radishes, parsley or tomato wedges for color and garnish.

# Hot Rolls

2 packages yeast, 4 cups flour, ⅓ cup sugar, ⅓ cup oil, 1 teaspoon salt, 2 well-beaten eggs, 1 cup warm water. Mix all together and let rise in warm place until doubled. Form into rolls by rolling out on floured board and cutting with biscuit cutter. Put dab of melted butter in each roll, then fold over and place in oiled pan. Put melted

butter on top of rolls and let rise again. Bake in moderate oven, about 375 degrees, until brown. This makes 6 dozen very small rolls. They can be frozen and reheated.

## Chocolate Mousse

12 ounces semi-sweet chocolate. ⅓ cup water. 7 eggs. Melt chocolate and water in top of double boiler, stir and set aside to cool. Beat egg yolks and add to cooled chocolate. Beat whites until very stiff. Use largest bowl of mixer to do this, then add chocolate mixture, blending on slowest speed, just until smooth. Put into 12 serving cups and refrigerate. Can be served with whipped cream.

Gene Richardson / *Diocese of Texas*

# An Elegant Dinner Party for Sixteen

* Stuffed Mushrooms
* Lamb Curry with Condiments
  Rice
* Green Salad with Citrus and Avocado
  French bread
* Frozen Grasshoppers

## Stuffed Mushrooms

| | |
|---|---|
| 64 mushrooms about the size of a quarter | 3 tablespoons minced scallions |
| | ¼ teaspoon garlic salt |
| 2 large packages cream cheese, room temperature | ½ teaspoon Worcestershire sauce |
| | ½ teaspoon salt |
| 1 10½-ounce can minced clams | Paprika for garnish |

Remove stems from mushrooms. Wash and dry caps. With fork mix cheese with remaining ingredients. Fill caps with stuffing. Place on cookie sheet. Bake 10-12 minutes at 350 degrees. Garnish with paprika. Serve hot. Serves 16.

117

# Lamb Curry

First, find a butcher who calls you "Hon" and will do absolutely anything in the world for you. Ask him to trim and cube: 8 pounds of lamb. Saute this in:

**¼ pound butter or margarine**

With:

**1 piece of ginger root, peeled and minced**

**3 chopped onions**
**2 cloves garlic, crushed**

Add:

**3 cups chicken broth**
**3 cups milk**
**2 bay leaves**
**1 teaspoon Worcestershire sauce**

**4 peppercorns**
**4 tablespoons catsup**
**5 teaspoons curry powder**

Blend well. Bring to a boil, then simmer at low, low temperature for 3-4 hours. May be thickened with flour (about ½ to 1 cup) mixed with stock and stirred in. More curry may be added if desired. Serves 16.

Serve with:  Uncle Ben's Wild-Long Grain Rice Mixture.
4 boxes cooked according to directions.

## Condiments for Lamb Curry

Serve in individual dishes. (It helps to have houseguests to do the chopping.)

**2 pounds diced crisp bacon**
**8 hard cooked egg yolks, diced or sieved separately**
**1 fresh coconut, shredded and may be toasted**
**8 green scallion tops, cut into small rings**
**2 cups finely chopped salted peanuts**

**2 cups pitted black olives, chopped (do not buy the already chopped kind)**
**2 large jars mango chutney**
**Optional: 2 cans Bombay duck shredded (this makes it "authentic," but I think it is terrible)**

## Green Salad with Citrus and Avocado

Wash, dry, tear up and store:

2 heads iceberg lettuce
1 pound fresh spinach

2 heads endive
6-8 scallions, chopped

Drain and have ready to throw in:

2 jars Kraft grapefruit sections      2 cans Mandarin oranges

When ready to serve, add:

2-4 avocados, sliced

Toss with Italian dressing. Sprinkle with celery seed.

## Frozen Grasshoppers

48 dark chocolate wafers
1 stick butter (or margarine)
   melted

Crush wafers and mix with butter. Put into paper cups in muffin tins.

Filling:   48 large marshmallows
           1⅓ cups milk
           ½ cup green creme de
              menthe
           4 tablespoons creme de
              cacao

Melt marshmallows with milk in top of double boiler. When dissolved, add liqueurs. Cool. Add 2 cups cream, whipped. Pour into cups. When time to serve, peel off paper and grate bitter chocolate over top.

Jean Trelease / *Diocese of Rio Grande (New Mexico)*

*We thank Thee, LORD for the sharing of this food and fellowship. Strengthen and nourish us that we may go forth to do Thy will.   Amen.*

119

# Carolina Buffet for 18

Country ham, sliced thin
* Shrimp Creole
Steamed rice
* Spinach-Cream Cheese Casserole
Salad (2 heads lettuce, 1 endive, 3
avocados, 4 cups fresh grapefruit
sections, Wishbone Italian
dressing)
Artichoke pickle
Buttered French bread
Lemon Chess Pie, page 236

## Shrimp Creole

1½ cups minced green pepper
¾ cup margarine
3 packages onion soup mix
1 tablespoon salt
¼ teaspoon pepper

½ teaspoon paprika
8 cups canned tomatoes
3 pounds cooked shrimp, shelled
and deveined

Saute pepper 5-10 minutes in margarine. Add soup mix, seasonings
and tomatoes. Simmer 15 minutes. Add shrimp just before serving
and heat through. Serves 18.

Serve over hot rice (3 cups raw rice, 4½ cups water, 3 teaspoons
salt).

## Spinach-Cream Cheese Casserole

9 packages frozen chopped
spinach
3 8-ounce packages cream cheese

Salt and pepper
Buttered crumbs

120

Cook spinach, drain well. Add cream cheese, salt and pepper to taste and mix well. Put in buttered casserole and top with buttered crumbs. Heat in 350-degree oven until hot through. Serves 18.

"Dink" Elebash / *Diocese of East Carolina*

# *Fiesta Menu for 20— Panamanian Style*

* Ceviche (Marinated fish appetizer)
* Caldillo (Spicy soup with shrimp)
* Arroz con Pollo (Rice with chicken)
* Platanos en Tentacion (Baked
    plantains)
  Tossed Green Salad
* Sopa Borracha (Dessert cake with
    prunes and raisins)

## Ceviche (Marinated fish appetizer)

5 pounds firm-fleshed white fish, filleted
Salt
2 tablespoons olive oil

Juice of 12 large lemons (about 3 cups)
1 pound onions, minced
Hot peppers, minced

Skin raw fish and cut into small pieces (½-inch squares). Place in glass bowl (not metal or aluminum). Salt to taste. Add olive oil and lemon juice in sufficient quantity to cover fish completely. Mix onion and peppers (to taste) into fish. Refrigerate for about 12 hours. The lemon juice "cooks" the fish during this time. Serve cold with crackers as an appetizer. Serves 20.

121

## Caldillo (Spicy soup with shrimp)

1 pound onions, sliced
1 pound green peppers, chopped
1 clove garlic, minced
1 pound fresh tomatoes, peeled
  and chopped

2 quarts chicken broth
2 teaspoons tomato paste
Hot pepper or Tabasco sauce
1 pint cream
2 cups small cooked shrimp

Cook vegetables in chicken broth until tender. Add tomato paste and hot pepper sauce or Tabasco to taste. Just before serving, add cream and shrimps and bring to boiling point. Serve very hot. Serves 20.

## Arroz con Pollo (Rice with chicken)

¾ pound lard
3 frying chickens, 2 or 3 pounds
  each, cut in serving portions
2 pounds fresh prok, diced
6 Spanish sausages, sliced
2 large onions, chopped
4 cloves garlic, chopped
3 cups canned tomatoes
2 cups tomato sauce
6 large sweet peppers, chopped

4 bay leaves
Salt and pepper to taste
1 teaspoon saffron
4 pounds rice, picked and washed
1 small bottle stuffed olives
2 small bottles capers, drained
2 small cans pimientos, sliced
4 cups cooked peas
Chopped parsley

Heat half the lard in a large heavy pot, add chicken, pork and sausage and saute till golden brown. Take out meats and saute onions and garlic. Add tomatoes, tomato sauce and peppers and simmer for a few minutes. Add pork, chicken, sausage, bay leaves, salt, pepper, 6 cups hot water and saffron. On low flame cook until chicken is nearly tender. Remove meats and measure liquid.

You need 1¾ cups liquid for each cup of rice, that is, 14 cups liquid for 4 pounds of rice. Add hot water to make up the necessary amount and bring to a boil. Meanwhile, heat the remaining lard in a large frying pan and fry the rice, turning it constantly, till a golden brown. Add the rice to the boiling liquid and cook, uncovered, over a medium fire till the liquid has evaporated. Put in olives, capers, and meats. Cover and turn fire very low. After ½ hour turn rice with fork. Cook until rice is done. Serve on a large platter, garnished with peas, pimientos and chopped parsley. Accompany with baked plantains. Serves 20.

## Platanos en Tentacion (Baked plantains)

| | |
|---|---|
| 5 pounds very ripe plantains or firm bananas | 2 cups brown sugar |
| | 2 teaspoons cinnamon |
| 2 cups water | 1 cup sweet sherry wine |

Place peeled plantains or bananas in greased baking dish. Combine water, sugar, cinnamon and sherry. Pour over plantains. Bake at 350 degrees, turning plantains every 15 minutes until golden brown and sauce is thick.

## Sopa Borracha (Dessert cake with prunes and raisins)

| | |
|---|---|
| 1 pound seedless raisins | 6 cups water |
| 2 pounds pitted prunes | 2 large sticks cinnamon |
| 2 cups sherry (sweet or cream) | 2 slices lemon or lime |
| 2 cups rum | Large sheet sponge cake |
| 3 pounds sugar | |

Soak raisins and prunes overnight in sherry and rum. Make a heavy syrup with the sugar, water, cinnamon and lemon slices. Remove raisins and prunes and add them to the boiling syrup. When syrup is cool add the sherry and rum. Cut sponge cake into 1-inch squares and dip in the syrup. Arrange on a platter with the prunes and raisins on top of the cake. Pour any remaining syrup over the top. Decorate, if you wish, with tiny colored and silver candies. This is a very rich and delicious dessert that is served at every wedding and special fiesta in Panama. Serves 20.

Olga Shirley / *Diocese of Panama and the Canal Zone*

# Cook Ahead Stew and a Good Dessert Too

Serves 20

* Cook Ahead Beef Stew
  Garlic Bread
  Big tossed salad
* Walnut Pie

## Cook-Ahead Beef Stew

6 pounds beef chuck or round
3 tablespoons Kitchen Bouquet
8 carrots, quartered, then halved
6 onions, sliced
3 cloves garlic, minced
1 tablespoon salt
¼ teaspoon pepper

½ teaspoon marjoram, crushed
½ teaspoon thyme, crushed
2 cups burgundy or other dry red wine
2 pounds mushrooms
2 large cans tomatoes, blended slightly in blender

Trim excess fat from meat. Cut into 1½-inch cubes. Place in large dutch oven or casserole and toss gently with Kitchen Bouquet, coating meat. Put in rest of ingredients and mix gently. Cover and bake at 275 degrees for 5 hours or until done. Best cooked day before and reheated. Serves 20.

## Walnut Pie

1½ cups margarine, at room temperature
3 cups dark brown sugar, firmly packed
3 cups dark corn syrup

12 eggs, lightly beaten
½ teaspoon salt
3 teaspoons vanilla
3 unbaked 8- or 9-inch pie shells
3 cups walnut meats

Preheat oven to 375 degrees. Cream together margarine and brown sugar in a mixing bowl. Blend in syrup. Beat in eggs. Add salt and

124

vanilla and pour into pie shell. Arrange walnuts over top and bake for 40 minutes, or until set. Each pie serves 6 to 8.

Marie Robinson / *Diocese of Western New York*

# A Parish House Reception for 30 or More

> Coffee    Tea    Sherry
> * Coca-Cola Punch
> * Tuna Mold
> * Shrimp Sandwiches
> * Spinach Sandwiches
> * Peanut Butter Sticks
> * Miniature Cheesecakes
> * Orange Balls

## Coca-Cola Punch

**1 dozen lemons**          **5 pints water**
**3 cups sugar**            **40 ounces Coca-Cola**

Grate rind of 8 lemons, then squeeze all the lemons. Boil water, lemon rind, and sugar until sugar is dissolved. Add juice to the boiled mixture and refrigerate. Add chilled cola just before serving. I freeze a mixture of this in a ring mold and let it float in the punch bowl to keep it cold without diluting. Serves about 20.

# Tuna Mold

1 package unflavored gelatin
2 7-ounce cans white tuna,
  drained
2 hard-boiled eggs, chopped
½ cup chopped olives
2 tablespoons capers

2 tablespoons grated onion
1½ cups mayonnaise
3 tablespoons lemon juice
1 teaspoon Worcestershire sauce
Few drops Tabasco sauce

In a bowl dissolve gelatin in ¼ cup cold water. Set bowl in a pan of warm water until clear. Mix with remaining ingredients. Put in lightly greased fish mold and refrigerate. Chill until firm. Unmold and serve with melba rounds.

# Shrimp Sandwiches

1 large can small shrimp
2 8-ounce packages cream cheese
2 tablespoons mayonnaise

Instant minced onion to taste
2 large loaves thin-sliced bread

Drain shrimp, reserving liquid, and chop shrimp fine. Mix chopped shrimp with cream cheese, mayonnaise and minced onion to taste. Add juice drained from shrimp and mix until smooth. Make sandwiches. Refrigerate 24 hours, then trim crusts and cut each sandwich into 3 finger-length sandwiches. These can be frozen. Makes 30 whole sandwiches—or 90 finger size sandwiches.

# Spinach Sandwiches

1 package frozen chopped
  spinach, thawed
½ can water chestnuts, chopped
2 tablespoons mayonnaise
1 tablespoon sour cream

3 scallions, chopped
½ teaspoon salt
Freshly ground pepper to taste
1 large loaf thin-sliced bread

Do not cook thawed spinach, but press thoroughly to free of all water. Mix spinach with water chestnuts, mayonnaise, sour cream and scallions. Season with salt and pepper to taste. Make sandwiches, trim crusts and cut each sandwich into 4 triangles for 40 small sandwiches.

## Peanut Butter Sticks

| | |
|---|---|
| 1 large loaf sliced sandwich bread | Wesson oil |
| 1 large jar creamy peanut butter | Fine toasted bread crumbs |

Cut crusts from bread. Cut each trimmed bread slice into 4 finger lengths, place in 250-degree oven and let dry out about 1 hour. If you wish, toast crusts as well, and use to make bread crumbs. Mix peanut butter with enough Wesson oil to give the consistency of glue (so it will stick to the bread). Dip bread sticks in peanut butter mixture, spread evenly on all sides with knife. Roll in fine toasted bread crumbs, and put aside for 3 days. Do not put in refrigerator. Makes about 80 sticks.

## Miniature Cheesecakes

| | |
|---|---|
| Soft butter | 3 egg whites |
| Graham cracker crumbs | ¾ cup sour cream |
| 2 8-ounce packages cream cheese | 2½ tablespoons sugar |
| ¾ cup sugar | 1 teaspoon vanilla |
| 3 egg yolks | Strawberry preserves |

Butter 4 miniature muffin tins (of 12 muffins each) and sprinkle with graham cracker crumbs until well coated. Preheat oven to 350 degrees.

Mix cream cheese and ¾ cup sugar until creamy. Add egg yolks and mix well. Beat the egg whites until stiff and fold into the cheese mixture. Fill muffin pans until almost full and bake for 15 minutes. Remove from oven and cool; they will fall or lose volume. Mix sour cream, 2½ tablespoons sugar and vanilla. Drop about 1 teaspoon of this mixture into the center of the cool cakes. Top each cake with a bit of preserves and bake again at 400 degrees for 5 minutes. Cool and remove from pans. These freeze well. Makes 48 cakes.

## Orange Balls

1 6-ounce can frozen orange juice, thawed

1 pound confectioners sugar

1 stick margarine, melted

1 12-ounce box vanilla wafers, crushed

1 can angel coconut

Combine all ingredients except coconut. Mix together well. Place in refrigerator until firm enough to handle. Roll into balls and roll in angel coconut. Store in closed container. These keep well and are better in flavor if allowed to season a day or so. Makes about 50 Orange Balls.

Ann Allin / *Dover House (1974–)*

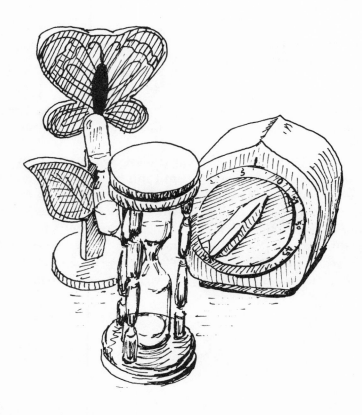

# Recipes from the Bishops' Wives

---

*A treasury of favorite recipes—from appetizers
for a parish reception to a Wassail Bowl for
Christmas Eve and preserves for the
Church Fair; a host of good main
dishes for dinner, lunch, and
potluck supper with soups
and breads, salads and
side dishes, cakes,
cookies, and
desserts.*

# APPETIZERS

## Avocado Dip

2 cups mashed avocado
¼ cup mayonnaise
2 tablespoons lemon juice
6 slices crisp bacon, crumbled
1 tablespoon finely chopped
   onion

¼ teaspoon chili powder
¼ teaspoon salt
¼ teaspoon garlic powder
Dash of hot pepper sauce

Blend avocado, mayonnaise and lemon juice. Add remaining ingredients, mix well and chill.

Louise Millard / *Diocese of California*

## Egg and Avocado Appetizer

6 hard cooked eggs, chopped
2 avocados, chopped fine
1 fresh chili pepper, chopped fine
   (or ¼ teaspoon dried ground
   chili)

1 onion, chopped fine
3 tablespoons chopped parsley
2 tablespoons vinegar
1½ teaspoons salt

Combine ingredients and mix well. Chill and serve on lettuce leaves or toast as a first course, or as a spread for crackers. Serves 6 to 8.

Peggy Rath / *Diocese of Newark (New Jersey)*

# Bean Dip

½ pound ground beef
¼ cup chopped onion
1 8-ounce can red kidney beans
¼ cup *hot* ketchup
1½ teaspoons chili powder
½ teaspoon salt

½ cup grated sharp American cheese
¼ cup chopped green onions, including stems
¼ cup sliced stuffed green olives

Brown the beef, stirring to keep it crumbly, and remove from pan. Gently saute onions in same pan until soft, adding oil if necessary. Put the beans with their liquid in blender. Add beef, onion, ketchup, chili and salt, and blend for 30 seconds until just well mixed.

Place in a chafing dish over hot water. Sprinkle cheese, green onions and olives on top. Serve as dip with corn chips or tortilla chips.

Janice Rusack / *Diocese of Los Angeles (California)*

# Winchester Dried Beef Dip

1 cup creamed cottage cheese
2 tablespoons skim milk
2 to 3 tablespoons horseradish

½ cup minced onion
2½ ounces dried beef, cut in small pieces.

Combine in blender. Refrigerate about an hour.

Jeanne Baden / *Diocese of Virginia*

# Nasturtium Blossoms

For special occasions, teas or cocktail parties.

Choose fresh nasturtium blossoms in assorted colors. Keep in water until ready to use.

Soften cream cheese with a little cream. Gently fill centers of the blossoms with this mixture. It is not only a beautiful hors d'oeuvre but good to eat.

Connie Hall / *Diocese of New Hampshire*

## Blue Cheese Ball

3 3-ounce packages cream cheese,
  softened
1 4-ounce package blue cheese,
  crumbled

2 teaspoons bourbon (optional)
¾ teaspoon dry mustard
2 tablespoons sesame seeds,
  toasted

Day before serving: In a small bowl with electric mixer at medium speed, beat together cream cheese and blue cheese until soft. Add bourbon and mustard; blend well. With hands, shape cheese mixture into a ball. Wrap with waxed paper or plastic wrap and refrigerate overnight.

At serving time: With hands, reshape ball and roll in sesame seeds. Serve with crackers. Makes about 32 appetizer servings.

Marge Fraser / *Diocese of North Carolina*


## Olive-stuffed Cheese Puffs

1 cup grated sharp cheese
¼ cup soft butter
½ cup flour, sifted

¼ teaspoon salt
½ teaspoon paprika
24 stuffed olives

About 4 or 5 hours ahead blend cheese with butter. Stir in flour, salt, paprika and mix well. Wrap 1 teaspoon of this dough around each olive, covering it completely. Arrange on ungreased cookie sheet. Refrigerate. About ½ hour before serving, bake puffs at 400 degrees for 10 to 15 minutes. Serve warm. Makes 24 canapes.

Elena Gooden / *Diocese of Panama and the Canal Zone*


## Cheese Crisps

2 cups grated cheddar cheese
2 sticks butter or margarine
2 cups flour
1 teaspoon salt

½ teaspoon red pepper
2 cups Rice Krispies
1 cup chopped pecans

Mix all ingredients together very well. I end up using my hands. Shape into small balls and put on a cookie sheet. Bake 10 to 15 minutes at 350 degrees. Place in tight tin. These freeze well. If you want them crisp after freezing, put them in a warm oven for a few minutes before serving. Makes about 90 pieces.

Helen Kellog / *Diocese of the Dominican Republic*

## Cheese Puffs

1 8-ounce stick sharp cheese, grated
1 3-ounce package cream cheese
4 tablespoons margarine
2 whites of eggs, well beaten
Bread slices, cut in cubes

Melt cheeses and margarine in double boiler, add beaten egg whites. Dip bread cubes in mixture and set on cookie sheet. Let stand overnight. Bake at 350 degrees for 15 minutes.

Hannah Lawrence / *Diocese of Western Massachusetts*

## Snappy Cheese Wafers

2 cups all-purpose flour
2 sticks margarine (I use corn oil margarine)
10 ounces sharp cheddar cheese (Kraft sharp or very sharp)
½ teaspoon salt
½ teaspoon cayenne pepper
2 cups Grape-Nuts

Mix softened margarine and flour thoroughly. Add finely-shredded or grated cheese and mix. Add salt, cayenne, and Grape-Nuts. Mix well. Chill dough for two hours. Pinch off small bits and place on ungreased cookie sheet. Press flat with tines of fork. Bake in 350-degree oven for 15 minutes. Can be made ahead and frozen. Yields about 10 dozen.

Marje Gosnell / *Diocese of West Texas*

## Cheese Straws

4 tablespoons chicken fat
1 cup grated sharp cheddar cheese
1½ cups flour
½ teaspoon salt
½ teaspoon sugar
Dash of cayenne pepper

Mix ingredients well. Mold into roll 1½ inches thick. Chill. Slice. Place on lightly greased cookie sheet. Bake for 10 to 12 minutes in 350-degree oven.

Martha Henton / *Diocese of Northwest Texas*

## Chicken Liver Paté

½ cup butter
1 3-ounce package cream cheese
½ pound chicken livers
1 small onion, quartered
2 tablespoons brandy or cognac

6 tablespoons chicken broth
½ teaspoon paprika
½ teaspoon curry powder
½ teaspoon salt
⅛ teaspoon cayenne pepper

Remove butter and cream cheese from the refrigerator one hour beforehand. Clean chicken livers, cut in half and remove tissue. Place livers, onion, brandy and broth in saucepan; bring to a boil and cook 5 minutes. Place mixture in blender, add seasonings, cover and blend on high speed. Slice in the cream cheese and butter. Blend. Pour into small crock or ramekin and chill 2 hours or more. May be frozen, but serve at room temperature. Makes 2½ cups.

Lota Hogg / *Diocese of Albany (New York)*

## Jellied Chicken Liver Paté

1 quart chicken livers
1 stick butter
Juice of 1 lemon
¾ teaspoon salt
1 clove garlic
2 hardcooked eggs

1 tablespoon mayonnaise
4 drops Tabasco
½ envelope gelatin
2 tablespoons cold water
1 tablespoon sherry or brandy

Saute livers in butter. Put in blender. Add lemon juice, salt, garlic, eggs, mayonnaise and Tabasco. Blend for 1 minute on and off. Soak gelatin in 2 tablespoons of water in measuring cup. Place cup in boiling water. When dissolved, add with sherry or brandy to mixture in the blender, and blend on and off for ten seconds, three or four times. Pour into mold or crockery dish and leave in refrigerator for 12 hours. Unmold and serve on melba toast.

Martha Henton / *Diocese of Northwest Texas*

## Eggplant Caponata

1 medium size eggplant,
  unpeeled
Salt
¾ cup olive oil
2 onions, chopped
2 cloves garlic, chopped
1 1-pound can strained tomatoes
2 stalks celery, chopped

8 large pitted green olives,
  quartered
2 tablespoons pine nuts or
  slivered almonds
2 tablespoons wine vinegar
¼ cup capers
Additional salt and pepper to
  taste

Wash eggplant, cut into 1-inch cubes, sprinkle with salt and let stand for 1 hour. Rinse and dry. Put cubes into heated oil, cook over low heat until soft. Remove eggplant from oil and set aside. Add onions, garlic, tomatoes, celery and green olives to pan with oil. Cook until celery is crisp-tender. Add eggplant, capers, pine nuts and vinegar to celery-onion-olive mixture. Season to taste with salt and freshly ground pepper. Chill thoroughly before serving. As an hors d'oeuvre serve with plain crackers or toast triangles. Also can be used as one section of a mixed salad plate or in Pita bread sandwiches.

Janice Rusack / *Diocese of Los Angeles (California)*

## Chicken Quiche

2 cups cooked chicken, cut up in
  bite-size pieces
Unbaked 9-inch pie shell
6 ounces Swiss cheese
3 tablespoons slivered almonds

3 eggs
½ cup milk
Pepper and salt
Parmesan cheese

Put chicken in unbaked pie shell. Grate Swiss cheese over the chicken. Sprinkle almonds on top. Beat egg yolks with milk. Add salt and pepper. Beat egg whites until stiff and fold in egg yolk mixture. Pour over chicken. Sprinkle top with Parmesan cheese. Bake at 350 degrees for 30 minutes or until filling is set.

Beth Murray / *Diocese of Central Gulf Coast*

# SOUPS

## Basic Soup Stocks—and soups to make from them

These soup stocks can be used for a number of soups. Add chicken pieces, noodles, barley, vermicelli—use your imagination. I make up a large batch of each kind and freeze it in quart jars so I can take what I need for a certain recipe.

### Basic Beef Stock

3 pounds short ribs
2 gallons cold water
1 large onion
2 cloves garlic
3 carrots
3 stalks celery

1 bunch parsley
2 tomatoes or 2 tablespoons
   tomato sauce
2 whole cloves (optional)
Salt and papper to taste

Put the short ribs and water in a large pot. When this begins to boil, skim any foam from the top until the liquid is clear. Now add the vegetables, cut in large pieces, and the parsley—well tied. The cloves, salt and pepper go in at this time, too. Cover the pot and let the stock simmer gently for 2½ to 3 hours. Cool the stock, discard the vegetables, and skim excess fat. Reserve the short ribs for they can be eaten either cold or simmered with potatoes, cabbage and a little soup stock.

## Basic Chicken Stock

1 stewing chicken
2 stalks celery
1 medium onion
2 cloves garlic

2 carrots
1½ gallons cold water
1 whole clove
Salt and pepper

Cut the chicken in half and the vegetables in large pieces. Cover them with the water in a large soup kettle. Add clove, salt and pepper. When the stock comes to a boil, reduce heat and simmer gently for about 2 hours. Remove and reserve the chicken; strain the stock and discard the vegetables and clove.

## Fried Vegetable Soup

2 cups vegetables (almost any
  vegetables can be used—such
  as celery, carrots, leeks,
  spinach, chard, cabbage,
  potatoes, turnips)

1 tablespoon olive oil
1 tablespoon flour
2 teaspoons tomato sauce
4 cups Basic Beef Stock
Salt and pepper

Chop the vegetables fine and fry them in the olive oil until they are limp. Stir in the flour and continue frying until the mixture is golden. Now stir in the tomato sauce and soup stock. Season gently and allow the soup to simmer for ½ hour. Serves 4-6.

## Vegetable Puree

2 medium potatoes
3 good-sized carrots

4 cups Basic Beef Stock
Salt and pepper

Peel and cut up the potatoes and carrots and simmer them until tender in the stock. Puree, season and serve. Serves 4-6.

## Onion Soup

4 medium onions
2 tablespoons olive oil
1 tablespoon flour
4 cups Basic Beef Stock or
  Chicken Stock

Salt and pepper
Croutons or small pieces of
  toasted bread

Peel onions and slice them as thinly as possible. Fry them gently in olive oil in a large soup pot until they are golden. Add the flour and continue frying for 1 or 2 minutes. Don't let the mixture brown! Add the broth and the salt and pepper. Bring the soup to a boil and then turn down the heat. Cover the pot and simmer the soup for 30 minutes. Serve and top with croutons or toasted bread. Serves 4.

Dee Frensdorff / *Diocese of Nevada*

## Black Bean Soup

3 pounds dry black beans
  (available in food specialty
  stores)
1 large onion, quartered
1 large green pepper, quartered
4 quarts water
1 medium onion, finely chopped
1 medium green pepper, finely
  chopped
1 6-ounce can tomato paste
1 tablespoon Worcestershire sauce

1 tablespoon garlic salt
1 tablespoon chopped parsley
1 teaspoon black pepper
1 teaspoon oregano
1 teaspoon thyme
2 teaspoons vinegar
2 teaspoons sugar
Green pepper strips
Hard-cooked egg slices or lemon
  slices
Fried rice (optional)

Thoroughly wash beans. (There's no need to soak them overnight.) Combine beans, quartered onion, quartered green pepper and water in 6-quart kettle. Bring to boil, reduce heat and simmer, covered, about 3 hours or until beans are nearly tender. Add chopped onion, chopped green pepper, tomato paste, Worcestershire sauce, garlic salt, parsley, black pepper, oregano, thyme, vinegar and sugar. Mix well. Bring to boil, reduce heat and simmer, covered, about 45 minutes or until beans are done, stirring occasionally. Taste during cooking period and add more of any one of the listed seasonings, if desired. Serve as a soup or on fried rice, if desired. Garnish with green pepper strips, egg or lemon slices. (Soup freezes nicely.) Makes 6 quarts.

Barbara Frey / *Diocese of Colorado*

## Hearty Soup with Italian Sausage

4 trimmed, sliced celery stalks
1 coarsely cut onion
2 tablespoons olive oil
2 cups chopped seeded, ripe
  tomatoes (or canned ones)
1 cup tomato puree
1 pound sweet Italian sausage, cut
  into 1-inch chunks
6 cups chicken broth

3 bay leaves
⅛ teaspoon thyme
½ teaspoon basil
1 cup chopped parsley
3 tablespoons sugar
Generous pinch of saffron
2 cups mashed potatoes
½ cup Madeira or Marsala

Saute celery and onion in oil until barely tender. Add tomatoes, tomato puree and sausage, and cook gently for 10 minutes. Add chicken broth, bay leaves, thyme, basil, parsley, sugar and saffron. Simmer 30 minutes. Blend mashed potatoes with some of hot soup and Madeira. Add to soup, stirring until smooth and hot. Remove bay leaves. If desired, garnish with slices of hard boiled egg.

This is a marvelous soup to take on skiing trips. It can be refrigerated and reheated, and it really is a meal in itself with fruit for dessert.

Janice Rusack / *Diocese of Los Angeles (California)*

## Lamb and Barley Soup

2 medium onions, sliced
2 carrots, sliced
2 stalks celery, sliced
1 small turnip, thickly sliced or
  cubed
4 tablespoons margarine
Leg of lamb bones and leftovers
1½ quarts water

1½ quarts soup stock (lamb,
  chicken or bouillon)
½ cup barley
1 bay leaf
Pinch of rosemary and thyme
Salt and freshly ground pepper to
  taste
Chopped parsley

Cook vegetables in fat until onion is transparent. Add bones and leftover lamb meat, barley and herbs. Simmer for about 2 hours over low heat. Remove bones, clean for useable meat which should be chopped and added to the soup. Add parsley just before serving. Serves 8 to 10.

Polly Keller / *Diocese of Arkansas*

## Chicken Corn Soup

1 chicken or chicken parts
2 slices bacon
1 medium-sized onion, chopped
4 cobs of corn or 1 can creamed or
    whole kernel corn

2 hard-cooked eggs, chopped
Salt and pepper to taste
Parsley, chopped

Boil chicken until tender in 2 quarts of water. Strain, cut meat into small pieces. Place in chicken broth. Fry bacon until crisp and crumbled. Add the chopped onion; saute until clear. Add bacon and onion to chicken. If you use fresh corn (which has been cut off cob) add to the chicken mixture and cook for 20 minutes. If canned corn is used just add and heat for 5 minutes. Add chopped eggs, salt and pepper to taste. When serving, sprinkle with parsley.

Doris Stevenson / *Diocese of Central Pennsylvania*

## Florida Keys Fish Chowder

¼ pound fat salt pork
2 onions, sliced
3 cups uncooked potatoes, cut
    into ½ inch cubes
4 cups boiling water
3 pounds assorted fish, boned

1¾ cups evaporated milk
1 teaspoon salt
⅛ teaspoon pepper
1 tablespoon minced parsley
1 tablespoon butter
1 tablespoon flour

Cut salt pork into small pieces, fry slowly in soup kettle. Add onions and cook five minutes. Add potatoes, boiling water and fish cut into small pieces. Simmer until potatoes are soft. Add milk, salt, pepper and parsley. Melt butter, add flour and blend thoroughly. Add gradually to soup until liquid is slightly thickened. Cook five minutes longer.

This serves about 8 people. I double or triple the recipe when needed. I serve it from a tureen with pilot's crackers, a tossed or simple salad plus some fruit. Good for a luncheon—or Sunday night supper—a cold weather dish, but all right too in warm weather.

Condie Lee Moody / *Diocese of Lexington (Kentucky)*

141

## Salmon Chowder

3 slices salt pork, diced
3 medium onions, minced
4 medium potatoes, cubed

1 pint milk
1 tall can salmon (red, preferably)
Salt and pepper to taste

Fry pork until crisp. Remove from pan. Fry onions in pork fat until golden. Add 1½ quarts water. Bring to boil. Add potatoes. When potatoes are tender, add 1 pint milk and salmon, including juice and minced bones. Heat until hot, but do not boil. Serve at once. Good as main dish for lunch or supper. Serves 6.

Frances Lewis / *Armed Forces*

## Hearty Shrimp Chowder

3 cups milk
1 pound Velveeta cheese, cut up
  or grated
5 large onions, peeled and thinly
  sliced
¼ pound margarine

1½ cups water
5 large potatoes, peeled and
  thinly sliced
Salt and pepper to taste
1 quart boiled shrimp, shelled
  and deveined

Heat milk, add cheese and stir until melted. Set aside. Lightly brown onions in margarine. Add water and potatoes, bring to boil and simmer until done. Add salt, pepper, cheese mixture and shrimp. Serve piping hot. Serves 6 to 8.

"Dink" Elebash / *Diocese of East Carolina*

## Crab Meat Bisque

1 can Campbell's Tomato Soup
1 can Campbell's Pea Soup
1 cup cream

1 6½ ounce can of crabmeat
½ cup sherry

Put soup in saucepan with cream, heat, and stir constantly. Add crab meat. Just before serving, add sherry gradually. Serve very hot. This is good for a Sunday night supper with a salad. Serves 4.

Margaret Esquirol / *Diocese of Connecticut*

142

## Dinner Party Consomme

4 cans consomme
2 cups V-8 juice
2 cups water

Dash of garlic salt and onion salt
Slices of lemon for garnish

Mix the first 4 ingredients in a saucepan; place on medium heat. When piping hot, garnish with lemon slices and serve. An easy first course before dinner. Great for a stormy winter day in front of a roaring fire. For extra flavor, add a dash of Tabasco and a couple of bouillon cubes. Serves 10.

Charlotte McNeil / *Diocese of Western Michigan*

## Egg and Lemon Soup

1 quart well-seasoned chicken
  broth

2 eggs
Juice of 1 large lemon

Just before serving, bring broth to boil in a saucepan. Remove from heat. In a bowl beat eggs until light and frothy. Add lemon juice. Beating constantly, add a cup of the hot broth to the egg-lemon mixture. Return saucepan of broth to low heat. Slowly pour in the egg-lemon-broth mixture, stirring constantly to prevent curdling. Heat through but do not allow to simmer. Serve immediately—in bouillon cups, mugs or Japanese soup bowls. Serves 4 to 6.

Patti Browning / *Executive Council*

## Squash Bisque

4 tablespoons butter
2 ribs celery with leaves, chopped
3 scallions or 1 medium onion,
  chopped
4 yellow crookneck squash or 4
  zucchini, sliced
1 large butternut or acorn squash

1 quart of chicken stock, fat
  removed
1 13-ounce can evaporated milk
½ teaspoon sugar
Salt and pepper
½ teaspoon nutmeg

Melt butter and add celery, onions, yellow or zucchini squash. Saute on low heat for 15 minutes. Bake butternut or acorn squash in oven at 375 degrees for 45 minutes. Halve the squash. Remove the seeds and scrape meat into saucepan with other squash. Add 3 cups of the chicken stock. Cook 10 minutes. Strain vegetables and blend with 1 cup of cold stock. Return stock and squash to saucepan. Heat. Add milk, soy sauce and sugar. Do not boil. Add salt and pepper to taste. Add nutmeg just before serving.

Martha Henton / *Diocese of Northwest Texas*

## Potato Soup

| | |
|---|---|
| 6 cups raw potatoes, peeled and sliced (about 5 large potatoes) | 2 tablespoons flour |
| ½ cup carrots, peeled and sliced | 4 cups milk |
| 5 slices bacon, cut in small pieces | 1½ teaspoons salt |
| 1 cup celery, chopped | ¼ teaspoon pepper |
| 1 cup onion, chopped | Grated cheese |
| | Parsley, chopped |

Cook potatoes and carrots in water until tender. Drain. Fry the pieces of bacon and set aside. Saute celery and onions in bacon fat. Mix flour in small amount of milk, then add to remaining milk. Combine all ingredients except parsley and cheese and simmer 30 minutes. Do *not* boil. Sprinkle grated cheese and parsley atop each serving. Serves 8.

Ruthie Gray / *Diocese of Mississippi*

## Lettuce Soup

| | |
|---|---|
| 3 to 4 cups romaine lettuce, chopped very fine | ½ cup cream or evaporated milk |
| 1 cup water | Nutmeg |
| 1 tablespoon chopped onion | Salt |
| 1 tablespoon butter | Pepper |
| 2½ cups chicken stock | Croutons for garnish |

Cook lettuce and water until lettuce is limp. Heat onion in butter and add to lettuce along with remaining ingredients, except the croutons. Bring to a boil, lower the heat immediately and simmer 10 to 15 minutes. Serve with browned, buttered croutons. Serves 6.

Evelyn Thayer / *Diocese of Colorado*

## Spinach Soup

1 10-ounce package of frozen
   spinach
3 tablespoons margarine
2 onions, chopped
1 rib of celery, chopped
1 quart of chicken stock, fat
   removed*
1 13-ounce can of evaporated milk

1 teaspoon of soy sauce
3 drops Tabasco
½ teaspoon anise flavoring
¼ teaspoon nutmeg
¼ teaspoon salt
¼ teaspoon white pepper (of
   course, black pepper will do)

Cook spinach according to directions. Do not drain, cool. Melt margarine in a 4-quart saucepan. Saute onion and celery on low heat until onion is translucent and celery soft. Do not brown. Put spinach in blender with onion and celery. Blend thoroughly. Return to sauce pan. Add other ingredients. Heat slowly. Do not boil. This can be served hot or cold, after simmering for 2 minutes. This can safely be added to with more chicken stock should it be necessary. Serves 6 in big bowls; 8 in cups or glasses; 10 in demitasse cups before dinner.

* Chicken fat tends to separate too much in the soups I make, unless it boils, and boiling soup hurts the flavor, which survives either short or long simmering.

Martha Henton / *Diocese of Northwest Texas*

## Cold Cucumber Buttermilk Soup

1-1½ cups cucumbers, seeded and
   grated
1 quart buttermilk
2 tablespoons chopped green
   onions

1 teaspoon salt
Cucumber slices and chopped
   chives for garnish

Mix the ingredients well and chill for 3 hours. Mix again when ready to serve. Place in chilled bouillon cups and garnish with a cucumber slice and chives. Serves 6 to 8.

Carolyn Leighton / *Diocese of Maryland*

145

## Cold Cucumber Soup

4 tablespoons butter
2 ribs of celery with leaves, chopped
3 scallions or 1 medium onion, chopped (leeks give wonderful flavor in place of onion. I use onion because they're cheaper and I always have them.)

4 cucumbers, sliced
1 quart chicken broth, fat removed
¼ teaspoon soy sauce
1 level teaspoon sugar
1 cup heavy cream (I substitute evaporated milk)

Melt butter in saucepan. Saute vegetables until soft over low heat, and onion is clear. Add chicken broth, soy sauce and sugar. Let simmer 25 minutes. Puree in blender. (My blender does not cooperate with hot things so I strain the stock and cool the vegetables by adding a little cold stock, then return vegetables to stock.) Bring pureed soup just to simmering point and add cream. Again bring barely to a simmer. Do not boil. Chill. I serve this sometimes in goblets or glasses before dinner. It serves 6. If you need it to serve 8, use smaller glasses.

Martha Henton / *Diocese of Northwest Texas*

# BREADS

## My Favorite Bread Recipe

½ cup yellow corn meal
⅓ cup brown sugar
1 tablespoon salt
2 cups boiling water
¼ cup cooking oil

2 packages active dry yeast
½ cup lukewarm water
¾ cup whole wheat flour
½ cup rye flour or wheat germ
4½ cups all-purpose flour

Place first five ingredients in large bowl. Thoroughly combine and cool to lukewarm. Soften yeast in the ½ cup lukewarm water and when proofed, add to first ingredients. Stir in whole wheat flour and rye flour or wheat germ. Mix well. Add all-purpose flour to make a moderately stiff dough. Turn out on lightly floured surface and knead 6 to 8 minutes until smooth and elastic. Place in greased bowl, cover and let rise in warm place till doubled in size. Punch down, divide into loaf sizes and shape loaves, placing them in well-greased pans. Let rise until double in size or almost double (brown bread should not be allowed to rise quite as high as white bread before baking). Bake at 375-400 degrees for approximately 45 minutes or until loaves sound hollow when tapped on top. Remove from pans and cool on rack. This bread freezes and maintains its moisture well. Because of the inclusion of the cornmeal, it makes elegant crisp toast. Makes 2 1-pound loaves and 1 small loaf.

Marilyn Jones / *Diocese of South Dakota*

147

## Sister Amelia's Shaker Daily Loaf

An old recipe from the Shaker community of North Union, where the city of Shaker Heights, Ohio now stands.

| | |
|---|---|
| ½ cake compressed yeast | 1 tablespoon sugar |
| ⅛ cup warm water | 1 teaspoon salt |
| 1 cup milk | 3-3½ cups all-purpose flour, |
| 1 tablespoon butter | sifted |

Dissolve yeast in warm water. Scald milk with butter, sugar and salt and stir until well mixed. When lukewarm, add yeast. Gradually add flour until sponge is stiff enough so it does not stick to hands. Place in buttered bowl and brush top with soft butter. Let rise to double its bulk. Knead lightly this time and shape into loaf in pan. Again brush with soft butter and let rise to twice its bulk. Bake in moderate 350-degree oven for 50 minutes. Test loaf by tapping top. If it sounds hollow, the loaf is done. Remove from pan immediately. Cover lightly, for steam must escape. This is an excellent loaf of wholesome, crusty bread. It must not be allowed to rise very fast or be baked in too hot an oven.

Martha Burt / *Diocese of Ohio*

## Trinity Wheat Bread

| | |
|---|---|
| 3 cups boiling water | 1½ packages dry yeast |
| ½ stick oleo | 4 cups whole wheat flour |
| 1 tablespoon salt | 1 cup rye flour |
| ½ cup honey or molasses | 4 or more cups white flour |

Combine water, oleo, salt and honey. Let cool to lukewarm. Add dry yeast and dark flours. Add white flour slowly until easy to work. Knead. Put to rise in greased bowl. When double in bulk, punch down. Work into 3 loaves and let rise until double in bulk. Bake in preheated oven at 350 degrees for about 40 minutes. I rub tops with oleo as I take from the oven for softer crust. I turn them out on cake racks and cover with tea towels until cool. Bread may be wrapped in aluminum foil and frozen. Makes 3 loaves.

Jeanne Baden / *Diocese of Virginia*

# Oatmeal Bread

| | |
|---|---|
| 2 cups boiling water | 4 tablespoons bacon drippings |
| 1 heaping cup regular oatmeal | 1 cake yeast dissolved in |
| 2 teaspoons salt | ¼ cup warm water |
| ½ cup molasses | 5-6 cups flour |

Pour boiling water over oatmeal, salt, molasses and bacon drippings. Let stand until cool. Add yeast dissolved in warm water. Add flour and knead until it doesn't stick to the board. Let rise in warm place until double in bulk. Form into two large loaves or four small ones. Let rise again. Bake at 350 degrees for 45 minutes. Give one loaf away.

This is a very old recipe. This last instruction is very important.

Katherine Appleyard / *Diocese of Pittsburgh (Pennsylvania)*

# Brown Rice Bread

| | |
|---|---|
| 1 cup white corn meal | ½ cup honey |
| 2½ teaspoons salt | 6½ cups unsifted flour |
| ¼ teaspoon baking soda | 2 cups cooked brown rice (at |
| 2 packages active dry yeast | room temperature) |
| ½ stick margarine, softened | |
| 2 cups warm tap water (120-130 | |
| degrees Fahrenheit) | |

In large bowl mix corn meal, salt, soda and yeast. Add margarine. Gradually add warm tap water and honey. Beat 2 minutes at medium speed of electric mixer, scraping bowl. Add ½ cup flour. Beat 2 minutes at high speed. Stir in rice and enough of remaining flour to make a stiff dough. Turn out on floured board and knead 10 minutes until smooth and elastic. Place in greased bowl, turning dough greased side up. Cover. Let rise in warm place until doubled in bulk. Punch dough down. Turn out on board; divide in half. Cover and let rest 15 minutes. Roll each piece and place in a greased bread tin. Cover. Let rise until doubled—about 1¼ hours. Bake at 350 degrees for 35 minutes or until done. Remove from bread tins and cool on rack.

I make this bread frequently and find it delicious and very filling. Makes 2 large loaves.

Elizabeth Corrigan / *Diocese of Colorado*

## Raisin Bread

| | |
|---|---|
| 1 yeast cake or 2 teaspoons dry yeast | 1 cup water |
| | 1 cup flour |

Dissolve yeast in lukewarm water. Add flour, mix well and let stand overnight.

| | |
|---|---|
| 1 cup milk | 1 teaspoon vanilla |
| 6 tablespoons butter or margarine | 6 cups flour |
| ⅓ cup sugar | 1 teaspoon mace |
| 1 teaspoon salt | 1 teaspoon nutmeg |
| 1 cup raisins | 1 teaspoon cinnamon |
| ¼ cup water | |

Warm milk, butter, sugar and salt. Let mixture cool, then add to above yeast mixture, stirring thoroughly. Boil raisins in ¼ cup water for 3 minutes. Drain, cool, then add with vanilla to milk and yeast mixture.

Sift 5 cups of the flour with spices, add to mixture, beating in well. Put dough in greased bowl and let stand for 3 hours in warm place (80-85 degrees) until doubled in bulk. Turn dough out onto a lightly floured board. Knead dough until smooth, adding any of the remaining cup of flour needed. Divide dough evenly and place in 2 well-greased bread pans. Let rise in warm place until doubled in bulk, about 2 hours. Bake in preheated 400-degree oven for about 10 minutes, reduce heat to 350 degrees and bake 45 minutes longer. Remove from pans and cool slightly. While still warm, spread with the following glaze:

| | |
|---|---|
| 2 tablespoons butter | 2 tablespoons water |
| 2 tablespoons sugar | |

Boil together until thick enough to spoon over bread or brush on with pastry brush.

Maria Walker / *Diocese of Washington*

## Dill Bread

2 packages dry yeast
½ cup lukewarm water (110 degrees)
1 16-ounce carton creamy cottage cheese
2 eggs
4 tablespoons sugar

2 tablespoons minced onion flakes
2 tablespoons melted butter
4 teaspoons dill seed
2 teaspoons salt
½ teaspoon soda
5 cups sifted flour

Dissolve yeast in lukewarm water. In large mixing bowl bring cottage cheese and eggs to room temperature by setting bowl in a pan of warm water. Add dissolved yeast and remaining ingredients except flour. Beat with a wooden spoon until thoroughly blended. Add flour to make a stiff dough. Let rise at room temperature for about 1½ hours until doubled in bulk. Beat down and knead very well. Place in 2 greased loaf pans. Brush tops with melted butter. Let rise 1 hour. Bake in a 350-degree oven for 40 minutes. Brush again with melted butter. Let cool on racks. Makes 2 loaves.

Kathleen Jones / *Diocese of Louisiana*

## Aunt Sarah Chapman's Saffron Bread

1 pint milk, scalded and cooled to lukewarm
3 tablespoons butter
1 teaspoon salt

2 eggs, beaten
1½ cups sugar
1 yeast cake dissolved in 1 cup of lukewarm water

At night, mix all the above together with enough flour to make a soft sponge. Steep ½ dram of saffron in 1 cup boiling water. Let stand in covered pitcher until morning.

In the morning, strain saffron tea into the sponge. Add ½ pound currants, ½ pound seeded raisins, ½ pound candied lemon peel cut in strips. Knead in enough flour to stiffen—not quite as stiff as bread. Let rise till it doubles in bulk. Put in pans and let rise for 1 hour. Bake; takes a little longer than plain bread.

Virginia Gray / *Diocese of Connecticut*

# Hot Rolls

| | |
|---|---|
| 1 cake compressed yeast | 4 eggs |
| 1 tablespoon sugar | ½ cup sugar |
| ½ cup warm water | 1 tablespoon salt |
| 2 cups milk | 6 to 7 cups flour |
| 1 cup shortening | ½ pound hot melted butter |

Combine the crumbled yeast with 1 tablespoon sugar and ½ cup warm water. Set aside. Heat the milk just to boiling; add the shortening; cool a little. Beat the eggs, sugar and salt in large bowl. Add cooled milk mixture. Add yeast and mix. Add enough flour to handle easily and blend well with hands. Cover and let rise in warm place for 2 hours. It will be at least doubled in bulk, maybe more.

Using about ⅓ of the dough at a time, pat out on floured surface to ¼ inch thickness. Cut into rounds with biscuit cutter or glass, 1½ inches in diameter. Dip each round in melted butter and fold in half. Place in three 13×9×¾-inch pans to rise for 10 minutes. Bake at 400 degrees for 10 to 15 minutes until browned. Brush with melted butter on one side. Freeze if desired. Thaw before reheating. Reheat on cookie sheets at 350 degrees until warm through. Yield 8 dozen.

Marie Louise Creighton / *Diocese of Washington, D.C.*

# Danish Kringle

| | |
|---|---|
| 2 cups flour | ½ cup milk |
| 1½ tablespoons sugar | 1 egg yolk |
| ½ teaspoon salt | 1 package dry yeast |
| ½ cup soft butter or margarine | ¼ cup warm water |

*Filling*

| | |
|---|---|
| ¼ cup butter or margarine | 1 cup chopped pecans |
| ½ cup brown sugar | 1 egg white |

*Icing*

| | |
|---|---|
| 1 cup confectioners sugar | ¼ teaspoon vanilla |
| ½ tablespoon milk | |

152

Mix together flour, sugar and salt. Cut in shortening until mixture is like coarse meal. Scald milk and cool slightly. Then stir in egg yolk. Add to flour mixture. Add yeast to water and let stand about 5 minutes. Add to batter and mix thoroughly. The dough will be quite soft. Cover tightly and chill at least two hours, and no more than 48 hours.

Prepare filling before shaping kringles. Cream butter and sugar until fluffy. Stir in pecans.

Divide dough into two 6×18-inch rectangles. Brush a 3-inch strip down the center with half the beaten egg white. Spread half the pecan mixture over the egg white. Fold over one side of dough and then the other with a 1½-inch lap to cover filling. Pinch dough to close fold. Arrange dough on baking sheet in horseshoe shape. Prepare and shape second kringle as first. Cover them and let rise about 1½ to 2 hours. Bake in a hot oven 400 degrees for 20-30 minutes, or until golden brown. Spread icing on kringles.

Cary McNairy / *Diocese of Minnesota*

## Favorite Coffee Cake

| | |
|---|---|
| ½ cup shortening | 2 cups sifted flour |
| ¾ cup sugar | 1 teaspoon baking powder |
| 1 teaspoon vanilla | 1 teaspoon baking soda |
| 3 eggs | ½ pint sour cream |

*Filling*

| | |
|---|---|
| 6 tablespoons butter | 2 teaspoons cinnamon |
| 1 cup firmly packed brown sugar | 1 cup chopped nuts |

Cream shortening, sugar, vanilla together. Add eggs 1 at a time, beating well after each addition. Sift flour, baking powder and baking soda together. Add to creamed mixture, alternating with sour cream, blending after each addition. Spread half of batter in 10-inch tube pan that has been greased and lined on the bottom with wax paper. Mix filling ingredients together. Spread half of filling on batter. Add rest of batter and top with filling. Bake at 350 degrees about 50 minutes. Cool cake in pan 10 minutes before removing. Serves 10.

Grace Maclean / *Diocese of Long Island (New York)*

153

## Fruit Nut Loaf

4 cups flour
4 teaspoons baking powder
½ teaspoon salt
1 cup sugar
1 cup raisins

1 cup broken walnuts
1 egg
2 cups milk
4 tablespoons melted butter

Sift flour, baking powder and salt. Add sugar, fruit and nuts. Mix well. Beat egg, add milk and melted butter. Add liquid to flour mixture. Stir till blended. Let stand for 30 minutes in greased loaf tin or tube pan. Bake at 350 degrees for 1 hour.

Jean Coggan / *Lambeth Palace, London, England*

## Bishop's Bread

½ cup soft margarine
¾ cup sugar
1 teaspoon vanilla
2 eggs
2¾ cups flour
3 teaspoons baking powder
½ teaspoon salt

1 cup milk
⅓ cup chopped nuts
⅓ cup candied cherries
   (maraschino cherries)
⅓ cup semi-sweet chocolate bits
⅓ cup raisins or dates

Blend together margarine, sugar, vanilla. Beat in eggs, one at a time. Sift together flour, baking powder and salt; gradually blend into margarine mixture alternately with milk. Stir in fruits, which have been lightly coated with flour. Add nuts and chocolate bits. Pour into a greased 9×5×3-inch loaf pan, bake at 350 degrees for 1 hour and 5-10 minutes. Cool and frost if desired.

This appropriately named recipe was discovered by two contributors. The second version uses 3 eggs and no butter.

Marge Gressle / *Diocese of Bethlehem (Pennsylvania)*
Cary McNairy / *Diocese of Minnesota*

## Cranberry Nut Bread

2 cups flour
1 cup sugar
1½ teaspoons baking powder
½ teaspoon soda
1 teaspoon salt
¼ cup margarine

1 egg
¾ cup orange juice
1 tablespoon grated orange rind
1 cup raw cranberries, coarsely
    chopped
½ cup chopped nuts

Sift together the dry ingredients. Cut the margarine into dry mixture as for pastry. Combine egg, juice and rind and pour over dry
ingredients, mixing just enough to moisten the whole. Fold in nuts
and cranberries. Place in two 4×8×2-inch greased loaf pans and
bake at 350 degrees about 50 minutes. These make lovely Christmas
gifts for the neighbors! Makes 2 loaves.

Louise Millard / *Diocese of California*

## Orange Date Bread

1 whole orange
1 cup dates
1 tablespoon melted butter
1 teaspoon vanilla
1 egg, beaten
2 cups flour

¼ teaspoon salt
1 teaspoon baking powder
½ teaspoon baking soda
1 cup sugar
½ cup nuts

Grate orange peel and grind dates. Fill 1 cup half full of orange juice
and finish filling with boiling water; pour over dates and peel. Stir
in melted butter, vanilla, egg and sifted dry ingredients. Add nuts
and pour into 1-pound baking tin. Bake 1 hour in 350-degree oven.
Cool in pan. Makes 1 loaf.

Evelyn Thayer / *Diocese of Colorado*

## Carrot Bread

1½ cups flour
1 cup sugar
1 teaspoon baking powder
1 teaspoon baking soda
2 eggs

¾ cup vegetable oil
¼ teaspoon salt
1 teaspoon cinnamon
½ cup nut meats
1 cup grated raw carrots

155

Combine all ingredients in bowl. Mix with electric mixer 3 minutes. Pour into greased bread pan. Bake 1 hour at 350 degrees. To make tea sandwiches, spread with cream cheese and orange marmalade. Makes 1 loaf.

Carolyn Butterfield / *Diocese of Vermont*

# Black Walnut Bread

4 cups flour
4 teaspoons baking powder
Pinch of salt
2 eggs

1½ cups sugar
1½ cups milk
1½ cups black walnuts, coarsely
    chopped

Sift dry ingredients together. Beat eggs; add sugar. Alternately add dry ingredients and milk. Stir in the walnuts and put into 2 bread pans that have been greased and dusted with flour. Let stand for 20 minutes before putting into 350-degree oven. Bake for 40 minutes. When cool slice thin and butter. Delicious with tea. Will freeze. Makes 2 loaves.

Mary Louise Creighton / *Diocese of Washington, D.C.*

# Carolyn's Lemon Bread
## Delicious at Christmas—or any other time

½ cup Crisco
1 cup sugar
2 eggs
½ cup milk
1½ cups flour

1 teaspoon baking powder
¼ teaspoon salt
½ cup ground pecans
Grated rind of 1 lemon

Cream the Crisco and sugar together. Add eggs and beat. Mix the dry ingredients together and add alternately with milk. Bake in bread loaf pan for 1 hour at 350 degrees.

*Topping:*

¼ cup sugar added to juice of 1 lemon; mix well. Pour over top of loaf when it comes from oven. Let loaf cool in pan.

Beth Murray / *Diocese of Central Gulf Coast*

## Three-Grain Peanut Bread

1 cup flour, fork-stir to aerate
  before measuring
½ cup quick-cooking oats
½ cup yellow cornmeal
½ cup nonfat dry milk
½ cup sugar

3 teaspoons baking powder
1 teaspoon salt
⅔ cup creamy peanut butter
1 egg
1½ cups milk

In a large bowl stir together first 7 ingredients. Cut in peanut butter until particles are small. Beat egg and milk to blend. Pour into flour mixture and mix well. Turn into a greased and floured 9×5×3-inch loaf tin and spread evenly. Bake in a preheated 325-degree oven about 70 minutes or until a cake tester inserted in center comes out clean. Place pan on wire rack to cool for 10 minutes. Loosen edges; turn out on wire rack; turn right side up and cool completely. Makes 1 hearty and especially nutritious loaf.

Elizabeth Corrigan / *Diocese of Colorado*

## Bran Muffins

3 cups All Bran
1 cup boiling water
1½ sticks oleo
1½ cups sugar
2 eggs

2 cups buttermilk
2½ cups flour
2 teaspoons salt
2½ teaspoons baking soda

Pour boiling water over 1 cup of the All Bran. Set it aside to soak. Cream oleo and sugar. Add eggs one at a time. Beat. Add buttermilk alternately with flour to which you have added salt and soda. Add remaining dry All Bran and soaked bran. Stir this together well. Bake in muffin tins for 18–20 minutes at 400 degrees. I like to use small 1½-inch tins. The dough can be stored in the refrigerator in a tight container with saran wrap over the dough for 10 to 12 weeks! Use as needed.

Martha Henton / *Diocese of Northwest Texas*

## Apple Muffins

| | |
|---|---|
| 1½ cups flour, sifted | ¼ cup soft shortening |
| ½ cup sugar | 1 egg |
| 2 teaspoons baking powder | ½ cup milk |
| ½ teaspoon salt | 1 cup chopped raw apple |
| ½ teaspoon cinnamon | |

Sift the dry ingredients together. Add the remaining ingredients and mix together until well blended. Fill muffin cups ⅔ full. Bake at 400 degrees for 20-25 minutes. (Can be topped with a mixture of cinnamon, sugar and nuts before baking.) Makes 12 muffins.

Mary Parsons / *Diocese of Quincy (Illinois)*

## Famous German Pancake

Thoroughly tested at our house and just great. Good with bacon or sausage and a great brunch concoction. We prefer lemon juice and powdered sugar on it rather than maple syrup or jelly.

| | |
|---|---|
| ½ cup flour | 4 large eggs |
| ½ cup milk | 1 tablespoon butter |
| Pinch of salt | 1 tablespoon shortening |

Mix flour, milk and salt together until smooth. Add eggs and mix well. Melt butter and shortening in a heavy frying pan (one with sloping sides is best) and pour in all the batter. Fry until golden brown. Turn with spatula and bake in a 425-degree oven for about 12 minutes; the pancake will begin to rise in about 7 or 8 minutes. Or may be cooked entirely in the oven—at 400 degrees for 18 to 20 minutes. Serves 4.

Ruth Hallock / *Diocese of Milwaukee (Wisconsin)*

---

*O God our Father*
*To all thou hast given us*
*We ask but one thing more*
*Give us grateful hearts.  Amen.*

# MAIN DISHES

## Meat Dishes

### Fat-Free Roast Beef

Strip a complete eye of the round roast of all external fat (the interior is exceptionally lean) and insert meat thermometer. Place in roasting pan on lower shelf of oven. Roast at 250 degrees for 1 hour, then turn down to 150 degrees and roast for another 8 to 10 hours. Turn up the heat the last twenty minutes or so if necessary to raise the heat reading of the meat thermometer to the desired reading. This slow cooking makes a delicious, tender, almost fat-free main course. Slice thin and serve with a green vegetable and a lettuce and tomato salad with oil and vinegar dressing.

Katherine Welles / *Diocese of West Missouri*

### Open House Buffet Sandwiches

**4 pound fresh beef brisket**

If possible, have butcher de-fat it. If not, slice off all fat you possibly can before preparing.

Sprinkle entire surface of both sides of meat lightly with salt, pepper, garlic powder, Accent and Adolph's meat tenderizer. (I use seasoned salt, instead of plain, on one side, and seasoned pepper on the other.) Place meat flat in roasting pan. Add ⅓ cup water to pan (not directly on meat). Cover. Bake at 175 degrees (yes, *one hundred and seventy-five degrees*) for approximately 24 hours. Check occasionally to make sure there is always some liquid in bottom of pan.

Remove from pan to cutting board. Let "set" a few minutes. Slice thinly across grain with a very sharp knife. (I like an electric knife for this.) Keep sliced meat on a platter on a warming tray, with a basket of soft, sliced bite-size rolls beside it.

Helen King / *Diocese of Idaho*


## Greek Stew

2 pounds top round beef, cut into
  small pieces
¼ pound margarine
2 tablespoons vinegar
2 large yellow onions, sliced
1 8-ounce can Hunt's tomato
  sauce

1 cup raisins
Dash of cinnamon
1 cup red wine
Salt to taste

Place meat in heavy skillet or casserole. Melt margarine and pour over meat. Cover and place over low heat. Do not fry or brown. When steaming, add vinegar and spread sliced onions over meat. Cover. After an hour's slow cooking, add tomato sauce, raisins and cinnamon. Keep covered. When meat is tender, add red wine. Serve with rice. Serves 6.

Katherine Appleyard / *Diocese of Pittsburgh (Pennsylvania)*


## Flank Steak Roll-ups

2 flank steaks, 1½ pounds each
Meat tenderizer
¼ cup soy sauce
¼ cup sherry
¼ cup vinegar
½ teaspoon pepper
3 tablespoons butter

⅔ cup chopped onion
⅔ cup chopped celery (or green
  pepper)
1 cup sliced mushrooms
1 tablespoon chopped parsley
Salt to taste

160

Prick steak with fork and add meat tenderizer. Combine soy sauce, sherry, vinegar and pepper. Pour over meat and let stand for 2 hours, turning occasionally.

Heat the butter and saute onions, celery and mushrooms; add parsley and salt. Take steak out of marinade and put mushroom mixture on surface of meat. Roll up and tie. Brush meat with marinade, place on foil and broil for 10 minutes or more on each side. Serve with baked tomato halves, topped with crumbs, grated cheese and a dab of butter, baked for about 15 minutes in a 350-degree oven. Serves 6 to 8.

Cary McNairy / *Diocese of Minnesota*

## Superb Spaghetti

3½ cups canned tomatoes
2 pounds ground beef
¼ cup butter
¼ cup margarine
2 medium onions, chopped fine
2 tablespoons salt

½ to ¾ pound Swiss cheese, chunked
¼ teaspoon paprika
3 cups spaghetti, broken, boiled in salt water, drained

Combine all ingredients in a 3- or 4-quart casserole. Bake in 375-degree oven until bubbly, about 1 hour, in the morning. Then bake again at 350 degrees for 1 hour before serving. The two bakings are very important. Serve with dark bread, green salad and fresh fruit. Serves 8 to 12 depending on the appetites.

Betty Powell / *Diocese of Oklahoma*

## Chili Casserole

3 pounds ground beef
3 cups chopped onion
3 packages chili seasoning mix
3 8-ounce cans tomato sauce
2 cups water
3 1-pound cans red kidney beans, drained

1 3¾-ounce package small corn chips
1½ cups sliced pitted ripe olives
2 cups shredded sharp cheddar cheese

161

In a large heavy kettle, cook meat until it is brown, breaking it up as it browns. Add the next 4 ingredients. Stir, bring to boil and simmer, covered for 15 minutes, stirring frequently to prevent sticking. In a 4-quart casserole, layer meat mixture with beans, corn chips, olives and cheese, ending with chips and cheese. Bake at 325 degrees for 50 to 60 minutes. Serves 12.

Katie Vogel / *Diocese of West Missouri*

## Arroz and Frijoles "Ole" (Rice and Beans)

We raise and eat a lot of rice in Arkansas. It's a great meat stretcher. Use it with leftovers and in soups. The brown rice is delicious. It should be cooked about twice as long as white rice. We like this recipe.

1 pound lean ground beef
½ cup celery, diced
½ cup green pepper, chopped
1 teaspoon each garlic and onion
  powders
1½ teaspoons salt
¼ teaspoon Tabasco

1 can cheddar cheese soup
1 can pinto beans, drained
2 medium tomatoes, cut in
  eighths
3 cups cooked rice
1 cup crushed corn chips

Saute meat, celery and green pepper with garlic and onion powders in lightly greased skillet about 10 minutes. Add remaining ingredients except corn chips. Turn into a greased 2-quart casserole. Top with corn chips. Bake at 350 degrees for 25 minutes. Serves 6.

Polly Keller / *Diocese of Arkansas*

## Beefburger Pie with Cheese Topping

2 tablespoons cooking oil or fat
2 tablespoons chopped onion
¾ pound ground beef
1 teaspoon salt
⅛ teaspoon pepper

2 tablespoons flour
2 cups canned tomatoes
½ teaspoon Worcestershire sauce
1 cup diced cooked carrots
1 cup cooked string beans, cut up

Melt fat in frying pan, add onion, meat; brown well. Mix salt, pepper, flour into the meat. Add tomatoes, Worcestershire sauce, and cook until slightly thickened. Add cooked carrots and beans; pour into a greased casserole. Prepare ahead, if you wish. Before baking spread with the following topping:

| | |
|---|---|
| 1 cup flour, sifted | 2 tablespoons shortening |
| 1½ teaspoons baking powder | ¼ cup grated sharp cheese |
| ½ teaspoon dry mustard | ½ cup milk |
| ½ teaspoon salt | |

Mix the dry ingredients together and cut in shortening. Add cheese and milk, blend to a soft dough. Spread topping evenly over the meat mixture. Bake 20 to 25 minutes in 350-degree oven. If doubled, it should be cooked in two equal casseroles. Serves 6.

Jean Weinhauer / *Diocese of Western North Carolina*

## Stuffed Cabbage Rolls

| | |
|---|---|
| 2 small heads cabbage | 1 teaspoon salt |
| ⅔ cup uncooked rice | ¼ teaspoon pepper |
| 1½ pounds ground beef | 1 medium can sauerkraut, drained |
| ½ pound ground pork | 5 strips bacon, chopped |
| 1 egg, slightly beaten | 2 10½-ounce cans condensed |
| 1 onion, chopped | tomato soup |
| 1 clove garlic, minced | 1 8-ounce can tomato sauce |
| 1 tablespoon chopped parsley | 2 soup cans water |

Core cabbage and place in rapidly boiling water for about 2 minutes to separate leaves. Drain. Cook rice, drain and rinse thoroughly. Combine meats, rice, egg, onion, garlic, parsley, salt, pepper, and mix well. Place a little of meat mixture on each cabbage leaf, roll leaf and push in ends tightly so mixture does not come out. Place half the sauerkraut and bacon in a deep pot. Add the cabbage rolls and place the rest of the sauerkraut and bacon on top. Combine tomato soup, tomato sauce and water in saucepan; bring to a boil. Pour this mixture over the cabbage rolls, making sure there is enough liquid to cover all. Simmer slowly, covered, for 1½ to 2 hours. Serves 8 to 10.

Katherine Appleyard / *Diocese of Pittsburgh (Pennsylvania)*

## Johnny Mazette

2 cups chopped green peppers
1 cup chopped celery
2 cups chopped onions
2 pounds ground beef
1 cup margarine
2 teaspoons salt
½ cup sliced stuffed olives

1 8-ounce can sliced mushrooms
1 10½-ounce can condensed
   tomato soup
1 8-ounce can tomato sauce with
   mushrooms
1 pound noodles
2 cups grated American cheese

In a large skillet saute peppers, celery, onions and meat in hot margarine. Add salt. Reduce heat and cook 5 minutes. Stir in olives, mushrooms and juice, soup and tomato-mushroom sauce. Cook 5 minutes longer. Cook noodles according to directions and drain well. Turn noodles into a 14 × 10½ × 1½ inch dish. Add sauce gradually, stirring well. Sprinkle cheese on top. Bake at 350 degrees for 35 minutes. This dish freezes well. Serves 12.

Virginia Turner / *Diocese of Kansas*

## Canton Tease Balls

1 pound ground beef
1 egg
1 teaspoon salt
1 tablespoon cornstarch

2 tablespoons chopped onion
Dash of black pepper
½ teaspoon monosodium
   glutamate (optional)

Combine ingredients and shape into 18 small balls. Brown in skillet.

1 tablespoon peanut or corn oil
1 cup pineapple juice
3 tablespoons cornstarch
½ cup sugar

3 tablespoons vinegar
1 tablespoon soy sauce
6 tablespoons water

Mix oil and pineapple juice; cook over medium heat. Mix the remaining ingredients, add to pineapple juice and cook, stirring constantly, until sauce thickens. Add the meat balls and heat thoroughly. Just before serving, add:

3 green peppers, cut into long
   strips

4 slices pineapple, chunked

Serve over hot rice. Serves 6.

Betty Powell / *Diocese of Oklahoma*

## Lasagne Casserole

Saute in oil for 10 minutes:

½ cup chopped onion
½ cup chopped celery

½ cup chopped green pepper

Add and fry until meat is brown

1 pound ground round beef

½ pound pork sausage meat

In a separate pan mix:

1 6-ounce can tomato paste
2½ cups whole tomatoes
1 8-ounce can sliced mushrooms
2 tablespoons sugar
1 teaspoon chili powder, or to
taste

6 drops Tabasco
Salt and pepper
1 clove garlic, crushed

Bring to boil. Add meat mixture and simmer for an hour, until the sauce is medium thick.

Cook according to package directions:

1 8-ounce package of lasagne

In 11 × 7-inch buttered baking dish, alternate layers of cooked lasagne, meat sauce, and

8 ounces mozzarella cheese, cut
up or grated

Finish with a layer of meat sauce and cheese. Bake for 1 hour at 350 degrees. Serves 6 to 8.

Helen Klein / *Diocese of Northern Indiana*

## Roast Pork Chinese Style (Cantonese Cha Siu)

1 pound boneless pork (mui tao
yuk)
2 tablespoons sugar
2 tablespoons light soy sauce
1 tablespoon soya bean paste
1 tablespoon salt
1 tablespoon rosé flavoring wine

1 teaspoon sesame paste
1 shallot, chopped fine
1 clove garlic, chopped fine
A dash of monosodium glutamate
1 tablespoon sesame oil
1 tablespoon honey

165

Wash the pork and cut into strips 14-inches long by 2-inches by 1-inch. Combine remaining ingredients, except for the sesame oil and honey, in an earthenware pot and mix thoroughly. Immerse the pork in the mixture. Stir well and marinate for at least 1 hour. Then thread pork strips onto skewers and grill for about 15 minutes. Combine honey and sesame oil and brush on pork strips. Grill a further 15 minutes. Serves 4.

Lily Pong / *Diocese of Taiwan*

## Macaroni Oriental

1½ pounds elbow macaroni
2 pounds boned pork loin, thinly
   sliced in bite-size pieces
½ cup butter or margarine
¾ pound fresh mushrooms,
   sliced
2 Bermuda onions, sliced
3 bunches green onions, sliced in
   1-inch pieces

6 cups celery, sliced diagonally
1 pound fresh spinach
3 5-ounce cans water chestnuts,
   drained and sliced
6 beef bouillon cubes, dissolved
   in 3 cups boiling water
3 tablespoons cornstarch
¾ cup soy sauce
¾ cup cooking sherry

Cook the macaroni until tender, drain and keep warm. Saute pork slices in butter for about 10 minutes, stirring to cook thoroughly. Cook the vegetables in bouillon, covered, for 3 minutes. Blend cornstarch and soy sauce, add to vegetables and cook 2 minutes. Add meat and sherry and serve over macaroni. Serves 12.

Betty Powell / *Diocese of Oklahoma*

## Pork Steak Casserole

1 8-ounce package egg noodles
1 pound pork steak, cubed
1 onion, chopped
1 can condensed tomato soup
1 can water

1 teaspoon salt
Pepper
¼ pound American cheese, cubed
⅔ cup buttered bread crumbs

Cook noodles as directed. Brown pork in a little butter. Add onion and brown. Add tomato soup, water, seasonings and cheese. Put in

2-quart casserole and cover with buttered crumbs. Bake at least two hours at 325 degrees. Should be moist; add water if necessary. This could be assembled ahead of time (except the bread crumbs) and baked in time for the meal. I have frozen the leftover portion. If reheating, add more water. A good meat stretcher. Serves 8 generously. Serve with tossed salad or cole slaw and crusty bread.

Polly Spofford / *Diocese of East Oregon*

## Chilis Rellenos (Stuffed Peppers)

| | |
|---|---|
| 6 chilis Guaques (dark green hot peppers) | ¼ pound chopped pickles, including pickled beets |
| ¾ pound ground pork | 2 eggs, well-beaten |
| 4 medium tomatoes | 2 tablespoons flour |
| 1 cup chopped cooked vegetables | Fat for frying |

Roast peppers for a few minutes so as to be able to remove skin. Remove seeds with care, keeping pepper whole. Stew pork with tomatoes for 15 minutes. Stuff the peppers carefully with the pork, vegetables and pickles. Make a batter with the eggs and flour, dip the peppers in the batter and fry in very hot fat. Serve very hot. Serves 6.

Berta Carral / *Diocese of Guatemala*

## Egg Sausage Souffle

Good for breakfast or brunch. It must be mixed up the night before, and can be stretched by adding more milk, eggs and bread. I serve it with a fresh fruit bowl and homemade biscuits or sweet rolls.

| | |
|---|---|
| 1 pound sausage, browned, drained and crumbled | 6 slices of bread, cubed |
| | 1 cup grated cheese |
| 2 cups milk | 1 teaspoon salt |
| 6 eggs, slightly beaten | 1 teaspoon dry mustard |

Mix all the ingredients together and refrigerate 12 hours. Bake in 1½-quart casserole 45 minutes to 1 hour at 350 degrees. Serves 6 to 8.

Gray Davis / *Diocese of Erie (Pennsylvania)*

167

## Sausage filled Crepes

**Filling:** 1 pound sausage
¼ cup onion, chopped
½ cup process cheese, shredded

1 3-ounce package cream cheese
¼ teaspoon dried marjoram

Cook sausage and onion; drain. Add shredded cheese, cream cheese and marjoram. Set aside.

**Crepes:** 3 eggs, beaten
1 cup milk
1 tablespoon cooking oil

1 cup all-purpose flour
½ teaspoon salt

Combine eggs, milk and oil. Add flour and salt. Blend until smooth. Pour 2 tablespoons batter into greased 6-inch skillet and tilt to spread batter. Cook on 1 side, invert on paper towelling. Repeat to make 16. Place 2 tablespoons sausage filling across each center; roll up. Place in flat buttered baking dish, cover and chill. Bake covered in 375-degree oven for 40 minutes. Mix sauce:

½ cup sour cream
¼ cup butter or margarine, softened

Spoon this sauce over the crepes and bake, uncovered, for 5 to 10 minutes more. These crepes may be made and frozen before baking. Serves 4 to 5.

Marilyn Jones / *Diocese of South Dakota*

## Stuff'N Such Ham Rolls

12 slices of boiled ham, thickness for easy rolling
½ small green pepper, chopped
1 small clove garlic, minced
5 tablespoons butter
1 6-ounce package Uncle Ben's Stuff'N Such Cornbread Stuffing

1 7-ounce can whole kernel corn, drained
Pepper to taste
½ cup dry white wine
1 tablespoon flour

Set ham slices aside. Cook green pepper and garlic in 3 tablespoons of the butter. Prepare box stuffing up to cooking point. Stir in green pepper mixture, corn and black pepper. Place ¼ cup of stuffing mixture at narrow end of ham slice and roll up. Arrange in baking dish, 12 × 18 × 2 inch. Heat wine in sauce pan, and pour over ham rolls. Dot with 1 tablespoon butter. Cover with foil and bake for 25 minutes in 350-degree oven. Remove rolls to serving platter, keep warm. Measure pan juice, add water to make ¾ cup liquid. Melt remaining butter, stir in flour, add pan juice liquid and cook until thick. Serve over ham rolls. Serve two to a plate with green beans and mushrooms and tossed salad. Serves 6.

Mabel Davies / *Diocese of Dallas (Texas)*

## Ham Loaf and Sauce

| | |
|---|---|
| 2 pounds fresh pork (ground with ham) | 2 eggs, beaten |
| | 1 cup milk |
| 1 pound smoked ham (ground with pork) | 1 teaspoon salt |
| | Pepper to taste |
| 3 cups rolled corn flakes | 2 teaspoons prepared mustard |

Mix the ground pork and ham thoroughly. Add the other ingredients and mix well. Put into loaf pan and bake for 1¼ hours at 375 degrees. Serve with sauce:

| | |
|---|---|
| ⅓ cup brown sugar | 2 tablespoons cornstarch |
| ⅓ cup vinegar | 2 tablespoons prepared mustard |
| ⅓ cup hot water | |

Cook over medium heat, stirring constantly, until thick. Serves 6 to 8.

Ida Lou Barnds / *Diocese of Dallas (Texas)*

## Ham Rolls with Cheese Sauce

| | |
|---|---|
| 1½ cups ham, chopped in blender | 2 cups flour |
| | ½ teaspoon salt |
| 3 tablespoons butter, softened | 4 teaspoons baking powder |
| 2 tablespoons prepared mustard | ¾ cup milk |
| 4 tablespoons shortening | |

Mix the chopped ham with the butter and mustard. Cut the shortening into the dry ingredients, add milk and mix. Turn out on a floured board and knead slightly. Roll out to ¼-inch thick, making

169

a rectangle approximately 10 × 12 inches. Spread with ham mixture. Roll up lengthwise and seal. Slice with a sharp knife in 1-inch pieces. Place on a cookie sheet and flatten slightly with a spatula. Bake at 400 degrees for 15 to 20 minutes until golden brown. Serve with cheese sauce. Follow the traditional cheese sauce method, combine:

2 tablespoons butter
2 tablespoons flour
2 cups milk

½ cup grated cheese
1 teaspoon salt

You may substitute 1 can of Campbell's Cheddar Cheese soup slightly diluted with milk instead. Serves 4 to 6.

Marilyn Jones / *Diocese of South Dakota*


## Braised Veal with Herbs

2 pounds veal cutlet
2 tablespoons vegetable oil
2 medium onions, cut into rings
1 clove garlic (optional)
¼ cup water

2 tablespoons lemon juice
1 teaspoon salt
½ teaspoon crushed oregano
2 tablespoons chopped parsley

Cut veal into serving pieces. Heat oil in large skillet. Add veal and cook until brown on both sides. Remove from pan. Add onions and garlic; cook until onions are tender. Remove garlic. Add veal, water, lemon juice, salt and oregano. Cover and simmer over low heat, turning meat occasionally, until meat is tender, about 20 to 30 minutes. Add additional water if needed. Serve with chopped parsley. Serves 6.

Jeanne Bigliardi / *Diocese of Oregon*


## Veal Croquettes

2 green peppers, chopped
2 onions, chopped
4 tablespoons butter
3 pounds veal, cooked and
  ground

Salt, pepper and celery seed
2 eggs, beaten
Cracker crumbs
Fat for frying

170

Saute peppers and onions in butter until vegetables are tender. Mix together with veal and seasonings. When cool, shape into long croquettes. Dip in beaten eggs and roll in cracker crumbs. Fry in deep fat. Makes about 40 croquettes. Serve with:

**Cream Dressing:**
¼ pound butter
8 tablespoons flour

2 quarts liquid (about 1 quart veal
   or chicken stock and 1 quart
   milk)
Salt and pepper

Melt butter, blend in flour. Add stock and milk slowly, stirring until smooth and thickened. Season to taste.

Eleanor Jackson / *Diocese of Louisiana*

## Lamb Curry

2 pounds of boneless lamb
1½ teaspoons salt
1 tablespoon flour
1 tablespoon curry powder
½ cup oleo
2 large onions, peeled and sliced
1 large or 2 small apples, pared,
   cored and chopped

1 small clove garlic, minced
2½ tablespoons brown sugar
1 tablespoon Worcestershire sauce
1 lemon, sliced
2 cups water
2 tablespoons shredded coconut

Cut lamb in serving pieces. Mix flour, salt and curry powder and dredge lamb in this mixture. Melt fat in a large, deep frying pan or Dutch oven. Add onions and fry until golden brown. Push the onions to one side and cook meat until delicately browned. Add the apples and cook three or four minutes. Add the remaining ingredients. Bring to the boiling point, cover and simmer gently until the meat is tender, approximately one hour. Yield: 4 to 6 servings.

Marie Louise Creighton / *Diocese of Washington, D. C.*

---

*We thank thee, our Heavenly Father,*
*For Thy hand that feeds us,*
*For Thy love that forgives us*
*And Thy grace that sustains us.   Amen.*

171

## Venison Roast

3 to 4 pound deer loin or saddle
  roast of venison
¼ pound fat, suet or pork fat
Salt and pepper to taste

1 cup red currant jelly
½ cup water
2 medium onions, quartered

Trim roast of all fat. Place on rack in shallow roasting pan, skin side up. Cut suet in pieces, and lay on top of roast. Roast in 325-degree oven ½ hour. Season with salt and pepper. Add other ingredients to pan. Continue roasting until done, about 1 hour longer. Baste every 15 minutes. Allow 20-25 minutes per pound. Do not overcook venison. Serves 6 to 8.

Evelyn Thayer / *Diocese of Colorado*

# *Poultry Dishes*

## Basic Poached Chicken

*There are so many uses for the versatile chicken. Its meat and broth are used in the recipes that follow. Flavorful chicken stock is the base for several soup recipes elsewhere in the book. Chicken livers (which freeze very well) make a good Chicken Liver Paté. Even chicken fat has many uses. It makes delicious Cheese Straws or superior flaky pastry for Chicken Pie, or patty shells for Chicken à la King.*

*First, poach your chicken. Here is the mother recipe that makes possible the ones that follow.*

2- or 3-pound chicken with
  gizzard, neck and heart
Salt, pepper, poultry seasoning
3 quarts water
1 tablespoon salt
1 medium onion, sliced or
  chopped

1 carrot, sliced or chopped
1 garlic clove, sliced
3 whole peppercorns
¼ tablespoon Tabasco sauce

Wash chicken under cold running water. Check to make sure no inedible parts remain inside. Pat dry with paper towels. Sprinkle inside with salt, pepper and poultry seasoning. Place chicken in salted water with remaining ingredients and simmer 1 hour. Do not boil. Allow chicken to remain in stock until cool enough to handle. Remove chicken from stock and remove meat from bones.

Reserve bones and skin, if you wish to make a little more stock. To them add 5 cups water, 3 or 4 bouillon cubes and the seasonings used to poach the chicken. Simmer for ½ hour or more.

Meanwhile refrigerate the stock in which the chicken was cooked. When it is cold, remove chicken fat with a spatula or spoon. Render it in a small saucepan over low heat. It keeps well, refrigerated, or can be frozen.

## Chicken-Filled Crepes

### The Crepes

3 eggs, beaten
1 cup milk
⅞ cup flour (1 cup minus 2
   tablespoons)

2 tablespoons melted margarine
or oil

Blend above to the consistency of heavy cream. Let stand for an hour or so. Heat crepe pan or griddle. When hot, pour a scant ¼ cup (3 tablespoons) into pan and tilt to spread batter and give crepe a good shape. When crepe is brown on underside flip with spatula. These may be done a day ahead. In that case, put wax paper between each crepe and wrap tightly in foil. Makes 16-18 crepes.

### The Filling

3 tablespoons butter
3 level tablespoons flour
¼ teaspoon salt
¼ teaspoon white pepper
⅛ teaspoon nutmeg
1¼ cups hot chicken broth
2 egg yolks or 1 egg
½ cup cream (canned milk is
   cheaper, but not quite so good)

3 cups cut poached chicken
Optional: chopped ripe olives,
   well-drained cooked spinach,
   sliced mushrooms, small ham
   strips
Swiss or Monterrey Jack cheese,
   shredded

Melt butter in saucepan (preferably Teflon-lined, enamel or stainless steel, not aluminum). Add flour, salt, pepper and nutmeg and blend. Add hot chicken broth (be sure it is well boiled down so that sauce will have a decided chicken flavor). Beat egg yolks or whole egg into cream and add some hot broth. Add egg mixture to remaining broth. Do *not* boil. Add cut chicken. Do not use large pieces. Finely cut gizzard and heart may be included, if desired. Taste for seasoning. Add any of the optional ingredients, if desired.

Place a spoonful of chicken filling near the lower edge of each crepe. Roll up and place, seam side down, closely together in a buttered 8 × 11-inch baking dish.

For the sauce, make a second recipe of the above sauce, without adding chicken or optional ingredients, or double the sauce recipe when you make it originally and reserve 2 cups. Cover the rolled up crepes with sauce. Cover baking dish with foil and bake in a 375-degree oven for 25 minutes. Uncover for the last 10 minutes and sprinkle with shredded cheese. Allow 2 crepes per person. Makes 16-18 filled crepes.

## Scalloped Chicken with Sauce

4 cups poached chicken, diced
2½ cups soft bread crumbs
3 cups cooked rice
¼ cup diced pimiento
1 teaspoon parsley flakes
½ cup sliced mushrooms,
    optional

4 eggs, beaten
2 teaspoons salt
¼ cup melted butter or margarine
3 cups milk or chicken broth
3 grinds black pepper
4 drops Tabasco sauce

Mix and pour in greased 3-quart ring mold. Bake at 325 degrees for 1 hour and 15 minutes. Remove from oven, let stand 10 minutes. Turn out on warm round platter. In the center of the ring place a bowl of the following sauce:

2 tablespoons butter or margarine
2 heaping tablespoons flour
1 cup chicken broth
1 egg yolk
¼ cup thick cream (canned milk
    of course is cheaper)

1 10½-ounce can condensed
    cream of mushroom soup
1 tablespoon lemon juice
½ teaspoon horseradish
Salt, pepper and Tabasco sauce to
    taste

Melt butter, add flour and hot chicken broth. Beat egg in cream and add. Do not boil. When smooth and thickened, add all other ingredients. Serve hot. Serves 10-12

## Creamed Chicken in Spinach Ring

*The Spinach Ring*

| | |
|---|---|
| 1 10-ounce package spinach | ½ cup hot chicken broth |
| 3 eggs, well beaten | ½ cup warm milk |
| ½ cup grated cheese | ½ teaspoon salt |
| ¼ cup chicken broth | ¼ teaspoon black pepper |
| 2 tablespoons butter | Sprinkle of cayenne pepper |
| 2 tablespoons flour | |

Cook spinach and drain well. Combine with eggs, cheese and ¼ cup chicken broth and set aside. Melt butter, add flour and stir on low heat for 2 minutes. Slowly add hot chicken broth, stir until smooth. Slowly add warm milk. Add seasonings and spinach mixture. Pour into greased 1½-quart ring mold. Place mold in pan of hot water. Bake in 325-degree oven for 30 minutes. Test for doneness by inserting toothpick which should come out clean. Remove from oven. Let stand 10 minutes. Unmold and fill center with bowl of creamed chicken.

*The Creamed Chicken*

| | |
|---|---|
| 1 10½-ounce can cream of chicken soup | 2 tablespoons lemon juice |
| 1 cup mayonnaise | ½ teaspoon salt |
| 1 cup buttermilk | Black pepper and Tabasco to taste |
| | 2 cups diced poached chicken |

Combine soup, mayonnaise and buttermilk in saucepan or double boiler. Add other ingredients. Heat but do not boil. Do not freeze. Place in a bowl in the center of the spinach ring.

## Tortilla Chicken Casserole

| | |
|---|---|
| 2½- or 3-pound chicken, poached (see Basic Poached Chicken, page 172) | 1 4-ounce can green chilis |
| | 2 cups grated cheddar cheese |
| 2 medium onions, chopped | 1 cup grated Swiss cheese |
| 2 stalks celery, chopped | 15 tortillas, torn into about 1-inch pieces—preferably flour tortillas; if not available, corn tortillas |
| ½ teaspoon salt | |
| 1 10½-ounce can condensed cream of chicken soup | |
| 1 10½-ounce can condensed cream of mushroom soup | 1 cup sour cream |
| | ½ cup mayonnaise |

175

Butter 3-quart casserole. Cut chicken into bite-size pieces with kitchen scissors or paring knife. Combine all ingredients but tortillas, sour cream and mayonnaise—a day ahead, if you wish. Mix last 3 ingredients just before baking and spread on top of casserole. Bake in a 350-degree oven for 45-50 minutes. Do not freeze.

Serve with tomato aspic or green salad and popovers. Serves 10, perhaps 12 at noon.

## Ring Around the Chicken

### Puff Pastry Ring

| | |
|---|---|
| 1 stick butter or margarine | Pinch salt and pepper |
| 1 cup water | 4 eggs |
| 1 cup flour | ½ cup grated cheese |

Heat butter and water until butter is melted and mixture boils. Add flour, salt and pepper all at once. Stir until mixture forms a ball in the center of the pan. Cool for several minutes. Beat in eggs one at a time, beating well after each addition. Stir in cheese. Reserve dough while making the filling.

### Chicken Filling

| | |
|---|---|
| 4 tablespoons butter or margarine | 1½ cups chopped poached chicken |
| 2 medium onions, chopped | 2 cups tomatoes, peeled, quartered and seeded |
| ½ pound mushrooms, sliced | ¼ cup shredded cheddar cheese |
| 4 tablespoons flour | 2 tablespoons chopped parsley |
| 1 cup hot chicken broth | |
| 1 teaspoon salt | |
| ¼ teaspoon black pepper | |

Melt butter, add onions and mushrooms. Cook over low heat for 2 minutes. Blend in flour, then add chicken broth, salt and pepper. Stir constantly until mixture boils. Simmer 4 minutes. Remove from heat. Add chicken and tomato quarters.

Shape puff dough around edge of pyrex pie plate or shallow baking dish. Place filling inside, sprinkle with cheese. Bake in a 400-degree oven for 40 minutes. Sprinkle with chopped parsley before serving. Do not freeze. Serves 4-6.

Martha Henton / *Diocese of Northwest Texas*

## Poulet et Artichauts à La Crème

2 packages frozen artichoke hearts
2 cups uncooked chicken breasts, cubed
2 cups cream of chicken soup
1 cup mayonnaise
1 teaspoon lemon juice

½ to 2 teaspoons curry powder
½ to ¾ cup shredded sharp cheese
½ cup bread crumbs
1 tablespoon melted butter

Cook artichoke hearts according to directions. Drain, put in casserole and top with raw chicken. Combine soup, mayonnaise, lemon juice and curry powder to taste. Pour over chicken. Sprinkle with cheese. Combine bread crumbs with butter and sprinkle over top. Bake at 350 degrees for 25 to 30 minutes. Serve over rice or noodles. Serves 5 or 6.

Helen Hines / *Dover House (1965–1974)*

## Maryland Fried Chicken

3 broiling spring chickens
6 tablespoons fat, melted
¼ cup flour
½ teaspoon salt
⅛ teaspoon white pepper

2 slices salt pork, cut fine
Dash nutmeg
3 cups cream (or evaporated milk)
Parsley

Cut whole chickens into quarters. Brush with fat and dredge with flour, salt and pepper. Fry salt pork until brown. Add nutmeg. Place chicken on pork and baste with melted fat. Cover the skillet and cook chickens about 30 minutes. When tender, pour 1 cup cream in the skillet. Remove cover and let cream cook down. When it is fairly thick, pour in the other 2 cups, cook until thick as you want it. Serve chickens with the cream gravy. Garnish with parsley. Serves 8 to 10.

Betty Cox / *Diocese of Maryland*

## Baked Chicken Parmesan

3 chickens, 2½ to 3 pounds each,
   cut up for frying
4½ cups fresh bread crumbs
1¼ cups grated Parmesan cheese
1 tablespoon salt
⅓ cup chopped fresh parsley

1½ cups butter
1 clove garlic, crushed
1 tablespoon Dijon mustard
1½ teaspoons Worcestershire
   sauce

Wash the chicken pieces and pat them dry. Prepare the bread crumbs in a blender, using day-old firm-type white bread with crusts removed, or use the fine side of a grater. Add the cheese, salt and parsley to the crumbs and mix well. Spread the mixture in a shallow pan. Melt the butter in a medium-sized saucepan. Add the garlic, mustard and Worcestershire sauce. Stir well and let the mixture cool until lukewarm but not congealed.

Preheat the oven to 350 degrees. Dip the chicken pieces into the butter mixture, then roll them in the crumb-cheese mixture. Be sure each piece is well coated; pat the coating on with your hands. Place the pieces of chicken on a large shallow baking tray. Pour remaining butter over the chicken. Bake until golden and tender, about 1 to 1¼ hours. Baste once or twice with the pan drippings. This dish is full of different flavors—cheese, mustard, garlic—that blend beautifully. Serves 8.

Susie Reed / *Diocese of Kentucky*

## Chicken Cacciatore

2 frying chickens
2-3 tablespoons flour
Olive oil for frying
½ large onion, chopped
2½ cups canned Italian tomatoes
1 can tomato paste
1 teaspoon salt
¼ teaspoon pepper

½ bay leaf
½ teaspoon oregano
Pinch thyme and marjoram, if
   desired
½ cup white wine
1 can mushroom stems and
   pieces, drained

Cut the chickens into serving pieces, dredge with flour and brown in skillet in olive oil. Remove to a large flat casserole. In the same skillet, brown the onion. Drain some liquid from the tomatoes, then add to the onions with the rest of the ingredients. Pour over the chicken. Bake at 350 degrees for about 1 hour. Good reheated; can be made ahead. Serve with tossed green salad and French bread. Serves 8.

Helen Putnam / *Diocese of Oklahoma*

## Oriental Chicken Casserole

2½ cups toasted bread cubes
2 cups bean sprouts
⅔ cup sliced water chestnuts
½ cup sliced mushrooms
1 teaspoon salt
2½ to 3 cups cooked diced
  chicken (or turkey)

¼ cup sugar
2 tablespoons cornstarch
¾ cup pineapple juice
¼ cup imported soy sauce
2 tablespoons vinegar
¼ cup toasted almonds

Preheat oven to 350 degrees. Combine bread cubes, bean sprouts, water chestnuts, mushrooms, salt and chicken. Set aside. Combine sugar and cornstarch in a small pan. Stir in juice and soy sauce. Bring to a boil, stirring, and cook 2 to 3 minutes once it is thickened. Remove from heat and add the vinegar. Place the chicken mixture in a greased 1½ quart casserole, pour sauce over and top with almonds. Bake 30 minutes. Serves 6.

Polly Keller / *Diocese of Arkansas*

## Chicken Casserole

2 cans cut string beans, drained
3 whole chicken breasts, cooked
  and cut into large pieces
1 can condensed cream of celery
  soup
1 can condensed cream of chicken
  soup

1 envelope Lipton's dry onion
  soup mix
1 pint sour cream
1 small package Pepperidge Farm
  herb flavored stuffing
¾ cup chicken broth or water
½ stick margarine, melted

In a 9 × 13-inch baking pan put the string beans, then cover with the chicken pieces. Mix the undiluted soups together and add sour cream; spread over the chicken. In a separate bowl mix the stuffing, broth and margarine. Cover the chicken with the dressing, place foil over the pan and bake at 350 degrees for 1 hour. Remove the foil for the last 15 minutes. Serves 10.

Florence Lichtenberger / *Dover House (1958–1964)*


## Chicken and Rice Casserole

4 whole chicken breasts
2½ cups water
Salt
1 teaspoon curry powder
2 bags saffron rice

1 pound hot sausage
1½ pounds mushrooms, sliced
3 tablespoons butter
1 can mushroom soup
Bread crumbs or potato chips

Cook chicken in water with salt and curry powder until tender; use enough water to have 2 cups remaining. Cook rice in this liquid. When rice is done, add chicken which has been cut into small pieces. Fry the sausage until crumbly. Drain off excess fat, leave a little for seasoning. Saute mushrooms in butter; mix with chicken, rice and soup. Put in a greased casserole, top with potato chips and dot with butter. Bake in oven about 30 minutes at 375 degrees until hot and brown. May be prepared a day in advance, then reheated to serve. Serves 16.

Nancy Gravatt / *Diocese of Upper South Carolina*


## Chicken-Broccoli Casserole

4 10-ounce packages frozen
   broccoli
4 cups chicken, boned and sliced
   (6 chicken breasts, cooked)
4 cans cream of chicken soup
2 scant cups mayonnaise

2 teaspoons lemon juice
1 teaspoon curry powder
1 cup shredded sharp American
   cheese
1 cup bread crumbs
2 tablespoons melted butter

Cook broccoli until almost tender. Drain. Place in 2 buttered casseroles. Cover with chicken slices. Combine soup, mayonnaise, lemon juice and curry powder. Pour over chicken. Cover with cheese and bread crumbs tossed with melted butter. Bake at 350 degrees for about 30 to 40 minutes. Serves 12.

Mary Alexander / *Diocese of Upper South Carolina*

180

## Chicken Singapore

½ boned chicken breast per
serving
6 tablespoons butter
¼ teaspoon pepper
½ teaspoon paprika
1 4-ounce can artichoke hearts
1 8-ounce can water chestnuts,
drained and sliced

¼ pound (or more) mushrooms,
sliced
2 tablespoons butter
2 tablespoons flour
1 cup chicken broth
1 tablespoon soy sauce
3 tablespoons white wine
¼ teaspoon rosemary

Brown chicken breasts in 6 tablespoons butter, sprinkle with pepper and paprika and arrange in a casserole with the artichoke hearts and water chestnuts. Saute the mushrooms in 4 tablespoons butter, sprinkle with flour and stir to blend. Add chicken broth and stir till sauce thickens. Add soy sauce, white wine and rosemary. Pour mushroom sauce over casserole and bake at 350 degrees for 1 hour. Serves 4-6.

Marjorie Bennison / *Diocese of Western Michigan*

## "Ordination" Chicken Casserole

1 5-pound stewing chicken,
cooked, meat cut in bite-size
pieces
1 12-ounce package noodles,
cooked and drained
3 large onions, diced and sauteed
until golden
1 pound mushrooms, sliced and
sauteed
2 green peppers, diced and
sauteed

1 small can pimientos, cut in
strips
5 tablespoons flour
3 cups chicken broth
½ cup heavy cream
Sherry to taste
Salt and pepper to taste
Buttered bread crumbs
Slivered almonds

Prepare the first 6 ingredients and mix together with gravy made of flour, chicken broth, cream, sherry, salt and pepper. Pour into 1 or 2 casserole dishes. Top with buttered crumbs and slivered almonds. Bake in 300-degree oven for 30 to 40 minutes until heated through. Serves 15.

Helen Loring / *Diocese of Springfield (Illinois)*

## Mexican Chicken

8 large chicken breasts
1 package Fritos or Doritos tortilla
chips
1 large onion, chopped
1 10½-ounce can condensed
cream of chicken soup

1 10½-ounce can condensed
tomato soup
1 cup milk
1 can Rotel tomatoes
4 ounces sharp cheese, grated

Poach chicken until tender. Reserve broth, cut chicken in bite-size pieces. Put 5 tablespoons chicken broth in bottom of casserole. Add layer of tortilla chips, then a layer of chicken pieces, then a layer of chopped onion. Repeat layers, ending with a layer of tortilla chips. Mix soups with milk, then add tomatoes. Pour over the casserole and sprinkle grated cheese on top. Cook 1 hour in a 300-degree oven. This dish has a Mexican flavor and can be used for luncheons or dinner parties. Serves 8-10

Warwick Brown / *Diocese of Arkansas*

## Chicken Pilau

1 hen, 4-5 pounds
1 quart salted water
¼ pound white bacon, diced
4 onions, cut fine
1-4 green peppers, diced
6 cups liquid (broth and water)
1½ tablespoons salt
1 teaspoon black pepper

1 teaspoon chili powder
1 small clove garlic, crushed
1 Datil (hot bird) pepper, cut
1 pinch allspice
5 tablespoons Worcestershire
sauce
8 ounces tomato catsup
4 cups raw rice

Cook chicken in salted water until tender. Remove meat from bones and leave in large pieces. Cut skin fine. Save broth.

Brown bacon, add onion, then green pepper when onion is almost brown. Add liquid, chicken pieces and skin, and all ingredients except rice. Bring to boil, add rice (which has been washed thoroughly) and bring to boil again. Stir, cover and steam over low heat until rice is done—40 minutes to 1 hour. Stir once or twice during cooking. Serves 12 to 15.

"Dink" Elebash / *Diocese of East Carolina*

# Captain's Chicken (and the beginnings of Shrimp Gumbo)

2 fryers, cut in pieces (no giblets)
Salt and pepper
¼ pound butter
1 large yellow onion, thinly sliced
1 green pepper, thinly sliced
2 cans (1 lb. 12-ounce each) solid packed tomatoes
½ teaspoon garlic powder

1 teaspoon salt
½ teaspoon pepper
1 tablespoon chopped parsley
½ teaspoon powdered thyme
½ teaspoon oregano
1 heaping tablespoon curry powder

Sprinkle chicken with salt and pepper and fry quickly in butter till brown—remove. Into butter put onion and peppers and fry until glossy. Mix remaining seasonings into undrained but chopped tomatoes; add this to onions and peppers and cook slowly for 5 minutes. In a 3-quart casserole arrange chicken, pour sauce over it, and refrigerate till baking time. Bake, covered, for 1¼ hours at 350 degrees. Serve with rice. Serves 6-8.

You will have about 2 quarts of sauce remaining as a start for an excellent gumbo. You may freeze this sauce and add the following ingredients when ready to make gumbo.

# Shrimp Gumbo

1 package frozen chopped okra
1 tablespoon butter
Thawed sauce

1 can cream of shrimp soup
2 6½-ounce cans shrimp or 1 pound frozen shrimp

Fry the okra in butter. Add the sauce, soup and shrimp. When very hot, serve over rice. Serves 6-8. Both of these dishes may be frozen.

Margaret Jones / *Diocese of Missouri*

# Chicken Breasts and Bacon

6 or 8 large chicken breasts, boned
6 or 8 slices of bacon

1 can mushroom soup
1 cup sour cream
½ cup mushrooms, sauteed

183

Wrap chicken breasts with bacon, and place in a flat casserole. Mix soup, cream and mushrooms and pour over chicken breasts. Leave in refrigerator overnight. Next day bake uncovered at 275 degrees for 3 hours. Serves 6 to 8.

Marion Craighill / *Diocese of Anking*


## Father Capon's Chicken

Truss two unstuffed broiling chickens (or split them down the back and flatten them); coat both the birds and the roasting pan with olive oil, then salt and pepper the birds and roast them in a hot oven (425 degrees) for 1¼ hours, basting occasionally with white wine or dry vermouth.

Meanwhile, make the sauce: Saute 1 cup of chopped onions and two cloves of garlic, crushed, in some olive oil until the onions are transparent. Add a can of tomato paste and sauté until the paste begins to brown a little on the bottom of the pan. Add a large can of tomato puree and simmer. Salt to taste.

In a mortar (or in a blender) pulverize 1 teaspoon each of dried rosemary and dried basil, and ¼ teaspoon dried thyme. Add this herb mixture to the pot, together with 1 piece of stick cinnamon and the grated rind of ½ lemon. Continue simmering.

Ten minutes before the birds are done, spoon the sauce around (not over) the birds in the roasting pan.

Bring the birds to the table in the pan and disjoint them, serving the pieces, plus some sauce, on top of hot, well-buttered pasta. Crusty bread, wine, a large green salad and a sweet for dessert will make a meal of it. Serves 8.

Chris Sherman / *Diocese of Long Island (New York)*

---

DEAR LORD
*We thank Thee for this food—may it nourish*
*our souls and bodies. As we gather together*
*as a family we ask Thy blessing on our love*
*for each other.   Amen.*

## Chicken and Chipped Beef Casserole

1 5-ounce package chipped beef
8 whole chicken breasts, boned
½ pint sour cream

1 10½-ounce can mushroom soup
3 tablespoons sherry

Line bottom of greased baking dish, 7 × 11 inches, with chipped beef. Lay chicken breasts over chipped beef. Mix together sour cream, mushroom soup and sherry. With a spatula, spread this mixture over the top of the chicken. Cover the baking dish with aluminum foil and bake at 350 degrees for about 45 minutes or until the chicken is tender. Serves 8.

Marge Fraser / *Diocese of North Carolina*

## Hot Chicken Salad

2 cups seasoned cooked chicken
2 cups chopped celery
½ cup slivered almonds
2 teaspoons grated onion
½ teaspoon salt

2 tablespoons lemon juice
1 cup salad dressing
1 cup crushed potato chips
½ cup grated cheese
½ teaspoon prepared mustard

Mix all ingredients together. Bake 30 minutes at 350 degrees. This dish has been received with great enthusiasm at church luncheons and at luncheons held at home. Serves 6.

Helen Klein / *Diocese of Northern Indiana*

185

## Quick and Easy Coq au Vin

4 chicken breasts
¾ cup vin rose
¼ cup soy sauce
¼ cup salad oil
2 tablespoons water

1 clove garlic, minced
1 teaspoon ginger
¼ teaspoon oregano
1 tablespoon brown sugar

Place chicken breasts in a casserole with cover. Mix liquids and condiments and pour over chicken. Bake covered for 1½ hours at 350 degrees. Serves 4.

Florence Moore / *Diocese of Easton (Maryland)*

## Easy Chicken with Onions

6 "meaty" chicken breasts
12 to 16 tiny whole white onions, peeled or use canned white onions
1 can cream of mushroom soup

⅛ cup sherry—or more
¼ pound cheddar cheese, freshly grated
Salt and pepper

Place chicken in baking dish. Add onions. Mix soup and sherry with salt and pepper to taste; pour over chicken. Sprinkle grated cheese over top. Refrigerate. When ready, place in 350-degree oven; bake covered for 45 minutes. Uncover and continue baking for a good 30 to 45 minutes more. Serves 6.

Janet Thomas / *Diocese of Pittsburgh (Pennsylvania)*

## Quick and Easy Chicken

6 chicken quarters
1 small jar apricot jam
1 bottle dark Russian dressing

1 envelope Lipton's dried onion soup

Place chicken pieces in casserole. Spoon apricot jam over chicken, then pour over Russian dressing, then sprinkle dried onion soup on top. Bake covered in 400-degree oven for 1 hour. It is good reheated at future date. Serves 6.

Helen Hatch / *Diocese of Western Massachusetts*

## After Holiday Turkey Hash

| | |
|---|---|
| 2 to 3 cups left-over turkey, cubed | 1 tablespoon brandy |
| 1 to 2 cups turkey gravy | 1 egg yolk, beaten |
| 1 cup sliced mushrooms | ⅓ cup thick cream |
| 3 tablespoons butter | ½ teaspoon mace |

Saute turkey lightly in 2 tablespoons butter. Blaze with brandy. Stir and add gravy. Saute mushrooms in remaining butter; add to turkey mixture. Heat but do not boil the egg yolk, cream and mace. Add to turkey. This may be "held" over very low heat, like a hot tray. Serves 8 to 10.

Betty Powell / *Diocese of Oklahoma*

## Roast Wild Duck

Pick, clean and singe duck, and wipe with damp cloth. Put quarter of pared apple in each duck. Place on rack in baking pan and roast, uncovered, in a very hot oven, 500 degrees.

> Black or Mallard ducks—roast 18-20 minutes
> Blue or Pintail ducks—roast 15-18 minutes
> Teals—roast 12-15 minutes

If you want stuffing for your duck, here is sufficient for 1 Mallard:

| | |
|---|---|
| 1 cup cooked wild rice | ¼ teaspoon salt |
| 1 tablespoon chopped celery | 1 pinch pepper |
| ½ apple, chopped | 1 tablespoon melted butter |

Combine ingredients, fill the duck with the stuffing and truss. Dot with butter and sprinkle with salt. Roast, uncovered, in hot oven, 400 degrees, basting frequently until desired doneness has been attained.

Betty Cox / *Diocese of Maryland*

## Doves or Quail for 12

Preheat oven to 300 degrees. Dust birds in flour, salt and pepper. Brown in butter in a heavy skillet. Set birds aside in a large dutch oven. Add 3 or 4 cans chicken broth to the skillet, bringing to a boil. Add 3 to 4 half pints of heavy cream, then add broth and cream to the birds. Scrape the skillet and add all the juices to the dutch oven. Liquid should almost cover the birds. Cover and bake for 1-1½ hours. Serve over toast or wild rice.

Marge Fraser / *Diocese of North Carolina*

## Pheasant in White Wine

Cut pheasant in serving pieces. Roll in seasoned flour and brown lightly in hot butter or cooking oil. Place in a casserole; add 1 small can of mushrooms, ½ cup white wine and 1 tablespoon minced onion; place some chopped parsley over this. Cover and cook for 2 hours in 350-degree oven.

Evelyn Thayer / *Diocese of Colorado*

# *Meatless Dishes*

## Cheese Bake-Souffle-Fondue-Chulf-Strata

Call it what you will, this bread-cheese-eggs-milk combination is a favorite with our contributors. It was the recipe most often sent in for the cookbook. Rather than print each variation, we offer you a composite version. Pick your own amounts and seasonings—they all turn out well. We like the idea that this meatless main dish embodies what we are striving for in this cookbook: thrifty recipes that taste good and are easy to prepare.

Bread—10 or 12 slices, crusts removed or not, use French bread if you wish

Butter—spread on bread, or skip butter; try sharp mustard instead

Cut bread slices in half or cubes or pull apart.

Layer bread in casserole with

Cheese—½ pound or 1½ cups, shredded or grated, cheddar or Swiss

Then mix together

Eggs—4 or 5 or 6 with

Milk—2, 2½, 3 or 5 cups of whole, evaporated or powdered milk, hot or cold

Season with any combination of

Salt, pepper, dry mustard,
  Worcestershire, paprika,
  cayenne, dried minced onion
Pour over bread and cheese and
  let stand for
½ hour, 1 hour, overnight

Bake in 325 or 350-degree oven
  for
25, 45 or 50 minutes or 1 hour or
  1½ hours.
Serves 6 to 8.

With thanks to these good cooks for their versions of this popular
dish:
Maureen Atkins, Diocese of Eau Claire (Wisconsin)
Alice Harte, Diocese of Arizona
Nan Hunter, Diocese of Wyoming
Carolyn Leighton, Diocese of Maryland
Mary Parsons, Diocese of Quincy (Illinois)
Betty Powell, Diocese of Oklahoma
Adele Reeves, Diocese of Georgia
Marie Robinson, Diocese of Western New York

# Gratin of Zucchini, Rice, Onions, Spinach and Cheese

2½ pounds fresh zucchini
½ cup rice
1 cup minced onion
6 tablespoons olive oil
2 cloves garlic, chopped
2 pounds fresh spinach

2 tablespoons flour
2½ cups hot liquid (zucchini
  juices plus milk, heated in a
  pan)
⅔ cup grated Parmesan cheese
Salt and pepper

Wash and grate zucchini coarsely onto a clean dish towel. Sprinkle
2 teaspoons salt over grated zucchini. Let stand for 15 minutes.
Gather up in dish towel and squeeze juices into a pan. Drop rice
into boiling salted water, and boil exactly 5 minutes. Drain. Fry
onions slowly in 4 tablespoons of oil for 8-10 minutes until tender
and translucent. Stir zucchini and garlic into onions, toss and turn
for 5-6 minutes until zucchini is almost tender. Wash spinach and
drop into boiling salted water for two minutes, until just limp.
Drain, chop and add to zucchini, onion, garlic mixture. Sprinkle in
flour, stir over moderate heat for 2 minutes and remove from heat.
When flour is well blended and smooth, gradually stir in hot liquid
and bring to simmer, stirring. Remove from heat and stir in
blanched rice and cheese. Salt and pepper to taste. Turn into gener-

189

ously buttered baking dish. Dribble with remaining olive oil. Bring to simmer on top of stove and then bake at 425 degrees for 25 minutes until brown and rice has absorbed liquid. Serves 8 to 10.

Janice Rusack / *Diocese of Los Angeles (California)*

## Eggplant Parmigiana

1 14½-ounce can Italian-style tomatoes
½ can tomato paste
½ teaspoon dried oregano
½ teaspoon dried basil

1 teaspoon sugar
¼ teaspoon salt
3 cloves garlic, crushed
2 tablespoons olive oil
Dash of red pepper, if desired

Combine above ingredients in a saucepan and cook 20-30 minutes over moderate heat.

2 medium eggplants, pared
3 beaten eggs
2 tablespoons milk
Olive oil
1 cup shredded mozzarella cheese
3-4 tablespoons grated Parmesan cheese

½ cup ricotta cheese
Optional: 1 pound ground beef or lamb. The addition of this ingredient makes a very hearty main dish.

Brown meat, if used, and set aside. Slice eggplant lengthwise ¼ inch thick. Sprinkle with salt; place in a colander with a heavy plate on top for 15 or 20 minutes and let drain. Wipe off excess salt. Dip eggplant in mixture of beaten eggs and milk; brown slices on both sides in hot olive oil. Drain on absorbent paper.

In a square casserole, alternate layers of eggplant, ground meat, if used, mozzarella, tomato sauce and Parmesan cheese, sandwiching the ricotta cheese in at least the first layer. Finish with top layer of tomato sauce and Parmesan cheese. Bake in 375-degree oven for 10 minutes or until bubbly. Serves 6.

May be done ahead and baked at last minute to heat through. Also, freezes well. I do two at one time and freeze one. If frozen, of course, the dish must be thawed to room temperature. The same if refrigerated, or it will not cook "bubbly" in 20 minutes.

Serve with a green salad with oil and vinegar dressing, garlic bread, fresh fruit in season, sliced with a little orange liqueur, or vanilla ice cream with creme de menthe.

Essie Haden / *Diocese of Northern California*

## Eggplant Lasagne

5 tablespoons butter
4 tablespoons flour
2 cups milk
Salt and pepper to taste
½ pound lasagne
8 tablespoons butter

6 to 8 ripe tomatoes (or use 2 cups canned tomatoes)
1 large eggplant
1 pound mozzarella cheese, cut in strips

Make a thick cream sauce with 5 tablespoons of the butter, flour, milk, salt and pepper. Cook the lasagne for 10 minutes in 2 quarts boiling salted water. Drain. Simmer the tomatoes with 1 tablespoon of butter, salt, pepper and ¼ cup water. Slice the eggplant with skin on, and saute slowly in the remaining butter. In a large shallow casserole dish put layers of sauce, lasagne, tomatoes and cheese, finishing with cheese and a few tomatoes. Place in 350-degree oven and bake for 25 to 30 minutes or until cheese melts. Serve immediately. Serves 8.

Clara Claiborne / *Diocese of Atlanta (Georgia)*

## Red Beans and Rice

1 pound dried kidney beans
4 tablespoons oleo or butter
1 cup finely chopped scallions, including 3 inches of green tops
½ cup finely chopped onion
3 cloves garlic, minced or run through garlic press

Ham hocks, or ham bone, or bacon grease
Salt and black pepper to taste
2 bay leaves
1 teaspoon Worcestershire sauce, optional
Dash Tabasco sauce, optional

Soak the dried beans overnight, covering well with cold water. Next morning, pour off remaining liquid, rinse beans. In a 4-quart saucepan put soaked beans well covered with fresh water. Bring to a boil, then keep on low simmer.

Saute in the oleo or butter the scallions, onion and garlic. Cook until soft and translucent but not brown. Add to the cooking red beans. Add ham bone, or ham hock. If neither is available, the beans can be flavored with bacon grease. Add the bay leaves. Cook slowly several hours until the beans are tender. Salt and pepper to taste. Add more water as needed throughout the cooking. Keep them always quite liquid. During the last 30 minutes of cooking, stir frequently and mash the softest beans against the sides of the saucepan to form a thick sauce for remaining beans.

If ham bone or hocks are used, remove to a plate. Cut meat away from bones. Remove and discard skin, bone, fat and gristle. Cut meat into small pieces and return it to the pot. Taste for seasoning. Worcestershire sauce and Tabasco may be added, if desired. Remove bay leaves.

Serve on freshly cooked rice. Chili sauce or tomato ketchup on top adds a good flavor. The red beans freeze well, but cook rice freshly each time. Serves 6.

Kathleen Jones / *Diocese of Louisiana*

## Spinach Casserole

4 packages frozen chopped
  spinach
4 tablespoons butter
1 large onion, chopped or 2 cans
  water chestnuts, sliced
½ pint half-and-half cream

Salt and pepper
3 hard-boiled eggs, sliced
  (optional)
2 cans cream of mushroom soup
½ pound sharp cheese, grated

Cook spinach, drain well. Saute onions or water chestnuts in butter. Combine with cream and spinach. Season to taste. In large casserole, make layers of spinach, egg, soup, and grated cheese, ending with cheese. Bake at 350 degrees for 20 to 30 minutes.

This adaptable casserole is nifty for pot luck suppers, or for a group at home. If the eggs are included, it makes a well-rounded meal with the addition of whole grain bread and fruit for dessert. Serves 12.

Barbara Smith / *Diocese of New Hampshire*

## Egg and Mushroom Casserole

5 hard-cooked eggs
¾ cup sliced mushrooms
3 tablespoons butter or shortening
2 tablespoons flour
1 cup milk
¼ teaspoon salt

¼ teaspoon onion powder
½ cup minced celery
½ cup poultry stuffing
½ cup grated sharp cheddar
    cheese

Slice the eggs into 2-quart casserole. Saute the mushrooms in 1 tablespoon of the butter; then sprinkle them over eggs. Melt remaining butter, stir in flour, gradually add milk and stir until blended and slightly thickened. Add salt and celery and pour over eggs. Mix stuffing with cheese and scatter over top. Bake for 20 minutes at 375 degrees or until bubbly. Serves 4 to 6.

Betty Powell / *Diocese of Oklahoma*

## Barley-Mushroom Casserole

½ pound butter or oleo
2 medium onions, coarsely
    chopped
¾ pound mushrooms, trimmed
    and sliced
1½ cups pearl barley

3 pimientos, coarsely chopped
3-4 cups vegetable broth (start
    with 3, add as needed while
    cooking)
Salt and pepper

Saute onions in butter until transparent, then mushrooms until tender. Add barley, cook until a delicate brown. Add pimientos and vegetable broth, salt and pepper to taste. Bake, covered, in a 2-quart casserole for about 2 hours at 350 degrees, until barley is tender and liquid absorbed.

Polly Keller / *Diocese of Arkansas*

---

*Let us all in full accord*
*Give grateful thanks unto the Lord—*
*A very kind and gracious Lord,*
*Who gives us more than our reward.   Amen.*

## Baked Grits à la Rosa

1 cup quick-cooking grits
4 tablespoons butter
⅓ pound sharp cheddar cheese,
  coarsely grated

6 tablespoons milk
2 eggs, beaten

Cook grits according to directions on package. Stir cooked grits, butter, cheese and milk together until cheese is melted and all ingredients are mixed and smooth. Cool slightly, add eggs and mix again. Pour into a 2-quart casserole dish and bake for 40 minutes at 400 degrees. Serve immediately. Serves 6.

Barbara Rivera / *Diocese of San Joaquin (California)*

## Hominy Casserole

1 can condensed cream of
  mushroom soup
1 cup light cream
1 teaspoon celery salt
1 teaspoon Worcestershire sauce
¼ teaspoon cayenne pepper

salt and pepper
1 can big hominy, drained
1 cup split blanched almonds
bread crumbs
margarine

In top of double boiler make sauce of soup, cream and seasonings. Heat and blend until smooth.

Combine hominy and almonds in buttered casserole and pour sauce over them. Cover with bread crumbs and dot with margarine. Cook for 30 minutes in 350 degree oven. Serves 6 as a meatless main course with fresh fruit salad and hot rolls.

Blossom Marmion / *Southwestern Virginia*

## Rice Verde

¾ to 1 pound Monterrey Jack
  cheese (or other mild cheese)
1 pint sour cream
1 can green chilis, chopped

3 cups cooked rice, seasoned to
  taste with salt and pepper
¼ cup grated cheddar cheese (I
  like a sharp one)

194

Cut cheese in strips. Combine sour cream and chilis. In a 2-quart casserole layer rice with sour cream mixture and cheese strips, in that order, ending with rice. Bake at 350 degrees about 30 minutes, or until heated through, sprinkling top with grated cheddar cheese about 10 minutes before the dish has finished baking.

Polly Keller / *Diocese of Arkansas*


## Dahl of Yellow Split Peas

¾ cup yellow split peas
2 cups water
1 teaspoon salt
2 tablespoons margarine
¼ teaspoon dry mustard
1½ teaspoons curry (or more according to your taste)

2 onions, chopped
2 tablespoons minced parsley
1 lemon, very thinly sliced and seeded

Wash split peas. Place in saucepan, add water and the salt. Boil gently until peas are tender. Do not cover. Melt margarine, add mustard and curry; fry just 1-2 minutes. Add onions and fry 5 to 10 minutes. Stir onions and curry into the peas. Cook gently for 15 minutes, stirring occasionally. Just before serving add parsley. Serve over rice with sliced lemon on top. Serves 4.

Martha Henton / *Diocese of Northwest Texas*


## Peanut Macaroni and Cheese

1½ cups elbow macaroni
3 tablespoons butter
½ cup minced onion
1 cup milk
1 cup peanut butter

2 cups shredded process cheese
½ teaspoon salt
½ teaspoon cayenne pepper
½ cup chopped peanuts

Cook macaroni according to the package directions; drain and set aside. In a saucepan melt butter, add onions and saute until tender. Add milk and heat almost to the boiling point. Blend in the peanut butter, stirring until smooth. Stir in cheese, salt and cayenne. Fold in drained macaroni and pour into a greased 2-quart casserole. Sprinkle chopped peanuts on top. Bake in 350-degree oven for 30 to 40 minutes or until hot and bubbly. Serves 6.

Claudia Gesner / *Diocese of South Dakota*

## Corn Pudding

3 eggs
2 cups half-and-half
1 tablespoon sugar
1 teaspoon salt
2 tablespoons melted butter
1/3 cup bread crumbs
1/2 cup grated sharp cheddar cheese

7-ounce jar pimientos, chopped
3 tablespoons onion, finely chopped
1/4 teaspoon pepper
17-ounce can creamed corn

Beat eggs until light and fluffy. Add all ingredients. Pour into 1½ quart greased casserole. Place casserole in pan of hot water. Place in pre-heated 350-degree oven and bake for 60 minutes or until custard is set.

Helen Haynes / *Diocese of Southwest Florida*

## Baked Eggs

For each serving, drop into a generously buttered 4-ounce baking dish or custard cup:

1 egg
2 tablespoons cream

1/2 teaspoon chopped fresh chives
Salt and pepper to taste

Cover with foil; bake for 20 minutes in 300-degree oven. These baked eggs make a simple main course for our Tuesday morning clergy breakfasts, accompanied by fresh fruit—half a grapefruit or melon, depending upon the season—and English muffins or pita bread toasted. The length of baking the eggs really depends upon how long the propers are for the Eucharist that morning.

Janice Rusack / *Diocese of Los Angeles (California)*

## Incarnation (Dallas) Cheese Dish

3 eggs, separated
½ pound Cheddar cheese, grated
½ pound Monterrey Jack cheese, grated

1 jalapeno pepper, chopped (no more as it will be too hot!)
1 large can evaporated milk

Beat egg yolks and egg whites separately. Mix all ingredients, folding the egg whites in last. Pour into a pan; the size depends on whether you want it thick or thin. Bake at 350 degrees about 30 minutes. Serves 6.

Ida Lou Barnds / *Diocese of Dallas (Texas)*

# *Seafood Dishes*

## Shrimp Newburg

1 pound raw shrimp
3 tablespoons butter
2 tablespoons flour
1 cup cream

3 tablespoons tomato catsup
2 teaspoons Worcestershire sauce
2 tablespoons sherry

To cook shrimp, cover with more than 4 cups water, season with 2 slices unpeeled lemon, ¼ cup vinegar, ¼ teaspoon red pepper, ½ teaspoon celery salt, and 1 teaspoon seasoned salt. Bring to rolling boil. Remove from heat. Cover and allow to cool. Remove shells and devein. Melt butter in heavy sauce pan, stir in flour until blended then slowly stir in cream. Place over medium heat. When sauce has thickened, add tomato catsup and Worcestershire sauce. Stir in shrimp. Heat well. Just before serving, add sherry. Serve with rice. Serves 4.

Holly Richards / *Pastoral Development*

## Shrimp Thermidor

| | |
|---|---|
| 2 cups boiled shrimp, deveined | Pepper to taste |
| 1 can mushrooms (or 1 cup fresh, | Juice of ½ lemon |
| sliced and cooked in butter) | 1 tablespoon butter |
| 4 teaspoons chopped parsley | ¼ cup sherry |
| 2 teaspoons paprika | 3 cups medium thick cream sauce |
| 1 teaspoon dry mustard | 4 hard-cooked eggs, diced |
| ½ teaspoon salt | 4 tablespoons Parmesan cheese |

Cut shrimp in half, if large. Combine with mushrooms, parsley, paprika, mustard, salt, pepper and lemon juice. Saute in melted butter. Remove from fire. Add sherry, cream sauce and eggs. Divide into 6 or 8 ramekins or baking shells. Sprinkle with the cheese. Bake in moderate oven until bubbly and brown. Serve at once. Serves 6-8.

Frances H. Lewis / *Armed Forces*


## Colombian Shrimp Pie

| | |
|---|---|
| 2 pounds shrimp, cleaned and | 10 slices bread |
| deveined | 1 to 1½ cups milk |
| 3 tablespoons butter or margarine | Salt and pepper to taste |
| 4 medium onions, sliced | |

Wash the shrimp and put aside. Melt the butter and fry the onions until transparent. Put into a large casserole. Put the bread in a bowl and pour over the milk, just enough to soak it through. Add the bread to the onions, then the shrimp. Cook in a very slow oven, add more milk when necessary and stir occasionally.

For variations: Add curry powder, or chopped green peppers and a little tomato sauce. Cut fresh tomatoes and mixed cooked vegetables may also be added. Serves 15.

Winifred Franklin / *Diocese of Colombia (South America)*

---

*O Lord, keep us from being like porridge, slow to warm up and hard to stir, but make us like cornflakes—always ready to serve. Amen.*

## Fish à La Grace

4 10½-ounce cans condensed
   tomato soup
1 pound Velveeta cheese
1½ quarts milk
¼ pound margarine
¼ cup Worcestershire sauce
2 pounds shrimp, shelled and
   deveined

3 pounds fish fillets, cut in
   serving pieces
2 cans lobster meat
1 can crabmeat
Salt and pepper
2 tablespoons cornstarch
Sherry to taste

Mix tomato soup and cheese together and heat until cheese is melted. Add all other ingredients except cornstarch and sherry. Mix cornstarch with a little cold water and stir into sauce to thicken. Cook briefly over low heat until shrimp and fish fillets are done. Just before serving, add sherry to suit your taste. Serve over rice. Serves about 30. Can be frozen.

               Grace Warnecke / *Diocese of Bethlehem (Pennsylvania)*

## Seafood Oriental

3 strips breakfast bacon
1½ pounds shrimp, shelled and
   deveined
1 medium onion, chopped
3 tablespoons browned flour
1 10½-ounce can diced clams

1 16-ounce can Chinese
   vegetables
1 10½-ounce can cream of
   mushroom soup
1 pound crabmeat, fresh or frozen
Salt and pepper to taste

In large skillet fry bacon until crisp. Remove from pan and set aside. Place shrimp in bacon fat, cover skillet and cook until they are light in color. Remove from skillet. Add onions and saute until tender. Stir in browned flour. Drain water from clams and Chinese vegetables into skillet and add cream of mushroom soup. Stir until blended. Return shrimp to skillet and heat for 2 minutes.

Just before serving, add diced clams and crabmeat; heat 2 minutes. Add Chinese vegetables; heat 2 minutes. Add salt and pepper to taste. Sprinkle in crumbled bacon. Serve with fluffy rice, crisp green salad and a chilled rose or white wine.

            Annelle Martin / *Diocese of Long Island (New York)*

## Egg and Shrimp Casserole

12 hard-boiled eggs
½ cup mayonnaise
Salt and pepper

1 or 2 boiled shrimp, shelled and
deveined

Cut eggs in half lengthwise, remove yolks. Moisten with mayonnaise, season with salt and pepper. Stuff the eggs and place in flat buttered baking dish. Cover eggs with shrimp and pour over the following white sauce:

2 tablespoons butter
2 tablespoons flour
2 cups milk
2 teaspoons Worcestershire sauce
½ teaspoon dry mustard
2 tablespoons chopped parsley

Small amount grated onion
½ teaspoon salt
Pepper to taste
¼ cup dry sherry
Paprika

Melt the butter, add flour and stir. Add milk, continue stirring until thick. Add seasonings. Pour over shrimp and eggs, sprinkle with paprika and bake at 350 degrees until heated through, about 20 minutes. Serves 6 to 8.

Mary Alexander / *Diocese of Upper South Carolina*

## Shrimp and Brown Rice Casserole

2½ cups cooked shrimp
3 tablespoons grated onion
3 tablespoons grated Bell pepper
2 cups cooked brown rice

½ cup chopped parsley
½ teaspoon salt
⅛ teaspoon pepper
1 cup mayonnaise

Mix well and top with bread crumbs. Bake 30 to 45 minutes at 350 degrees. Serves 4 to 6.

Ann Wood / *Executive Council*

## Easy Crab and Shrimp Casserole

6 cans cream of shrimp soup (do
   not dilute)
6 tablespoons sherry
3 8-ounce cans mushrooms
2 5-ounce cans slivered blanched
   almonds

2 pounds of crab (fresh)
2 bags (deveined and cleaned)
   frozen shrimp (24-ounce bag)

Mix all ingredients and put in buttered casserole. Put in moderate oven until bubbly. Grated cheese can be sprinkled on top. Serve with rice, a tossed green salad and French bread. Serves 20-25.

Carolyn Leighton / *Diocese of Maryland*

## Baked Crab and Shrimp

1 cup cooked shrimp
1 cup crabmeat
1 cup mayonnaise
1 cup chopped celery
1 chopped green pepper

1 medium onion, minced
1 tablespoon Worcestershire sauce
1/2 teaspoon pepper
Salt to taste
1 cup dry bread cubes, buttered

Mix all but final ingredient in a 2-quart casserole. Sprinkle with bread crumbs. Bake in 350-degree oven for 30 minutes.

Good with fresh fruit salad and hot rolls. Serves 4.

Marge Gressle / *Diocese of Bethlehem (Pennsylvania)*

## Casserole of Baked Crab Imperial

4 tablespoons butter or margarine
4 tablespoons flour
2 cups milk
1 teaspoon salt
1/8 teaspoon pepper
1/2 teaspoon celery salt
Dash of cayenne
1 egg yolk, beaten

2 tablespoons sherry
1 cup soft bread crumbs
1 pound crab flakes
1 teaspoon minced parsley
1 teaspoon minced onion
1/4 cup buttered bread crumbs
Paprika

Melt butter or margarine, add flour and blend. Gradually add milk and seasonings and cook over low heat, stirring constantly until thickened. Gradually add egg yolk and cook two minutes more.

Remove from heat and add sherry, soft bread crumbs, crab meat, parsley and onion. Gently mix and pour into well-greased 1½-quart casserole. Top with buttered crumbs and sprinkle with paprika. Bake in 400-degree oven for 20 to 25 minutes. Serves 6.

Etta M. Miller / *Diocese of Easton (Pennsylvania)*

## Chesapeake Bay Crab Cakes

| | |
|---|---|
| 1 pound blue crab meat | ½ teaspoon salt |
| 2 tablespoons chopped onion | Dash pepper |
| 2 tablespoons butter, melted | Dash cayenne pepper |
| 1 egg, beaten | ½ cup dry bread crumbs |
| ½ teaspoon powdered mustard | Fat for frying |

Remove any shell or cartilage from crab meat. Pick over carefully. Cook onion in butter until tender. Combine all ingredients except crumbs. Shape into 6 round cakes and roll in crumbs. Place cakes in a heavy frying pan which contains about ⅛ inch of fat, hot but not smoking. Fry at moderate heat. When cakes are brown on one side, turn carefully and brown the other side. Cooking time approximately 5 to 8 minutes. Drain on absorbent paper. Serves 6.

Betty Cox / *Diocese of Maryland*

## Maryland Crab in Ramekins

| | |
|---|---|
| 1 1-pound can of fresh backfin lump crab meat | 1 cup heavy mayonnaise |
| | 1 beaten whole egg |
| ¼ teaspoon salt | Dash of paprika |

Remove all shell from each lump of crab meat. Do this gently so as not to break the lumps. Place crab meat in bowl and add the salt and pepper over all. In another bowl, beat the egg, add the mayonnaise and stir strongly. Place enough of this dressing mixture in the crab meat to allow it to stick together. Pack the crab meat lightly in shells for baking. (Do not pack down, keep as light as possible). Try to have a high oval top with a thick coating of the dressing mixture. Place shells in a shallow pan and put in a pre-heated oven (275 to 350 degrees) for 30 minutes. Remove from oven and sprinkle top with paprika. Serve while hot. Serves 4-5.

Anne Taylor / *Diocese of Easton (Maryland)*

## Salmon Loaf

2 eggs
1 medium-sized onion, chopped
½ green pepper, chopped
¼ lemon, juiced and a little
   grated rind

1 cup chopped celery
¾ cup milk
1 teaspoon salt
Pepper to taste
1 tablespoon soft butter or oleo

Put above ingredients in blender and mix well. Gradually add 1 cup bread crumbs.

Remove from blender and carefully fold in 2 cups flaked salmon (1 pound can). Put into greased 1-quart loaf pan. Bake at 375 degrees for 45 minutes.

(This is almost a souffle, and if put into a souffle dish can pass as such. To make it "company"—serve with a medium white sauce to which are added chopped, hard-boiled eggs.) Serves 4-6.

Rosemary Atkinson / *Diocese of West Virginia*

## Salmon Souffle

2 cups soft bread crumbs
1 cup scalded milk
1 teaspoon salt
¼ teaspoon dry mustard

¼ pound sharp cheese, cut in
   pieces
3 eggs, separated
2 cups (1-pound can) salmon

Soak bread crumbs in milk, add salt, mustard and cheese; heat until melted. Cool, add egg yolks and then salmon. Fold in egg whites that have been beaten stiff. Pour into buttered casserole and bake in slow oven of 325 degrees for 45 minutes. Serves 6.

Grace Warnecke / *Diocese of Bethlehem (Pennsylvania)*

## New England Clam Souffle

½ pound minced clams, fresh or
   canned
2 cups Ritz crackers, rolled fine
2 cups milk
½ cup melted butter

2 eggs, beaten
¼ teaspoon tarragon
1 teaspoon sugar
Salt and papper to taste

203

Mix all the ingredients together. Let stand in bowl for 30 minutes. Stir and pour into buttered casserole. Bake at 350 degrees for 45 minutes or until firm. Serve with favorite fish sauce if desired. Serves 4 to 6.

Etta Miller / *Diocese of Easton (Maryland)*

## Spaghetti With Minced Clams

1 pound thin spaghetti
2 7½-ounce cans minced clams
1 clove garlic, crushed

6 tablespoons butter
2 tablespoons olive oil

Cook spaghetti according to package directions until barely tender; do not overcook. Drain in a colander. To the clean empty cooking pot, add the clam liquid with the garlic, butter and olive oil. Place over low heat until butter melts; add the cooked spaghetti, cook gently, tossing, until clam liquid is absorbed. Add clams when liquid is partially absorbed. Makes 6 servings.

Catherine Sterling / *Diocese of Montana*

## Tuna Casserole

2 pounds egg noodles
2 cans celery soup
4 15-ounce cans tuna
3 cans mushroom soup
½ cup chopped onions

½ cup chopped green peppers
½ cup chopped red peppers
Salt to taste
2 cups milk
3 teaspoons paprika

Cook noodles for ten minutes and drain. Mix all ingredients except milk and paprika. Place in three large casseroles. Pour milk over the tops and sprinkle with paprika. Bake in 350-degree oven for 45 minutes to 1 hour. Serves 30.

Jeanne Baden / *Diocese of Virginia*

## Tuna Fish Casserole

6 cups flaked tuna
4 cans mushroom soup
   (undiluted)
2½ cups diced celery
¼ cup chopped onions
2 teaspoons salt

2 tablespoons lemon juice
3 cups mayonnaise
1 dozen hard-boiled eggs,
   chopped
3 cups crushed saltines
Potato chips for topping

Mix and place in a large 12 × 18-inch pan. Cover top with crushed potato chips. Bake at 400 degrees until bubbly and brown. This can be made with diced chicken. Serves 25.

Helen Van der Horst / *Diocese of Tennessee*

## Friday Tuna Burgers

1 cup grated processed cheese
3 hard-boiled eggs, chopped
1 can tuna fish
2 tablespoons chopped onions
2 tablespoons chopped stuffed
   olives

½ cup mayonnaise
4 hamburger rolls or English
   muffins

Combine all the ingredients except the rolls. Spread mixture on rolls or muffins and broil until heated through. Serves 4.

Marion Higley / *Diocese of Central New York*

## Haddock with Scallops

2 pounds haddock or other white
   fish
1 pound scallops
8 tablespoons butter
9 tablespoons flour
1 cup evaporated milk
1½ cups milk
1 cup consomme
2 tablespoons cornstarch
1 tablespoon lemon juice
1 tablespoon Worcestershire sauce

4 tablespoons catsup
1 tablespoon horseradish
1 clove garlic, crushed
¼ cup sherry
4 teaspoons prepared mustard
½ teaspoon salt
1 teaspoon soy sauce
¼ teaspoon cayenne pepper
4 tablespoons chopped parsley
Buttered bread crumbs

Simmer fish and scallops for 10 minutes or until lightly cooked and flaky. Melt butter and add flour to make a thick roux. Heat evaporated milk with milk and consomme and add to roux; stir constantly until thick. When thick, add cornstarch blended with a little milk. Add the remaining ingredients except for bread crumbs and heat. Add fish to the sauce; place in greased casserole. Cover with buttered bread crumbs. Bake about 30 minutes in 400 degree oven. Can be refrigerated before baking; if cold, bake longer until bubbly.

Janice Rusack / *Diocese of Los Angeles (California)*

## Halibut Steaks, Kodiak Style

**2 pounds fresh halibut steaks**　　**¼ pound oleo**
**Dry bread crumbs, flavored as**
　**desired**

Preheat oven to 500 degrees. Shake halibut steaks in bag with dry bread crumbs. Line with foil a baking pan large enough to hold the halibut steaks. Melt oleo in the pan and roll the crumbed halibut in it until well coated. Place the pan in 500-degree oven and bake for about 15 minutes or until fish flakes easily. Serve sizzling hot with tartar sauce. Serves 4.

Mary Cochran / *Diocese of Alaska*

## Whole Fish Baked with Cheddar Cheese Soup

This is an excellent method of cooking any large fish, such as cod, haddock, blue, bonito, or striped bass. A 4-5 pound fish makes a good main course for four people.

**1 whole fish, 4-5 pounds**　　**½ cup milk**
**Bacon or salt pork**　　**1 can cheddar cheese soup**

Grease the pan lightly, or put a strip or two of bacon or pork under the fish. Fasten a few strips of bacon and/or pork on top of the fish. You can fill the body cavity, if you like, with a bread or cracker stuffing spiced with chopped onions—or prepared Pepperidge Farm stuffing—and sew or skewer the cavity shut.

Spread a layer of undiluted soup, about ½ can, all over the fish like a frosting. Put it in a hot steady oven, about 350 degrees. As the fish cooks baste it two or three times with the remaining ½ can of the soup which has been diluted with the milk. This builds up an outer crust. For the remaining 15 minutes of cooking time use up all the soup over and around the fish.

The time of baking varies with the size of the fish and temperature of the oven. A 4 pound fish requires 45 to 60 minutes in a 350-degree oven. The fish is done when the meat leaves the bone readily. The dish is done when only the bones are left.

Martha Porteus / *Diocese of Connecticut*

## New England Turkey Dinner

"Believe it or not, it can be good!"

Soak salt cod overnight. (As much of it as you can afford). Stew cod the next day until soft. Add boiled potatoes and boiled onions, carrots and turnips or any other root vegetable available. Mix "The Whole Kit and Boilin' Bottle" of these ingredients and serve with fried pork scraps floating in bacon fat as hot sauce.

N.B. Evidently the supply of wild turkey did not last indefinitely after the landing in Plymouth.

Katy Dun / *Diocese of Washington, D.C.*

# VEGETABLES

## Baked Acorn Squash

3 acorn squash, cut in halves and
   seeded
6 teaspoons butter
6 teaspoons brown sugar

6 teaspoons bourbon whiskey
1 teaspoon salt
¼ teaspoon nutmeg

Place squash in flat pan. Fill each half with butter, sugar and bourbon. Sprinkle with salt and nutmeg. Place a little water in pan and cover with foil. Bake at 400 degrees for 1 hour or until soft. Serves 6.

Carolyn Leighton / *Diocese of Maryland*

## Broccoli-Onion Deluxe

2 10-ounce packages frozen cut
   broccoli
2 cups whole white onions,
   cooked and peeled (or use
   canned white onions)
4 tablespoons margarine
2 tablespoons flour

Salt and pepper to taste
1 cup milk
1 3-ounce package cream cheese,
   cut up
1 cup soft bread crumbs
¼ cup grated Parmesan cheese

Cook broccoli until just tender, drain and combine with onions. Melt 2 tablespoons margarine, blend in flour, salt and pepper. Add milk all at once; cook until thick and bubbly. Reduce heat, blend in cream cheese and cook until smooth. Stir in vegetables and turn into a 1½-quart casserole. Bake at 350 degrees for 20 minutes. Melt remaining butter, toss with bread crumbs and cheese, sprinkle over casserole. Bake 15 to 20 minutes longer. Serves 10.

Virginia Turner / *Diocese of Kansas*

## Carrot Pudding from the Virgin Islands

½ cup butter or margarine
⅔ cup sugar
1½ cups raw carrots, scraped and
   grated
⅞ cup flour
½ teaspoon salt

1 teaspoon baking powder
½ teaspoon cinnamon
½ teaspoon nutmeg
¼ teaspoon cloves
1 cup seeded raisins

Cream the butter and sugar. Add the grated carrots. Sift flour with salt, baking powder and spices. Add to butter mixture and mix well. Add raisins. Pour into a greased and floured tube pan and bake in a moderate oven, 325 degrees, for about 40 minutes. Cool and serve. This is a cake-like dish which is served as a vegetable in the Virgin Islands. Serves 12-16.

Shirley Turner / *Diocese of the Virgin Islands*

## Cauliflower with Sour Cream

1 cauliflower, broken into
   flowerets
2 tablespoons butter or shortening
2 tablespoons onion, minced
1 teaspoon dill weed

1 tablespoon flour
1 cup sour cream
Lemon juice to taste
Salt and pepper to taste

Cook cauliflower in boiling water until barely tender. Drain and cool. Heat butter and saute onion. Add dill weed and flour. Stir and cook gently, then add sour cream and heat until smooth. Season to taste with lemon juice, salt and pepper, and pour over cauliflower, stirring gently until coated. Serves 6.

Betty Powell / *Diocese of Oklahoma*

## Corn Fritters

6 ears of corn
¼ cup milk if corn is dry
1 tablespoon sugar
3 tablespoons flour

Salt and pepper to taste
3 eggs, separated
Fat for frying

209

Cut corn from cooked ears, put in bowl with sugar, flour, salt and pepper. Add well-beaten egg yolks and fold in stiffly beaten egg whites. Fry in shallow fat using half vegetable oil and half butter, over medium heat. Serves 4.

Marie Louise Creighton / *Diocese of Washington, D.C.*

## Cucumber Scallop

4 large cucumbers
1½ cups sliced celery
3 tablespoons margarine
3 tablespoons flour
1 teaspoon salt

¼ teaspoon pepper
1½ cups milk
¼ cup mayonnaise
½ cup buttered bread cubes

Pare cucumbers, quarter lengthwise, remove seeds and cut into 1-inch pieces. Cook with celery in boiling salted water until just tender; drain well. Watch that it isn't overcooked. Place in buttered baking dish.

Melt margarine over low heat in saucepan. Stir in flour, salt and pepper. Cook, stirring constantly, just until mixture bubbles. Stir in milk slowly; continue cooking and stirring until sauce thickens and boils one minute. Remove from heat, blend in mayonnaise. Pour sauce over vegetables and sprinkle bread crumbs over top. (This much can be done ahead but cover and chill until ready to use.) Bake at 350 degrees for 30 minutes or until bubbly-hot and golden on top. If casserole has been chilled, bake a longer time. Serves 6.

Katherine Appleyard / *Diocese of Pittsburgh (Pennsylvania)*

## Eggplant Gratin

2 1-pound eggplants
Olive oil for frying
2 eggs
½ cup light cream
Salt and pepper to taste

1 cup tomato sauce
⅓ cup bread crumbs
2 to 3 tablespoons freshly grated
    Parmesan cheese
1 tablespoon chopped parsley

Peel eggplants and cut in ⅓-inch slices. Sprinkle with salt and let drain for at least 1 hour. Rinse off salt, dry the slices and dust with

210

flour. In a large skillet, saute the slices in ⅛-inch hot olive oil until they are browned on both sides. Drain on paper. Arrange slices in an oiled oval gratin dish.

In a bowl beat eggs with light cream and season lightly with salt and pepper. Pour custard over the eggplant and bake in a 375 degree-oven for 25 minutes, or until the custard is set. Spread tomato sauce over the custard. Sprinkle with bread crumbs and Parmesan cheese. Put under the broiler until the topping is browned. Sprinkle the dish with parsley and serve. Serves 4 generously.

Connie Hall / *Diocese of New Hampshire*


## Glazed Bermuda Onions

6 large Bermuda onions
2 tablespoons butter
¼ cup honey
½ teaspoon paprika

½ teaspoon salt
⅛ teaspoon pepper
3 tablespoons water

Peel and halve the onions; place cut side up in a covered casserole. Top with remaining ingredients. Cover and bake at 350 degrees for 1½ hours, basting occasionally.

Carolyn Butterfield / *Diocese of Vermont*


## Potatoes au Gratin

3 cups cooked potatoes, diced
6 tablespoons butter
3 tablespoons flour
1½ cups milk

¼ pound sharp cheddar cheese, grated
Salt and pepper to taste
¾ cup soft bread crumbs

Place cooked potatoes in shallow baking dish. Melt 3 tablespoons butter in saucepan. Blend in flour. Add milk gradually and cook, stirring constantly until thick and smooth. Add cheese and stir until melted. Season with salt and pepper. Pour sauce over potatoes and stir with a fork. Melt remaining butter and mix with bread crumbs. Sprinkle over potatoes. Place under broiler and broil until golden brown or bake in 350-degree oven until done. A good dish for a covered dish dinner. Can be made ahead. Serves 6.

Mabel Davies / *Diocese of Dallas (Texas)*

## Green Rice Casserole

| | |
|---|---|
| 1 cup rice | 1 small green pepper, chopped |
| ¼ pound butter | Handful of dry parsley |
| ½ pound sharp cheddar cheese, cubed | 2-3 eggs |
| | 1 cup milk |
| 1 medium onion, chopped | ½ teaspoon salt |

Cook rice in boiling salted water according to directions on box. Drain, and while still hot add butter and cubed cheddar cheese. Add onion and green pepper to mixture along with dry parsley. Beat and add eggs, milk and salt. Place mixture in medium-size casserole and bake at 325 degrees about an hour—should be like a custard. Makes 6 generous servings.

Catherine Sterling / *Diocese of Montana*

## Orange Rice

| | |
|---|---|
| ½ pound margarine | 2 cups cooked rice |
| ½ cup celery | Salt and pepper |
| 1 cup mandarin orange sections | |

Melt margarine in skillet; cut celery in ½-inch pieces; saute in margarine. Add drained oranges; combine with rice; season to taste with salt and pepper. Serves 6.

Ruth Quarterman / *Diocese of Northwest Texas*

## West Indian Rice

*West Indians love starches. Often at a single meal several starchy vegetables will be served. With many it is a "must" to have rice at every meal. Yet the handsome tall and slender figure of the native belies the high carbohydrate content of his diet.*

| | |
|---|---|
| ¼ pound salt pork or ham | 2 tablespoons shortening |
| 1 small onion, minced | 3 cups boiling water |
| 1 clove garlic, minced | Salt to taste |
| ¼ cup tomatoes, or 1 teaspoon tomato paste | 1½ cups rice |

Saute pork or ham, onion, garlic and tomatoes in shortening. Add 3 cups boiling water, boil rapidly; season to taste with salt. Add rice and cook covered for the first 10 minutes. Remove cover and allow to dry, turning the rice over now and then. Yield: About 6 cups.

Shirley Turner / *Diocese of the Virgin Islands*

## Spinach-Cottage Cheese Casserole

| | |
|---|---|
| 1 package frozen chopped spinach | 3 dashes nutmeg |
| 1 cup cottage cheese | ¼ teaspoon caraway seeds |
| 2 eggs, beaten | 2 tablespoons Parmesan cheese |
| ½ teaspoon seasoned salt | 1 tablespoon butter |
| ⅛ teaspoon pepper | ¼ teaspoon paprika |

Cook the spinach lightly and drain. Add cottage cheese, eggs, salt, pepper, nutmeg and caraway seeds to the spinach and mix. Put in a small shallow casserole, sprinkle with paprika, Parmesan cheese and dot with butter. Bake for about 20 minutes at 350 degrees. May be used as a meatless main dish. Serves 4.

Catharine P. Cole / *Diocese of Upper South Carolina*

## Southern Spoon Bread

An old family recipe

| | |
|---|---|
| 1 cup cornmeal, yellow or white | 1 teaspoon salt |
| 1 quart milk | 1 level teaspoon baking powder |
| 1 "lump" of butter, about 1 ounce | 2 eggs |

Cook the cornmeal and milk together until thick and gently boiling. Remove from heat and add other ingredients. Mix well, pour into greased 1-quart baking dish and bake 350 degrees for about 45 minutes. Cannot be made much ahead or it collapses. Serves about 6 people, depending on appetites!

Katherine Lawrence / *Diocese of Massachusetts*

213

## Stuffed Zucchini

4 small zucchini, uniform size
1 egg white, slightly beaten
Worcestershire sauce
seasoning salt
Bread crumbs
Butter

Boil squash only 3 to 5 minutes. Cut in half lengthwise and scoop out centers. Cut centers in small pieces and mix with egg white, Worcestershire, seasoning salt to taste, and a few dry bread crumbs to make proper consistency. Sprinkle shells lightly with seasoning salt. Fill shells and place in baking dish. Cover each squash with buttered bread crumbs. Bake at 350 degrees for about 20 minutes. Serves 4.

Mary Alexander / *Diocese of Upper South Carolina*

## Fig-Yams Casserole

4 medium sized yams
1/2 cup chopped dried figs
1/4 cup melted butter or margarine
1/2 teaspoon salt
1/8 teaspoon pepper
1/2 teaspoon grated orange rind
1/4 cup orange juice

Cook yams, peel and mash. Add rest of ingredients and mix well. Place in shallow baking dish and bake in moderate oven, 350 degrees, for 20 minutes. Serves 6.

Evelyn Thayer / *Diocese of Colorado*

## Curried Four-Fruit Bake

1/3 cup butter or margarine
3/4 cup brown sugar, packed
4 teaspoons curry powder
1 16-ounce can pear halves
5 maraschino cherries (optional)
1 16-ounce can cling peach or apricot halves
1 20-ounce can pineapple slices or chunks

Start heating oven to 325 degrees. Melt butter; add sugar and curry. Drain and dry fruits; place in 1 1/2-quart casserole; add butter mixture. Bake 1 hour uncovered. Flavor will be even better if dish stands covered, in refrigerator, and is then re-heated. It may be re-heated several times using a 350-degree oven for 30 minutes. Serve with ham, lamb, or poultry. Serves 12.

Dottie Hall / *Diocese of Virginia*

214

# SALADS

## Shrimp Mousse Salad

1 can tomato soup
2 3-ounce packages cream cheese
3 envelopes plain gelatin
1½ cups cold water
1 cup mayonnaise

¼ cup chopped onions
¼ cup chopped green peppers
1 cup chopped celery
1 or 2 cans small shrimp
Salt and pepper to taste

Heat soup and cream cheese until creamy. Add gelatin dissolved in the cold water. Add the mayonnaise, chopped vegetables and shrimp. Season to taste. Pour into any type of mold. Serve on lettuce plate.

Mabel Davies / *Diocese of Dallas (Texas)*

## Tuna Fish Mold

2 envelopes unflavored gelatin
2 cans or 1 large can flaked tuna
2 chopped hard-boiled eggs
½ cup chopped olives (green with pimiento)

2 tablespoons capers
2 cups stiff mayonnaise

Soften gelatin in ½ cup cold water. Place over hot water until dissolved, then add to fish, and stir lightly with fork. Don't break fish. Add to chopped eggs, olives, capers, and mayonnaise. Mix all together and put in ring mold. Gently rinse mold with cold water before putting mixture in it. Chill until firm. Place towel dipped in hot water over mold to loosen it when unmolding. Place fish mold on large plate, surround with lettuce leaves and watercress or parsley. Fill center of ring with small curd cottage cheese, about 1 quart. Decorate cheese with paprika and serve.

215

This dish can be made a day ahead and placed in refrigerator until ready to unmold. Serve with potato chips and fresh green peas for a summer luncheon dish.

Martha Porteus / *Diocese of Connecticut*

## Sarah's Salad Bowl

1 head lettuce, chunked
½ cup mayonnaise
1 sweet Bermuda onion, sliced
    paper thin
2-3 teaspoons sugar
1 cup frozen green peas, lightly
    cooked

¾ pound Swiss cheese, cut in
    thin strips
2-3 slices bacon, crisply cooked
    and crumbled

In a large wooden bowl, place a layer of chunked lettuce. Spread with mayonnaise and add a layer of onion slices. Lightly sprinkle with sugar. Add a layer of lightly cooked peas and a layer of Swiss cheese. Do *not* use salt or pepper! Do *not* toss! Place in refrigerator 1½-2 hours—no more! When ready to serve, top with bacon. This salad is not sweet; the sugar causes the onion to "weep" and this, with the mayonnaise, makes the dressing. Good for pot luck suppers. Serves 10.

Betty Powell / *Diocese of Oklahoma*

## Bean-Beet Salad

2 16-ounce cans dilled cut
    green beans
2 16-ounce cans pickled curly cut
    bits of beets
5-7 green onions, chopped
1 cup mayonnaise

5-6 hard boiled eggs, grated
1½ teaspoons sugar
Salt and pepper to taste
½ teaspoon paprika
1-2 tablespoons chopped parsley

Drain the vegetables. In a large glass bowl, place a layer of beans, then a layer of beets, and sprinkle with onions and ½ teaspoon sugar. Repeat until all the vegetables are in bowl. Spread mayonnaise on top. Season eggs with salt and pepper and sprinkle on top. Refrigerate 6 hours or overnight to allow flavors to blend. Garnish with paprika and parsley. Serves 10-12.

Billie Gross / *Diocese of Oregon*

## Korean Spinach Salad

1 pound spinach
2 hard-boiled eggs
8 slices crisp bacon, crumbled

1 can water chestnuts
1 can bean sprouts

Toss with following dressing just before serving:

1 cup oil
¼ cup vinegar
⅓ cup catsup

⅔ cup sugar
1 medium onion, chopped fine
Salt to taste

Serves 8.

Alice Harte / *Diocese of Arizona*

## Vegetable Bouquet Salad

1 1-pound can cut green beans,
   well drained
1 1-pound can red kidney beans,
   well drained
1 7-ounce can pitted ripe olives,
   well drained
1 6- or 8-ounce can whole or sliced
   mushrooms, well drained
1 4-ounce jar diced pimiento, well
   drained
1 15-ounce can artichoke hearts,
   well drained

1½ cups sliced diagonally celery
1 medium onion, sliced thin
¼ cup tarragon vinegar
1½ teaspoons Accent
1¼ teaspoons salt
1 teaspoon sugar
1 tablespoon fines herbes
¼ teaspoon Tabasco
½ cup salad oil
¼ cup chopped parsley
2 tablespoons chopped capers

Combine drained vegetables, celery and onion. For dressing, measure vinegar, spices and oil; beat or shake until blended. Pour over vegetables and refrigerate several hours or overnight. Turn into serving bowl and sprinkle with chopped parsley and capers. Serves 20-25.

Marie Louise Creighton / *Washington, D.C.*

## Bright Pink Molded Salad

6 medium beets
2 tablespoons mayonnaise
1 package unflavored gelatin
1½ cups boiling water

1 teaspoon salt
¼ teaspoon thyme
¼ teaspoon marjoram

217

Boil beets until tender. Drain, cool, peel and slice. Place mayonnaise in blender and add beets a few at a time. Add ⅛ cup water, then rest of beets, blending gradually. Soften gelatin in ¼ cup cold water, add 1½ cups boiling water and stir until dissolved. Add beets and spices to gelatin mixture, stir and pour into a 4-cup mold. Chill until firm. To serve, turn out of mold and garnish with lettuce and mayonnaise. Serves 6.

Berta Carral / *Diocese of Guatemala*

## Molded Vegetable Salad

1 can Campbells tomato soup
1 envelope gelatin
6 to 8 ounces cream cheese
¼ cup chopped celery
¼ cup chopped green pepper
¼ cup grated carrots

¼ cup chopped scallions or
  grated white onion
1 cup mayonnaise
2 teaspoons Worcestershire sauce
4-5 shakes Tabasco

Heat tomato soup undiluted. Add gelatin which has been softened in a little water. Bring to boil. Pour over cream cheese, and stir until dissolved. Add vegetables. When cool, add seasonings, and place in mold. When a ring mold is used, it may be filled with cooked shrimp. Serves 10-12.

Beth Murray / *Diocese of Central Gulf Coast*

## Molded Mustard Ring

1 cup weak vinegar (half vinegar,
  half water)
¾ cup sugar
Salt and pepper to taste
½ teaspoon turmeric
3 tablespoons dry mustard (use
  hot mustard for a sharper taste)

4 eggs, well beaten
1 tablespoon gelatin
  softened in
½ cup cold water
1 cup whipping cream

Mix vinegar, sugar, salt, pepper, turmeric, and mustard. In the top of a double boiler add this mixture to the well-beaten eggs. Cook over low heat until thick, like custard. Remove from heat and add the softened gelatin. Put over a pan of cold water to cool. When cool, fold in the cream, whipped firm, but not dry. Pour into mold. This amount fills an 8-inch ring mold. Spraying mold with Pam first helps in unmolding. Garnish with tomato and avocado wedges or fill center with coleslaw. Excellent served with ham, especially smoked Virginia ham. This may be made ahead. Serves 6-8.

Rachel Watson / *Diocese of Utah*

## Cranberry-Orange Salad

| | |
|---|---|
| 1 cup cranberries | ⅔ cups sugar (scant) |
| 1 large apple | 1 package orange Jello |
| 1 orange and peel | 1⅔ cups boiling water |

Grind cranberries, apple, orange and peel; add sugar and let stand one hour. Stir the orange Jello into the boiling water; when cool, add the fruit and pour into a wet mold. Chill until firm. Serves 6.

Evelyn Thayer / *Diocese of Colorado*

## Alice's Fancy Lime-Pear Salad for 50 people

For the bottom layer:

8 packages lime Jello (24 ounces)
6 cups boiling water
½ cup lemon juice
4 16-ounce cartons cream style
  cottage cheese

4 cups chopped celery
1 quart mayonnaise
5 tall cans evaporated milk
4 cups chopped pecans or walnuts

Follow directions to make Jello and cool until slightly thickened. Add rest of ingredients and pour into two large pans (11½ × 19½ × 2-inch)

For the top layer:

8 or 9 cans pear halves
8 packages lime Jello (24 ounces)
10 cups liquid (boiling water and
  pear syrup)

½ teaspoon green food coloring
50 maraschino cherries

Drain the pear halves and reserve the liquid. Mix the Jello in the hot liquid, stir until dissolved and cool until thickened. When bottom layer is almost set arrange pear halves, round side down, and press down slightly. Drop a maraschino cherry into center of each pear half. When Jello mixture is of correct consistency, pour over bottom layer and set until firm.

Barbara Rivera / *Diocese of San Joaquin (California)*

## Tropical Buffet Salad

1 3-ounce package lime Jello
1 3-ounce package lemon Jello
1 large can crushed pineapple
1 cup cottage cheese

1 cup mayonnaise
½ cup chopped pecans
2½ tablespoons fresh horseradish
2 tablespoons chopped pimiento

Dissolve Jello in 2 cups boiling water, then cool it. When it just begins to jell, add all other ingredients. Set in mold. Serves 12.

Nancy Gravatt / *Diocese of Upper South Carolina*

# Pink Molded Salad

1 3-ounce package raspberry Jello
1 envelope gelatin
1½ cups hot water (scant)

2½ cups crushed pineapple
1 pint cottage cheese (small curd)
1 pint Cool Whip

Mix ingredients together. After all is assembled, mixture will be smoother if beaten with egg beater before putting in mold. Serve on a lettuce leaf, with mayonnaise if desired. Serves 8 or 10.

Lillian Curtis / *Diocese of Olympia (Washington)*

# Frozen Fruit Salad

1 8-ounce package cream cheese
1 cup mayonnaise
1 tablespoon unflavored gelatin
¼ cup fruit juice
3 to 4 cups sliced, mixed fruits, drained of juice

¼ cup chopped nuts; pecans, walnuts or almonds
2 tablespoons chopped chutney or use chopped crystallized ginger
1 cup heavy cream, whipped

Mix cream cheese and mayonnaise in large bowl. Soak gelatin in fruit juice, dissolve over pan of hot water. Prepare fruit. Use any combination that tastes good to you . . . . . fresh fruits in season, partially thawed frozen fruits, drained canned fruits, pineapple, blueberries, mandarin oranges, grapes, cherries, strawberries, sliced bananas. (This is a good way to "store" seasonal fruit for future use.)

Add gelatin and fruits, nuts, chutney to the cream cheese mixture. Fold in whipped cream; place in containers to freeze. Use small containers so it can be sliced. Freeze until firm. It will keep 6 weeks or longer. To serve: remove from freezer, slice, place on lettuce and garnish with fresh or frozen fruit slices. Serve with poppy seed dressing. Serves 10 to 12.

Fran Rose / *Diocese of Southern Virginia*

---

*As you have so graciously provided food for our bodies, so dear God grant us nourishment for our souls, through Jesus Christ our Lord. Amen.*

221

## Poppy Seed Dressing

1 cup salad oil
½ cup sugar or honey
⅓ cup vinegar
1 tablespoon grated onion
1 teaspoon powdered mustard

1 teaspoon salt
1 or 2 tablespoons poppy seed
1 teaspoon grated crystallized
   ginger or minced chutney

Roast the poppy seeds slightly or crush to bring out the flavor. Mix all ingredients. An electric blender is great for combining flavors and textures.

Fran Rose / *Diocese of Southern Virginia*

## Green and Gold Papaya Salad

1 cup salad oil
⅓ cup tarragon vinegar
¼ cup sugar
1 tablespoon lime juice
¼ teaspoon paprika

½ teaspoon each: salt, dry
   mustard and instant minced
   onion
1 papaya, peeled cubed
4 cups salad greens

Place salad oil, sugar, vinegar, lime juice, paprika, salt, mustard and onion in blender. Add 1½ tablespoons papaya seeds and blend until seeds are size of coarsely ground pepper. Combine cubed papaya and greens. Toss lightly with the dressing. Serves 8.

Evelyn Thayer / *Diocese of Colorado*

## Cottage Cheese Dressing with Buttermilk

½ cup cottage cheese
½ cup buttermilk
3 hard-cooked egg yolks
¼ cup lemon juice
1 teaspoon salt

½ teaspoon paprika
⅛ teaspoon garlic powder
½ green pepper, cut in pieces
4 radishes, trimmed

Blend all the ingredients together in the blender until green pepper and radishes are finely chopped, but still show color in dressing. Lovely on salad greens and loved by weight-watchers.

Betty Powell / *Diocese of Oklahoma*

# DESSERTS

## *Cakes*

### Applesauce Cake

1 cup shortening
2 cups sugar
2 eggs
3 cups unsweetened applesauce
1 teaspoon soda
½ cup hot water
5 cups flour

2 teaspoons cinnamon
1 teaspoon nutmeg
1 teaspoon cloves
1 teaspoon salt
2 cups raisins
1 cup nuts, well floured

Cream shortening with sugar and eggs. Add the other ingredients in order given. 1 cup maraschino cherries may be added. Bake in moderate oven (350 degrees) for 1 hour. This recipe makes 3 loaves. If desired, add whipped cream to each serving. Great for a Guild meeting.

Charlotte McNeil / *Diocese of Western Michigan*

### Hot Milk Cake

4 eggs
2 cups sugar
2 cups flour
2 teaspoons baking powder

½ teaspoon salt
1 cup boiling milk
2 teaspoons butter
1½ teaspoons lemon extract

Beat eggs well, add sugar. Add flour sifted twice with baking powder and salt. Add hot milk with butter melted in it. Add flavoring. Bake for about 45 minutes in a slow oven (325 degrees) in a large size pan. Frost with Spicy Nutty Frosting:

223

| | |
|---|---|
| 4 tablespoons butter | ½ teaspoon cinnamon |
| 4 tablespoons hot cream | 2⅔ cups sifted confectioners |
| ¼ teaspoon salt | sugar |
| 2 teaspoons vanilla | ⅔ cup broken nuts |

Mix ingredients and beat well. Let stand 5 minutes. Beat until creamy. If the frosting seems a little stiff, add more cream.

Ida Lou Barnds / *Diocese of Dallas (Texas)*

## Kernstown Sponge Cake

| | |
|---|---|
| 12 eggs, separated | Scant weight of 6 eggs in flour |
| Weight of 11 eggs in sugar | Grated rind and juice of a lemon |

Beat egg yolks and whites separately, add sugar to yolks, then lemon, then beaten egg whites, and gently stir in flour. Bake in an ungreased mold at 325 degrees for approximately 50 to 60 minutes.

Eleanor Jackson / *Diocese of Louisiana*

## Orange Marmalade Cake

| | |
|---|---|
| ½ cup shortening | ½ teaspoon allspice |
| 1 cup sugar | ½ teaspoon nutmeg |
| 2 eggs, well-beaten | ½ cup buttermilk |
| 1½ cups flour | ½ cup orange marmalade |
| ½ teaspoon soda | ½ cup chopped pecans |
| ½ teaspoon cinnamon | ½ cup candied fruit (citron or |
| ½ teaspoon cloves | orange peel) |

Cream the shortening, add sugar gradually, then the well-beaten eggs. Sift flour once before measuring. Sift the flour, soda and spices together and add alternately with the buttermilk. Add marmalade, then nuts and fruit. Pour into well-greased and floured 9-inch square pan. Bake about 45 minutes at 350 degrees.

Note: As substitute for marmalade and candied fruit, sour orange, kumquat, limequat, grapefruit, alone or combined may be used.

Serve plain or iced with following icing:

*Icing for Marmalade Cake*

| | |
|---|---|
| 1½ cups sugar | 2 egg whites |
| 4 tablespoons orange juice | ½ teaspoon lemon rind |
| 1 tablespoon lemon juice | 1 tablespoon orange rind |

Mix in top of double boiler. Beat over boiling water until icing stands in peaks (about 7 minutes).

Mary Alexander / *Diocese of Upper South Carolina*

## Queen Elizabeth II's Cake

This recipe is not to be given away, but must be sold *only* for charitable purposes and priced at 25 cents. It is understood that this recipe is for the only cake that the Queen herself makes. She goes into her own kitchen and makes it there.

| | |
|---|---|
| 1 cup sugar | ½ teaspoon baking powder |
| ¼ cup butter | ½ cup crushed nuts |
| 1 beaten egg | 1 cup boiling water |
| 1 teaspoon vanilla | 1 cup dates, chopped |
| 1½ cups flour | 1 teaspoon soda |

Pour boiling water over dates and soda and let stand. Cream sugar and butter. Add beaten egg and vanilla. Sift flour and baking powder together and add alternately with dates mixture and nuts. Bake 35 minutes in moderate oven (350 degrees) in pan 8 × 10-inches. Ice with the following icing:

| | |
|---|---|
| 5 tablespoons brown sugar | 2 tablespoons butter |
| 5 tablespoons cream | |

Boil gently for about 3 minutes until sugar is dissolved, then spread on cake. Garnish with coconut and additional nuts.

Hannah Lawrence / *Diocese of Western Massachusetts*

## Scripture Cake

1  4½ cups I Kings 4:22
2  1½ cups Judges 5:25
3  2 cups Jeremiah 6:20
4  2 cups I Samuel 30:12
5  2 cups Nahum 3:12
6  ½ cup Judges 4:19
7  1 cup Numbers 17:8
8  2 tablespoons I Samuel 14:25
9  Season to taste II Chronicles 9:9
10  Six of Jeremiah 17:11
11  A pinch of Leviticus 2:13
12  2 tablespoons Amos 4:5
13  Follow Solomon's prescription for making a good child (Proverbs 23:14) and you will have a good cake.
See answers page 250.

Ann Allin / *Dover House (1974—)*

# *Cookies*

## Mother's Cookies

1 stick butter
1 stick margarine
1 cup sugar
1 egg yolk

2 cups flour
1 teaspoon vanilla
1 egg white
Chopped pecans

Cream butter and sugar, add egg yolk, flour and vanilla. Mix well. Spread on greased jelly roll pan (10×15-inch). Pat evenly. Brush slightly beaten egg white over mixture. Sprinkle chopped pecans over top. Bake at 325 degrees for 30-40 minutes. Cut into 48 squares before it cools.

"Dink" Elebash / *Diocese of North Carolina*

## Orange Ginger Cookies

1 cup butter
1½ cups granulated sugar
1 egg
2 tablespoons light corn syrup
3 cups flour
2 teaspoons soda

2 teaspoons cinnamon
2 teaspoons ginger
½ teaspoon cloves
2 tablespoons grated orange peel
¼ cup orange juice

Thoroughly cream together butter and sugar, egg and syrup; beat well. Sift together dry ingredients. Mix into creamed mixture along with orange juice and orange peel. Shape into 2 9-inch rolls about 2 inches across. Wrap in waxed paper. Chill several hours or overnight. Slice about ⅛ inch thick and place 2 inches apart on cookie sheet. Bake in 400-degree oven 8 to 10 minutes; watch them closely. Makes 4 dozen cookies.

Evelyn Thayer / *Diocese of Colorado*

## Cranberry Cookies

½ cup butter or margarine
1 cup granulated sugar
¾ cup brown sugar, firmly
    packed
¼ cup milk
2 tablespoons orange juice
1 egg, beaten

3 cups flour
1 teaspoon baking powder
¼ teaspoon baking soda
½ teaspoon salt
1 cup chopped nuts
2½ cups coarsely chopped fresh
    cranberries

Cream butter and sugars together. Beat in the milk, orange juice and egg. Sift together flour, baking powder, baking soda and salt. Combine dry ingredients with creamed mixture and blend well. Stir in chopped nuts and cranberries. Drop by teaspoonsful onto greased cookie sheet. Bake in preheated 350-degree oven for 10 to 15 minutes. Makes about 12 dozen cookies.

Susie Reed / *Diocese of Kentucky*

## Tea Gems

1 cup butter
1 cup sugar
½ teaspoon vanilla
2 tablespoons beaten egg
2 cups flour

Pinch of baking soda and a pinch
    of salt
Blanched almond halves or slices,
    or pecan halves

227

Cream together butter and sugar, add vanilla and 2 tablespoons beaten whole egg and beat well. Add flour, soda and salt gradually. Divide mixture into two parts. With your hands form each into a long sticklike form about 1 inch in diameter. Wrap each roll separately in waxed paper. If you wish, shape the rolls by placing them in cardboard tubes left from paper towels. These will keep in the refrigerator for several weeks.

When preparing to bake, cut ¼-inch slices, place on cookie sheet ¾ inch or more apart, and pat out lightly with one finger. Decorate with nut halves or nut crumbs, candied cherries or citron bits, or mark with side of fork or other two-pronged object. Paste to hold decorations is made of beaten egg and a little water. Use sparingly. Bake at 375 degrees about 10 minutes.

Harriet Chilton / *Diocese of Virginia*

## Lemon Squares

Work till mealy:

¾ cup flour
½ cup oleo

Pinch of salt
¼ cup powdered sugar

Press above mixture into 9 × 9-inch pan. Bake at 350 degrees for 15 minutes. Then mix:

2 eggs with

1 cup sugar

Add

⅓ cup lemon juice
1 lemon rind, grated

3 tablespoons flour

Pour this mixture over hot crust. Return to oven for 25 minutes at 350 degrees. Cool. Sprinkle with powdered sugar. Cut in squares. We often serve these and brownies for dessert at buffet to give choice.

Beth Murray / *Diocese of Central Gulf Coast*

## Brownies

A favorite dessert for buffet . . . no plate needed. Serve it with coffee.

| | |
|---|---|
| 1 small package chocolate bits (semi-sweet) | ½ cup flour |
| | ½ teaspoon baking powder |
| ⅓ cup oleo | ¼ teaspoon salt |
| 2 eggs, well-beaten | 1 teaspoon vanilla |
| ½ cup sugar | ½ cup chopped pecans |

Melt chocolate bits and oleo in top of double boiler over hot water. Beat eggs and sugar till thick. Add flour, baking powder and salt. Add melted chocolate mixture. Add vanilla and stir in nuts. I line an 8 × 8-inch square pan with aluminum foil. It helps get it out! Bake 25 minutes at 350 degrees.

My oven cooks these on the underdone side and they are moist and chewy. If your oven makes yours too dry, cook shorter time or lower temperature. Cool, lift out by aluminum foil. Cut in squares. Makes 9-12. Can multiply recipe. I always make by double batches.

Beth Murray / *Diocese of Central Gulf Coast*

## Brownies, War Time Recipe

This is a war time recipe that requires no eggs, butter or sugar.

| | |
|---|---|
| 16 graham crackers, crumbled | 1 can sweetened condensed milk |
| 1 package chocolate bits | |

Mix well. Bake at 350 degrees about 30 minutes or till light brown in 9 × 9-inch pan.

Hannah Lawrence / *Diocese of Western Massachusetts*

## Currant Cookies

| | |
|---|---|
| ½ pound butter | 1 teaspoon vanilla |
| ½ pound margarine | 3 cups flour |
| 2 cups sugar | 1½ cups currants, washed and drained |
| 1 egg, well-beaten | |

229

Cream butter and margarine until well blended. Add sugar slowly, then well-beaten egg and vanilla. Slowly add flour and mix well. Fold in currants and mix well. Drop from teaspoon on cookie sheet. Bake until lightly browned on edges, about 10 minutes in a 325-degree oven.

Virginia Turner / *Diocese of Kansas*

## Butterscotch Drops

2 6-ounce packages butterscotch
   bits
2 3-ounce cans chow mein
   noodles

1 cup nuts

Melt butterscotch bits in top of double boiler until melted. Quickly stir in noodles and nuts. Stir until well coated. Drop from teaspoon on wax paper. Chill. Makes about 3 dozen.

Virginia Turner / *Diocese of Kansas*

## Applesauce Cookies

½ cup butter
1 cup sugar
1 egg
1 cup applesauce
1 teaspoon soda
1 teaspoon cinnamon

¼ teaspoon cloves, allspice and
   salt
2 cups flour
1 cup raisins
1 cup nuts

Cream butter and sugar. Add beaten egg and applesauce, to which soda has been added. Add spices and salt to flour and mix. Add raisins and nuts and drop by teaspoonsful on greased cookie sheet. Bake at 350 degrees for 10 minutes. While warm, ice with confectioners sugar glaze. Makes 6 dozen.

At Christmas, candied fruit and dates may be added to dough. Decorate frosting with red or green cherries.

Ruth Quarterman / *Diocese of Northwest Texas*

## Kisses

3 egg whites
1¼ cups sugar
3 teaspoons baking powder

Pinch of salt
1 teaspoon vanilla or almond
    extract

Beat egg whites until stiff, add sugar *very* slowly, using the ¼ cup of sugar at the end with the baking powder and salt in it. Add flavoring. Beat very dry. Line cookie sheet with brown paper. Drop batter with a dessert spoon, spreading to a medium thickness. Bake very slowly at a very low (150 degree) heat until dried out.

Eleanor Jackson / *Diocese of Louisiana*

## Lillie's Cookies

Boil 1⅓ cups raisins in ⅔ cup of water until almost dry. Cool. Cream ⅔ cup margarine with 1 scant cup sugar. Add 2 well-beaten eggs and 1 teaspoon vanilla. To 2⅓ cups sifted flour, add 1 scant teaspoon salt, 1 scant teaspoon soda and 1 scant teaspoon baking powder. Sift and add to first mixture together with the raisins. Roll in balls, 1 teaspoonful for each cookie, then roll each ball in mixture of sugar and cinnamon. Cook for about 10 minutes in 375-degree oven. Makes about 3 dozen cookies.

These cookies are good for church receptions and like occasions. They can be made in advance and keep well.

Claudia Gesner / *Diocese of South Dakota*

## Russian Wafers

1 cup butter
½ cup powdered sugar

2 cups flour
¾ cup chopped pecans

Cream butter, sugar and flour. Add pecans. Roll into balls and bake in 325-degree oven until light brown—20 to 40 minutes. While warm, roll in powdered sugar and then roll again when cool. Makes about 36 wafers. A delicious Christmas cookie.

Marion Higgins / *Diocese of Rhode Island*

# Dessert Cakes

## Toffee Torte

1 14½-ounce box chocolate
covered almond toffee, crushed
2 cups heavy cream, whipped

1 8-inch loaf angel food cake,
split lengthwise

Reserve ¼ cup crushed toffee. Fold remaining toffee into whipped cream. Spread frosting between layers and over top of the cake and sprinkle remaining toffee on top. Chill.

Helen Hines / *Dover House (1965—1974)*

## Blitz Torte

½ cup butter
½ cup sugar
3 egg yolks, well-beaten

3½ teaspoons milk
½ teaspoon baking powder
¾ cup flour

Cream together butter and sugar. Add egg yolks, milk and baking powder sifted with flour. Beat well. Bake in 2 round cake tins in quick oven (375-400 degrees) until light brown. Remove from oven and spread with the following meringue:

3 egg whites
1 cup sugar

1 cup walnuts, finely chopped

Beat egg whites until stiff. Gradually add sugar. Continue beating until sugar is incorporated and egg whites stand in peaks. Fold in walnuts. Return cakes to oven and bake again until light brown. Put two layers together with the following custard filling:

2 cups milk
2 egg yolks
¾ cup sugar

2 dessertspoons cornstarch
Lump of butter
1 teaspoon vanilla

Mix milk, egg yolks, sugar and cornstarch together and cook over low heat until thick. Add butter and vanilla.

Beverly Varley / *Diocese of Nebraska*

## Ginger Walnut Roll with Molasses Cream

| | |
|---|---|
| 7 eggs, separated | 2 teaspoons ground ginger |
| ⅓ cup sugar | Salt |
| ¾ cup ground walnuts | Confectioners sugar |

Butter a jelly roll pan, 11 × 16 inches, line with wax paper and butter the paper. In bowl beat egg yolks until frothy. Gradually add sugar and continue to beat for several minutes or until it ribbons when beater is lifted. In another bowl beat egg whites with pinch of salt until they hold stiff peaks. Add ¼ of the whites to yolk mixture and fold them in gently but thoroughly. Pour yolk mixture over remaining whites and sprinkle it with a mixture of ground walnuts and ground ginger. Gently fold mixture together until there are no traces of egg white. Pour batter into prepared pan and spread evenly. Bake at 350 degrees for about 25 minutes or until lightly browned. Loosen wax paper from side of pan with a knife and invert cake onto baking sheet covered with a sheet of wax paper. Let cake cool and peel off top layer of paper. Spread the cake with molasses cream, (see below) reserving ½ cup. Roll the cake up lengthwise lifting it with the wax paper beneath the roll and finishing with the seam side down. (Cake may be rolled short way making a long 16-inch roll.) Dust the roll with confectioners sugar. Use ½ cup of the molasses cream mixture to decorate cake: fill a pastry bag and pipe across the top of roll. Serves 10.

*Molasses Cream*

| | |
|---|---|
| 1 teaspoon gelatin | ¼ cup molasses |
| 3 tablespoons water | |
| 2 cups heavy cream or 9-ounce carton Cool Whip | |

Sprinkle the gelatin over the cold water. When it has softened, beat the mixture over hot water until gelatin is dissolved and liquid clear. In a chilled bowl beat cream until it begins to thicken and pour in the gelatin mixture in a stream. Pour in molasses and continue to beat the cream until it is stiff.

Mary Alexander / *Diocese of Upper South Carolina*

## Linaskoog, a Swedish dessert

1 cup dark brown sugar
½ cup chopped pecans
1 16-ounce can fruit cocktail
  (heavy syrup)
1 cup flour

1 cup granulated sugar
1 teaspoon soda
½ teaspoon salt
1 egg white, beaten stiff
1 teaspoon vanilla

Mix brown sugar and pecans together. Drain fruit cocktail, reserving juice. In a bowl sift together the flour, granulated sugar, soda and salt. Add the drained fruit with 3 tablespoons of its juice, the beaten egg white and the vanilla. Pour quickly into well-greased cake pans, 8 × 8 inches and 5 × 7 inches if a thin cake is desired, or a single 8 × 8-inch pan for a thicker cake. Sprinkle with nut and sugar mix. Bake in a 325-degree oven for 50 to 60 minutes. Cool in pan. Cut in squares and serve with whipped cream.

Hannah Wright / *Diocese of East Carolina*

## Pumpkin Squares

Mix together and pat into buttered baking dish (13½ × 9 × 2):

24 single graham crackers,
  crushed (about 1¾ cups
  crumbs)

⅓ cup sugar
½ cup melted butter

In a separate bowl, beat until light and fluffy:

2 eggs
¾ cup sugar

8 ounces cream cheese, softened

Pour over crust. Bake in 350-degree oven for 20 minutes. Remove from oven and set aside.

In top of double boiler, combine:

2 cups cooked pumpkin
3 egg yolks
½ cup sugar

½ cup milk
½ teaspoon salt
2 teaspoons ground cinnamon

Cook over boiling water, stirring often. Cook until thick, about 5 minutes.

In small saucepan, sprinkle:

1 envelope unflavored gelatin on
  ¼ cup cold water

234

Stir over low heat just until dissolved. Stir into pumpkin mixture. Cool.

Beat until foamy:

**3 egg whites**

Gradually beat in:

**¼ cup sugar**

Beat until stiff and glossy. Gently fold into cooled pumpkin mixture. Pour over baked mixture. Refrigerate until chilled and firm. To serve, cut into 24 squares. Garnish with whipped cream.

Jane M. Hosea / *Diocese of Lexington (Kentucky)*

# Pies

## Shoo-Fly Pie

| | |
|---|---|
| ¼ cup shortening | ¼ teaspoon salt |
| 1½ cups flour | ¾ cup molasses |
| 1 cup brown sugar | ¾ cup hot water |
| ¾ teaspoon baking soda | A little ginger, cinnamon and |
| ⅛ teaspoon nutmeg | cloves |

Work shortening, flour and brown sugar together. Mix remaining ingredients together and add hot water. Into an unbaked pie shell, combine the sugar mixture and liquid in alternate layers with the sugar mixture on bottom and top. Bake 15 minutes at 450 degrees, then 20 minutes at 350 degrees.

Doris Stevenson / *Diocese of Central Pennsylvania*

## Vinegar Pie

Revolutionary times recipe from the Jarrett House, Dillsboro, N.C.

| | |
|---|---|
| 3 eggs, slightly beaten | 1 teaspoon vanilla extract |
| 1½ cups sugar | 1 stick melted butter |
| 2 teaspoons flour | 1 unbaked pie shell |
| 2 teaspoons vinegar | |

RECIPES FROM THE BISHOPS' WIVES

Mix all ingredients and pour into unbaked pie shell. Bake slowly at 250 degrees for about 1 hour. Serves 6 or 8.

This pie is very much like chess pie—rich and delicious!

Clara Claiborne / *Diocese of Atlanta (Georgia)*


## Pecan Tarts

*Crust:*

| | |
|---|---|
| 3 ounces soft cream cheese | 1 cup flour, sifted |
| ½ cup soft butter | |

*Filling:*

| | |
|---|---|
| 2 eggs, slightly beaten | 1½ cups light brown sugar |
| 2 tablespoons soft butter | ⅛ teaspoon salt |
| 2 teaspoons vanilla | 1⅔ cups chopped pecans |

Cream cheese and ½ cup butter together. Add flour. Chill 3 hours. Press with fingers in muffin tins. Mix next 5 ingredients together. Put ½ nuts in muffin tins on top of crust. Then put filling on top of nuts till ½ full. Then sprinkle rest of nuts on top. Bake 25 minutes at 375 degrees. Cool slightly. Remove.

Can freeze or keep in refrigerator. Number of servings depends on size of your muffin tins.

Beth Murray / *Diocese of Central Gulf Coast*


## Lemon Chess Pie

| | |
|---|---|
| 1 stick butter or margarine | Rind of 1 lemon, grated |
| 2 cups sugar | Juice of 2 lemons |
| 6 eggs | 2 unbaked pie shells |

Cream butter and add sugar gradually. Cream well. Add eggs singly and beat well after each. Add grated lemon rind and lemon juice. Pour into 2 unbaked pie shells, medium size. Bake at 350 degrees for 25 minutes or until the filling doesn't shake "wet."

Nancy Gravatt / *Diocese of Upper South Carolina*

## Buttermilk Chess Pie

½ cup unsifted flour
1 stick margarine
3 eggs, well-beaten
2 cups sugar

2 cups buttermilk
Juice of 1 large or 2 small lemons
2 unbaked pie shells

Cream flour and margarine together thoroughly. In another bowl, add sugar gradually to well-beaten eggs. Combine with first mixture; add buttermilk and lemon juice. Pour into 2 unbaked pie shells, medium size. Bake 15 minutes at 425 degrees. Reduce heat to 350 degrees and bake 30 minutes more or until brown.

Nancy Gravatt / *Diocese of Upper South Carolina*

## Coconut Pie (no crust)

1 stick softened margarine
2 cups sugar
4 eggs, well-beaten
Juice of 1 lemon

½ cup self-rising flour
2 cups milk
1 can coconut
1 teaspoon vanilla

Mix all ingredients well. Pour into 2 9-inch buttered pie plates. Bake at 350 degrees for 35 minutes or more until brown.

Note: If you use ½ of recipe, all ingredients may be put in blender together and beaten well. It's really good!

Nancy Gravatt / *Diocese of Upper South Carolina*

## Easy Cream Cheese Pie

3 eggs
⅔ cup sugar
½ teaspoon almond extract
1 pound cream cheese

1 pint sour cream
3 tablespoons sugar
1 teaspoon vanilla
½ cup chopped nuts

Beat eggs, sugar, almond extract and cheese until smooth and thick. Pour into a buttered 9-inch pie plate. Bake at 350 degrees for 25 minutes, then turn oven off, open door and let pie cool 20 minutes in oven. Beat sour cream, sugar and vanilla together. Remove pie from oven and turn oven to 350 degrees again. Pour frosting over pie until it reaches edge of plate. Return to oven and cook 15 minutes. Remove and sprinkle nuts on top.

Martha Porteus / *Diocese of Connecticut*

## Peach Glaze Pie

1 quart sliced peaches
¾ cup water
1 cup sugar
3 tablespoons cornstarch
1 tablespoon lemon juice

1 tablespoon butter
Dash salt
Baked 9-inch pie crust
Whipped cream

Chop 1 cup peaches. Add water. Boil 4 minutes. Mix sugar and cornstarch and add to peaches. Cook until thick and clear. Add lemon, butter and salt. Cool. Arrange remainder of peach slices in pie shell. Pour glaze over peach slices. Chill and serve with whipped cream. Serves 6.

Peggy Rath / *Diocese of Newark (New Jersey)*

## Gooseberry Pie

3½ cups gooseberries (fresh or canned)
2 tablespoons quick-cooking tapioca
1½ cups sugar
¼ teaspoon salt

1 teaspoon grated orange rind
2 tablespoons melted butter
Pastry for 2 crust pie
Whipped cream or hard sauce for garnish

If using fresh gooseberries, remove stem and blossom ends. Wash and drain. Add tapioca, sugar, salt, orange rind and butter. Let stand for 15 to 20 minutes. Line a 9-inch pie plate with pastry. Fill with gooseberry mixture and moisten edge of pastry with water. Adjust the top crust and press edges firmly together. Make several slits to permit the escape of steam. Bake in a hot oven (450 degrees) for 10 minutes, then decrease to moderate (350 degrees) and continue baking 30 minutes. Serve cold, with or without whipped cream, or serve warm with hard sauce.

238

This was the dessert for a luncheon which Lord Peter Wimsey shared at Simpson's-on-the-Strand with Miss Pamela Dean. They were secretly being watched by a furtive young man on this occasion. The rest of the menu was as follows:

Steaming joints of roast saddle of mutton with red currant jelly
Round yellow balls of new potatoes
Cauliflower (Lord Peter had peas)

The young man also drank Lager beer with his meal (Pilsener Light).

Anne Taylor / *Diocese of Easton (Maryland)*


## Cranberry Chiffon Pie

2 cups raw cranberries
½ cup water
1½ cups sugar
3 eggs, separated
1 envelope unflavored gelatin

2 tablespoons cold water
1 tablespoon lemon juice
1 9-inch pie shell, baked
½ cup heavy cream, whipped

Cook cranberries in water until skins burst. Put through sieve and add to beaten egg yolks with 1 cup sugar. Cook over hot water until thickened. Add gelatin softened in water and lemon juice. Cool. Fold in stiffly beaten egg whites with remaining sugar. Fill baked pie shell. Chill until firm. Top with whipped cream.

Helen Ludlow / *Diocese of Newark (New Jersey)*


## Rum Cream Pie

6 egg yolks
1 cup sugar
1 tablespoon gelatin
½ cup water

1 pint heavy cream, whipped
½ cup rum
2 graham cracker crusts

Beat egg yolks and sugar until light. Soften gelatin in water and heat over boiling water until gelatin is dissolved. Pour into egg mixture, beating briskly. Let cool. Fold whipped cream into egg mixture. Add rum. Pour into graham cracker crust. Place in refrigerator to set. Grate bittersweet chocolate on top before serving. Makes 2 pies.

Jane Hosea / *Diocese of Lexington (Kentucky)*

# Puddings

## Indian Meal Pudding

1 heaping tablespoon yellow corn
meal
1 heaping tablespoon minute
tapioca
⅓ cup sugar
¼ teaspoon ginger

¼ teaspoon cinnamon
¼ teaspoon salt
⅔ cup dark molasses
4 cups cold milk
Small lump butter
1 egg

Mix dry ingredients, plus molasses in bowl. In double boiler, put 2 cups cold milk and add above mixture. Stirring constantly, cook until it thickens. Put 2 cups cold milk and lump of butter in 2-quart baking dish. Turn mixture from double boiler into baking dish and add 1 beaten egg. Bake in slow oven (300 degrees) for 2½ hours. Serve steaming hot or cold. Add a dab of ice cream if you wish. Serves 6.

Carolyn Hutchens / *Diocese of Connecticut*

## Grapenut Pudding

| | |
|---|---|
| 2 teaspoons grated lemon rind | 2 tablespoons flour |
| 4 tablespoons butter or margarine | 4 tablespoons Grapenuts |
| 1 cup sugar | 1 cup milk or ½ cup canned milk |
| 2 egg yolks, well-beaten | and ½ cup water |
| 3 tablespoons lemon juice | 2 egg whites, stiffly beaten |

Add lemon rind to butter and cream well. Add sugar gradually, blending after each addition. Add egg yolks and beat thoroughly. Stir in lemon juice. Add flour, Grapenuts and milk. Mix well. Fold in egg whites. Turn into greased baking dish and place in pan of hot water. Bake in slow oven (325 degrees) 1 hour and 15 minutes. When done, pudding has crust on top, jelly below. Serve cold with whipped cream. Serves 6.

Dee Frensdorff / *Diocese of Nevada*

## Cranberry Pudding and Butter Sauce

| | |
|---|---|
| 3 tablespoons melted butter | ¼ teaspoon salt |
| ¾ cup sugar | 1 cup milk |
| 2 cups flour | 2 cups raw cranberries, washed |
| 3 teaspoons baking powder | |

Mix all ingredients, turn into greased 12 × 8 × 2-inch baking dish. Bake 40-45 minutes at 350 degrees.

*Butter Sauce:*

| | |
|---|---|
| 1 cup brown sugar | ¾ cup evaporated milk |
| ½ cup butter | |

Bring ingredients to boil and stir until sugar is dissolved. Serve hot over cranberry pudding.

Maureen Atkins / *Diocese of Eau Claire (Wisconsin)*

## Lemon Sponge

| | |
|---|---|
| ¾ cup sugar | 2 eggs, separated |
| 3 tablespoons flour | Juice of 1 lemon |
| ½ teaspoon salt | 1 cup milk |
| Rind of 1 lemon, grated | 3 tablespoons melted butter |

241

Mix sugar, flour, salt and grated lemon rind. Beat egg yolks and lemon juice and add to sugar mixture. Stir in milk and melted butter. Fold in stiffly beaten egg whites. Bake in pudding dish in a pan of hot water in a 350-degree oven for ¾ to 1 hour.

Virginia Huntington / *Diocese of Anking (China)*

## Chocolate Creme de Menthe Pudding

1 cup small semi-sweet chocolate
  bits
1 egg

2 tablespoons creme de menthe
¾ cup scalded milk

Combine all ingredients in blender and blend until smooth. Pour into 6 demi-tasse cups, cover with plastic wrap, and chill in refrigerator at least 3 hours. Serves 6.

Janet Campbell / *Diocese of West Virginia*

# *Gelatin Desserts*

## Coffee-Chocolate Mousse

1½ envelopes unflavored gelatin
3 teaspoons instant coffee (or
  Sanka)
6 squares unsweetened baking
  chocolate
4 cups milk
2 cups sugar

12 tablespoons flour
1 teaspoon salt
8 egg yolks, beaten
1 cup heavy cream, whipped
4 tablespoons butter
4 teaspoons vanilla
Ladyfingers

Soak gelatin in ¼ cup water. Add to coffee, chocolate and milk in top of double boiler, over hot water. When chocolate is melted add sugar, flour and salt and beat with egg beater till blended. Cook stirring over hot water until mixture is thickened. Cook 10 more minutes. Pour chocolate mixture over beaten egg yolks. Put back in double boiler. Cook 2 minutes. Add butter and vanilla. Cool. Fold in whipped cream.

I put in flan pan lined with ladyfingers so can unmold later . . . and garnish with whipped cream when unmolded. You can line silver bowl or china bowl with ladyfingers and pour in chocolate mixture and garnish with ladyfingers and/or whipped cream when served. Or you could mold in individual cups. Delicious and rich. Serves 10-20 depending on how you serve and how much they eat!

Beth Murray / *Diocese of Central Gulf Coast*

## Lemon Bisque

1 13-ounce can evaporated milk
1 package lemon flavored gelatin
1¼ cups boiling water
⅓ cup honey

⅛ teaspoon salt
3 tablespoons lemon juice
Grated rind of 1 lemon
2½ cups vanilla wafer crumbs

Thoroughly chill can of milk in refrigerator overnight. Dissolve gelatin in boiling water and add honey, salt, lemon juice and rind. When gelatin has congealed slightly, beat milk until it is stiff and whip gelatin mixture into it. Spread half of crumbs in a large pan (10 × 13½-inch) and pour lemon mixture over it. Top with remaining crumbs and set in refrigerator to chill (approximately 3 hours). May be served plain or with whipped cream.

125-144 calories per serving. Source of vitamin A. This can be prepared the day before it is to be served. A very economical dessert to serve a crowd. Serves 15-18.

Minnie Hargrave / *Diocese of Southwest Florida*

## Murray Lemon Charlotte

1 envelope plain gelatin
¼ cup water
6 egg yolks
1 cup sugar
1 cup lemon juice
Rind of 1 lemon, grated

1 can condensed milk
1 cup heavy cream, whipped
1 pack graham crackers (3 packs
 to box of Nabisco grahams)
1 stick margarine, melted

Soften gelatin in water. Beat egg yolks till pale and lemon colored. Slowly add sugar. Beat till light. Add lemon and rind. Combine

243

with softened gelatin in top of double boiler and cook till thick. Stir in condensed milk. Cool, then fold in whipped cream. Mix crushed graham crackers with melted margarine.

I line a pretty bowl with the crumbs, saving some for top, then pour in lemon mix. Sprinkle crumbs on top. Cool in refrigerator overnight. Garnish with strawberries and whipped cream if desired. Serves 12.

Beth Murray / *Diocese of Central Gulf Coast*

## Creme de Menthe Mold

2 packages lime Jello
2 cups hot water
Juice of 1 lemon
¼ cup green creme de menthe

½ cup cold pineapple juice
¾ cup heavy cream, whipped
½ cup crumbled macaroons

Dissolve Jello in hot water. Stir in lemon juice. Pour slightly less than half the Jello in the bottom of a mold or molds and chill until thickened. To remaining Jello add creme de menthe and pineapple juice. Chill until syrupy, then fold in whipped cream and crumbled macaroons. Pour over thickened Jello in mold. Chill until firm. Unmold and serve with a dab of whipped cream and a green cherry.

Jane M. Hosea / *Diocese of Lexington (Kentucky)*

## Fruit Jello for 60

3 large packages cherry Jello
2 cups peaches, sliced
1 can whole cranberries
1 can pineapple slices, cut up

1 can grapefruit sections
2 cans mixed fruit cocktail
8 red delicious apples
½ cup coconut

Dissolve Jello in 6 cups boiling water. Allow to cool. Drain fruit and save juices for 6 cups fruit juice. Cut up apples but do not pare. Combine all ingredients and allow to jell. Serves 60.

Jeanne Baden / *Diocese of Virginia*

244

# *Fruit Desserts*

## Grape and Nectarine Compote

2 cups white seedless grapes
6-8 nectarines
1 7-ounce bottle cold gingerale

1 pint sherbet: orange, lemon or
lime

Just before serving, slice nectarines and combine with grapes and gingerale in a serving bowl. Spoon sherbet over the top. Serves 10-12.

Connie Hall / *Diocese of New Hampshire*

## Blushing Peaches

4 large ripe peaches, peeled,
halved, pitted, and brushed
with orange juice to retard
browning
½ cup heavy cream
1 tablespoon confectioners sugar

1 tablespoon cognac
1 10-ounce package frozen
strawberries, thawed and partly
drained, or 1 pint fresh berries
and sugar to sweeten
Whipped cream for garnish

Arrange peach halves, pitted side up, in dessert dishes. Put cream, sugar and cognac in an electric blender. Cover and blend on low until thick. Pour into peach halves and refrigerate.

Just before serving, puree berries in blender. Pour puree over each peach, and top with whipped cream.

Polly Keller / *Diocese of Arkansas*

## Fruit Casserole

2 cups canned pears
2 cups canned pineapple
2 cups canned peaches
2 cups canned apricots
2 cups spiced apples

¼ pound butter
½ cup sugar
2 tablespoons flour
1 cup milk or sherry

Drain fruit, cut in bite-size pieces and place in baking dish. Combine butter, sugar, flour and milk or sherry and cook over low heat until thickened. Pour over fruit and let stand overnight. The next day, cook for 45 minutes in a 350-degree oven. Serve warm. Serves 20.

Nan Hunter / *Diocese of Wyoming*

## Lemon Sauce and Fruits (My Mother's)

This sauce can be made ahead of time and keeps well. It is equally good over plain spongecake, a mixture of canteloupe, peaches and grapes, or the fruit combination below.

(for four-six serving recipe)

1 can drained chunk pineapple
3 bananas
1 large can drained pitted black
   cherries
Mix at last minute, as cherries stain other fruit.

| *four servings* | *six-eight servings* | *twelve servings* | *twenty-five servings* |
|---|---|---|---|
| 2 egg yolks | 3 egg yolks | 4 egg yolks | 6 egg yolks |

Beat until thick. Add gradually:

| | | | |
|---|---|---|---|
| ⅓ cup sugar | ½ cup sugar | ¾ cup sugar | 1 cup sugar |

Beat well. Gradually add, still beating slowly:

| | | | |
|---|---|---|---|
| ⅓ cup melted butter or oleo | ½ cup melted butter or oleo | ¾ cup melted butter or oleo | 1 cup melted butter or oleo |
| 1 tablespoon grated lemon rind | 1½ tablespoon grated lemon rind | 2 tablespoons grated lemon rind | 3 tablespoons grated lemon rind |
| 2 tablespoons lemon juice | 3 tablespoons lemon juice | 4 tablespoons lemon juice | 6 tablespoons lemon juice |

Whip and fold in:

| | | | |
|---|---|---|---|
| ⅓ cup heavy cream | ½ cup heavy cream | ¾ cup heavy cream | 1 cup heavy cream |

Rosemary Atkinson / *Diocese of West Virginia*

# Ice Cream Desserts and Dessert Sauces

## Ice Cream Pudding

**Shortbread cookies**
**1 package instant vanilla pudding**
**1 pint butter pecan ice cream,**
  **softened**

Crumble cookies into the bottom of a small oblong baking dish. Mix instant pudding with softened ice cream. Spread over crumbled cookies. Let stand in refrigerator a few hours until firm. Serves 6.

Janet Campbell / *Diocese of West Virginia*

## Eggnog Tortoni

**1 cup dairy eggnog**
**1 slightly beaten egg yolk**
**1 tablespoon brandy or rum**
  **flavoring**
**¼ teaspoon almond flavoring**
**¼ teaspoon salt**

**⅓ cup vanilla wafer crumbs**
**¼ cup chopped toasted almonds**
**¼ cup chopped toasted coconut**
**1 stiffly beaten egg white**
**2 tablespoons sugar**
**½ cup heavy cream, whipped**

Combine eggnog and slightly beaten egg yolk. Cook and stir just until mixture starts to bubble. Cool. Add flavorings and salt. Stir in crumbs, almonds and coconut. Beat egg white to soft peaks. Gradually add sugar and beat to stiff peaks. Fold into eggnog mixture. Fold in whipped cream. Spoon into cups. Freeze firm. To serve, sprinkle on a few toasted almonds and top with a cherry. Makes 8 demitasse cups or pots de creme.

Katherine Appleyard / *Diocese of Pittsburgh (Pennsylvania)*

## Brandy Ice

1 pint vanilla ice cream
1 ounce brandy

1 ounce creme de cacao
Nutmeg

Let ice cream soften a bit, then mix with brandy and creme de cacao until consistency of a thick malted. Place in 4 pot de creme pots and freeze until firm. Sprinkle nutmeg on top.

Evelyn Thayer / *Diocese of Colorado*

## Heavenly Sauce for Ice Cream

1 cup white sugar
1 cup brown sugar
1 cup water
1 cup strawberries (fresh, frozen
  or jam)
1 cup bourbon whiskey

1 cup chopped nut meats
1 orange, juice and rind ground
  fine
1 lemon, juice and rind ground
  fine

Boil white and brown sugars with water to the soft ball stage. Remove from fire. Add rest of ingredients and mix thoroughly. Refrigerate, covered, for at least 48 hours.

Absolutely lovely over vanilla ice cream. Good on pound cake, too.

Jeanne Masuda / *Diocese of North Dakota*

## Banana Sauce Foster

1 cup light brown sugar
¾ stick butter
3 bananas, mashed
1 teaspoon cinnamon

2½ teaspoons banana liqueur
2 teaspoons lemon juice
1 ounce cognac
1½ ounces rum

Combine all the ingredients except the rum, cook in heavy skillet or chafing dish until sugar has dissolved and all is well blended. Pour heated rum over sauce, and flame. Serve over vanilla ice cream. Serves 6.

Polly Keller / *Diocese of Arkansas*

## Hot Fudge Sauce

3 squares unsweetened cooking
  chocolate
1½ cups granulated sugar
Pinch of salt

1/16 teaspoon cream of tartar
1 cup evaporated milk (I use
  skimmed evaporated milk)
1 teaspoon vanilla

Melt chocolate over low heat. Stir in sugar, salt, and cream of tartar. Gradually add milk, stirring constantly over low heat. Continue to full bubbling boil. Remove from heat and add vanilla.

May be used cold, but is elegant when used warm. (Can be re-heated by placing container for 20 minutes in pan of hot water.)

Lillian Curtis / *Diocese of Olympia (Washington)*

## Grandmother Thayer's Brandy Sauce

Put in bottom of bowl butter the size of two eggs, over it two cups sugar, into center of which break two unbeaten eggs. Set over hot water until butter is melted and sugar warm. Beat it thoroughly and pour over it a little boiling water, enough to dissolve sugar; or instead of water a cup of sherry.

This sauce is delicious and is always used on our Christmas Plum Pudding.

Evelyn Thayer / *Diocese of Colorado*

## Apricot-Orange-Pineapple Topping

1 pound dried apricots, put
  through fine grinder
3 oranges, juice and rind, put
  through fine grinder

3½ cups crushed pineapple
Sugar

Mix fruits together, measure and for every cup of fruit add a cup of sugar. Leave in a bowl overnight and stir now and then. Do not refrigerate.

Use your imagination with this one. You can add nuts. It's good on ice cream or a bit on the top of a sweet potato casserole, on a hot biscuit or on your English muffin.

Jeanne Masuda / *Diocese of North Dakota*

249

## Scripture Cake Answers

1 Solomon's provision for one day was 30 measures of fine flour and 60 measures of meal.

2 He asked water and she gave him milk, she brought him curds in a lordly bowl.

3 To what purpose does frankincense come to me from Sheba, or sweet cane from a distant land?

4 And they gave him a piece of cake of figs and two clusters of raisins.

5 All your fortresses are like fig trees with first-ripe figs.

6 And he said to her, Pray give me a little water to drink for I am thirsty. So she opened a skin of milk and gave him a drink.

7 Behold, the rod of Aaron for the house of Levi had sprouted and put forth buds, and produced blossoms, and it bore ripe almonds.

8 And all the people came into the forest and there was honey on the ground.

9 Then she gave the king 120 talents of gold, and a very great quantity of spices and precious stones.

10 Like the partridge that gathers a brood which she did not hatch, so is he who gets riches but not by right.

11 You shall season all your cereal offerings with salt.

12 Offer a sacrifice of thanksgiving of that which is leavened.

13 If you beat him with the rod you will save his life from Sheol.

# PRESERVES AND PICKLES

Beach Plums grow on the dunes at Cape Cod; have a lacy white bloom in Spring, and in late August bear berries from which the following two items can be made.

## Beach Plum Jelly

Stew ripe red beach plums until stones leave fruit. Do not add water. Strain juice. Balance equal parts juice and sugar. Boil until it forms soft ball in water. Pour into glasses. Seal when cool with paraffin wax. Jelly can also be made with Certo. Follow directions found on bottle. It is easier to make several small lots than one large amount.

## Beach Plum Cordial

Fill one quart jar (mayonnaise or other wide neck jar) with ripe beach plums. Work in one cup sugar and one cup either gin, rum, or vodka. Screw on top. Keep until Christmas.

Martha Porteus / *Diocese of Connecticut*

## Rhubarb Jam

5 cups rhubarb, cut fine
3½ cups sugar

1 cup crushed pineapple, drained
1 package strawberry Jello

Bring to a boil the first three ingredients. Boil gently for 12 minutes. Remove from stove and stir in the Jello until dissolved. Put in half pint mason jars and seal. This makes 3 pints.

Grace Warnecke / *Diocese of Bethlehem (Pennsylvania)*

## Pepper Jelly

¾ cup ground green pepper
¼ cup ground hot pepper
6½ cups sugar

1½ cups apple cider vinegar
1 6-ounce bottle Certo

Grind peppers in food grinder or chop in blender. Drain and reserve juices. Measure peppers to above proportions. Heat sugar and vinegar until sugar is melted. Add peppers and juices. Bring to a rolling boil. Remove from heat, wait 10 minutes. Stir in Certo. Put in sterilized jars. Seal. Work quickly because this jells in a hurry. Makes about 10 half-pint jars. Serve with any meat or with cheese and crackers.

Make this in the summer when peppers are plentiful and you will have nice economical gifts for friends or for the church fair.

Ann Allin / *Dover House (1974–)*

## Frederick County Eight Day Pickle

4 quarts pickling cucumbers,
   whole, 2- to 4-inch length

Place washed cucumbers in enamel or stainless steel container. Each day for 4 days pour over them enough boiling water to cover. (A short cut is to do this morning and evening for 2 days.) Allow boiling water to remain over cucumbers. Drain when ready to add fresh boiling water. Place a plate or tile on top of cucumbers to push them down under the liquid. The last time add ¼ cup salt (not iodized) to the boiling water.

On the 5th day, prepare a syrup and bring to a boil, using:

2 cups vinegar
3 cups sugar
¾ teaspoon turmeric
3 tablespoons minced dry onion
   flakes, or fresh onion cut fine

2 teaspoons celery seed
1 tablespoon mustard seed
1 teaspoon whole cloves and 2
   tablespoon pickling spice, tied
   in a cheesecloth bag

Pour over cucumbers. Each day for next 2 days drain syrup and reheat to boiling, adding:

½ cup vinegar

1 cup sugar

Pour back over cucumbers. On the last day, while syrup is heating to boiling, place cucumbers, whole or sliced, in sterilized jars. Pour boiling syrup over cucumbers, taking out spice bag. Seal jars. This makes a nice crisp pickle.

Jeanne Baden / *Diocese of Virginia*

## Chili Sauce

This recipe has been in use since 1882.

| | |
|---|---|
| 35 ripe tomatoes, peeled and chopped | 2 tablespoons prepared mustard |
| 7 onions, peeled and chopped | 3 teaspoons celery seed |
| 7 green peppers, chopped | 2 cups vinegar |
| 1 cup sugar | ½ teaspoon each of ground |
| 1 tablespoon salt | cinnamon, cloves and allspice |

Mix and place in large roasting pan in oven and set temperature at 200 degrees. Can be cooked down overnight. Seal in morning.

Charlotte McNeil / *Diocese of Western Michigan*

## Mango Chutney

This is for those who live where good mangoes can be bought cheaply, or even picked.

| | |
|---|---|
| 7 cups brown sugar | 3 cloves garlic, minced |
| 3 cups vinegar | 3 small chilis (hot!), chopped |
| 1 tablespoon salt | 1 large piece ginger root, chopped |
| 8 cups mangoes, not quite ripe but not green, peeled, seeded and cut up. | 1 cup raisins |

Put sugar, vinegar and salt into large pan; bring to a boil and simmer for 15 minutes. Add mangoes, garlic, chilis, ginger, and toward the end of the cooking, raisins. Boil until thick. Put in jars, seal with hot paraffin.

Helen Kellog / *Diocese of Dominican Republic*

# BEVERAGES

## Grace Church Christmas Wassail

6 quarts of water
3 pounds of sugar
1 tablespoon whole cloves
15 cinnamon sticks

2 large cans frozen lemonade
4 cans frozen orange juice
3 gallons sweet cider
1 or 2 fifths of rum (preferably 2)

Combine water and sugar in a kettle. Put spices in a bag and tie to the edge of the kettle. Bring slowly to the boil and boil for 10 minutes. Cover and let stand for one hour. Strain. Add lemonade, orange juice, cider, and rum. Heat but do not let mixture boil. Serves about 100.

Jane Cadigan / *Diocese of Missouri*

## White Wine Punch for 50

3 tablespoons Soochong tea
2 quarts boiling water
1 cup sugar
1 can (6 oz) frozen orange juice
1 can (6 oz) frozen lemonade

1 fifth cognac
1 gallon Chablis
4 quarts soda water
grenadine syrup (optional)

Measure the tea into a large teapot and pour freshly boiling water over it. Cover and brew for 5 minutes. Strain into a large pitcher and stir in the sugar. When it has dissolved add the concentrated fruit juices. Divide the mixture between two 1-gallon jugs and add half the wine and cognac to each. If the season calls for a bright red punch, add a little grenadine syrup. Cap and store in a cool place.

Place a block of ice in a punch bowl. Pour half the contents of one jug over the ice and add 1 quart of soda water. Repeat as necessary. Serves 50 liberally.

## Tea Punch for 150

40 teaspoons tea
6 quarts boiling water
10 pounds (20 cups) sugar
7 cans (6 oz) concentrated orange
  juice

2 cans (6 oz) concentrated
  lemonade
8 quarts ginger ale
orange slices

Place the tea in a large non-metal pitcher or bowl. Cover and let stand 5 minutes. Place the sugar in a large container and strain the tea over it. Stir until the sugar dissolves. Add the fruit juices, diluted according to directions on the cans. Divide into 3-quart portions and store in gallon containers (milk cartons do very well). At time of serving, pour 3 quarts of the mixture over ice in a punch bowl. Add 2 quarts of ginger ale and garnish with orange slices. Replenish the bowl as necessary. Yield: 300 glasses or punch cups.

## Wedding Punch for 300

1 bottle (½ pint) Rose's Lime
  juice
6 6-ounce cans frozen orange
  juice

6 6-ounce cans frozen lemon juice
7 bottles (fifths) apricot brandy
2 bottles (fifths) white rum
6 gallons Chablis

Mix all the ingredients and divide them in 3-quarts lots and store them in gallon containers. This can be done several days in advance. Cover and keep in a cool place. For every 3 quarts poured over ice in a punch bowl add 2 quarts of soda water. Garnish with small fresh strawberries, small orange slices or sliced maraschino cherries.

Jane Cadigan / *Diocese of Missouri*

## Wine and Champagne Punch

2 12-ounce cans frozen lemonade
1 pint brandy
1 gallon sauterne

6 quarts champagne
4 quarts soda water (club soda)

Mix undiluted lemonade, brandy, and sauterne ahead of time. Add champagne and club soda when ready to serve. All ingredients should be *well chilled*. Serves 75 or more.

Carolyn Leighton / *Diocese of Maryland*

## Bishops' Downfall

6 small oranges
⅓ cup whole cloves
1 gallon apple cider

4 sticks cinnamon
1 fifth dark rum

Stick oranges generously with cloves and roast in a 350-degree oven for 1 hour. Heat cider and cinnamon sticks together. Prick hot oranges with fork and put into a punch bowl. Add rum. Pour on hot cider and serve warm. Makes 5 quarts.

Jeanne Bigliardi / *Diocese of Oregon*

## Frozen Daiquiris

1 fifth white bacardi rum
2 cans frozen limeade
2 cans frozen lemonade

2 scant cups powdered sugar
1 juice-can fresh lemon juice
8 cans water

Place in freezer. Use as needed. Should be made in blender.

Nell Noland / *Diocese of Louisiana*

## Instant Sparkling Punch

1 12-ounce can frozen orange
   juice
1 small can frozen sweetened
   lemonade
1 quart pale dry gingerale

½ pint lemon or orange sherbet
Maraschino cherries and juice,
   plus water, frozen in a small
   ring mold, optional

In a large container put orange juice, plus 2 cans of water. Add lemonade, plus two cans of water. Stir until melted. Add a few ice cubes and stir. Pour mixture into punch bowl. Add gingerale and sherbet. Add ring mold, if desired, and ice cubes. Serves 15.

Carolyn Hutchens / *Diocese of Connecticut*

## Clarabelle's Punch

1 big package cherry Jello (add
   boiling water as directed)
1 12-ounce can frozen orange
   juice

1 46-ounce bottle cranberry juice
1 12-ounce can frozen lemonade
1 32-ounce bottle gingerale

Combine. Add ice.

Mary Cochran / *Diocese of Alaska*

## Spiced Tea Mix

1 27-ounce bottle Tang
4 ounces Nestea, lemon-flavored
  ice-tea mix

¼ cup sugar, optional
2 teaspoons ground cloves
2 teaspoons ground cinnamon

Mix ingredients thoroughly. Keep in closed container. Use 1-2 teaspoons of mix to 1 cup of boiling water.

Betty Powell / *Diocese of Oklahoma*

## A Morning Starter For One

1 cup orange juice
1 cup buttermilk

1 raw egg

Put in blender for a few seconds. And for all the buttermilk haters out there . . . a sprig of mint or a squish of lime does wonders.

Beatrice Sims / *Diocese of Atlanta (Georgia)*

# INDEX

259

264